PARTICIPATORY RESEARCH IN HEALTH

Issues and Experiences

Edited by
Korrie de Koning and Marion Martin

Zed Books Ltd
London & New Jersey

NPPHCN
Johannesburg

Participatory Research in Health: Issues and Experiences was published in Southern Africa
by National Progressive Primary Health Care Network (NPPHCN),
PO Box 32095, Braamfontein 2017, Johannesburg, South Africa and in
the rest of the world by Zed Books Ltd, 7 Cynthia Street, London N1 9JF
and 165 First Avenue, Atlantic Highlands, New Jersey, 07716, in 1996.

Cover design by Andrew Corbett
Typeset by Paula Waugh
Printed and bound in the United Kingdom by
Redwood Books, Kennet House, Kennet Way, Trowbridge, Wiltshire, BA14 8RN

A catalogue record for this book is available from the British Library
US CIP data is available from the Library of Congress

ISBN 1 85649 351 2 hb
ISBN 1 85649 352 0 pb

South African ISBN
0 620 19460 X

Contents

Notes on the contributors

Susanta Adhikari has been since the early 1970s the director of the Christian Commission for Development in Bangladesh (CCDB).

Margaret Bentley Ph.D. is currently Associate Professor, Division of Human Nutrition, Department of International Health, Johns Hopkins University School of Hygiene and Public Health. She is a medical anthropologist with extensive experience in women's reproductive health and infant and young child feeding. She has worked in India, Peru, Guatemala and Nigeria.

Maurice Bloem is a cultural anthropologist/medical sociologist who received his degree from the University of Leiden in the Netherlands. He has been working as a consultant for the Christian Commission for Development in Bangladesh (CCDB) since 1993 and is responsible for research and HIV/AIDS activities.

Dulal Biswas worked as an information officer for the CCDB until 1994 and is currently teaching at the Rajshahi University, Bangladesh.

Andrea Cornwall is a social anthropologist and has worked as a trainer in participatory learning methods in several African countries. She is currently working on a study of strategies for success and survival among Yoruba women in southwest Nigeria.

Lynn Dalrymple is Professor and Head of the Department of Drama, University of Zululand. She was a post-doctoral Research Fellow at the University of the Witwatersrand between 1990 and 1991 and is Director of the DramAide programme. She has published in the *South African Theatre Journal.*

Grindl Dockery has been working as a freelance community research and training consultant for the last 3 years, based in Liverpool. She worked in Papua New Guinea for 10 years coordinating a district health service, before coming to the UK. Her main interests are in developing research and training frameworks which facilitate greater participation, in her work both with under- and post-graduate students and with local communities. Much of her research in the UK has been commissioned by the Liverpool Health Authority and the Liverpool Family Health Services Authority.

Annie George is a researcher in women's health. Her area of research interest is the interface between gender, women's health and empowerment. She has published articles on women and menstruation and on sexism in medicine.

Lisa Howard-Grabman received her BA degree in Psychology from Oberlin College and her MA degree in International Affairs from Ohio

University. She has worked in the public health sector as a USA Peace Corps volunteer in Zaire, and since then principally in the US, Nigeria and Bolivia. The work on which her chapter is based was conducted with Save the Children/Bolivia from 1989 through to 1994.

Shubhada Kanani is a reader at the Department of Food and Nutrition, M. S. University of Baroda, India. Her interests include: promoting the integration of research in public health nutrition. Dr Kanani is also actively engaged in working towards partnership between researchers and programme implementors to bring about improvements in the health of disadvantaged communities.

Renu Khanna has a postgraduate degree in management from Delhi University. Over the last 11 years she has been working as an activist-trainer in women's issues especially health issues and the question of empowerment. Her main concern in recent years has been to find workable alternatives for women's health programmes.

Korrie de Koning is a behavioural scientist and educationalist, and works as a lecturer in health promotion at the Liverpool School of Tropical Medicine, UK. She has worked in the Netherlands, Papua New Guinea, Asia and Africa. Her work is focused on developing participatory approaches in teaching and research. Most of her work relates to improving communication between health workers and communities, community development, women's health issues and empowerment.

Patricia Maguire is an educator, community activist and mother of two daughters. She is Associate Professor of Education and Psychology at Western New Mexico University. Pat is working with a multicultural group to research and design a master's programme integrating Western and traditional Navajo approaches to mental health. She has trained for participatory education and research in Jamaica, West Africa, South Africa and the USA and is author of many publications including *Doing Participatory Research: A Feminist Approach* (1987).

Ravai Marindo-Ranganai is a lecturer in the Department of Sociology, University of Zimbabwe. She is currently studying for a doctorate in Medical Demography at the London School of Hygiene and Tropical Medicine, UK.

Marion Martin has worked and researched in community health and higher education and has published on participatory research and adult learning in health and professional education. She has worked in the UK, rural south India and Tanzania. Marion is co-coordinator of the M.Ed in Education for Primary Health Care (PHC) and Gender, Education and PHC courses at the Centre for Adult and Higher Education, University of Manchester, UK.

Dileep V. Mavalankar is professor at the Public Health Systems Group, Indian Institute of Management, Ahmedabad. He received his basic medical degree from Gujarat University, India, later completing his master's degree in Public Health, and doctorate, at Johns Hopkins University, USA. His current interests include micro-level planning in primary health care, improving management and quality of care in family-planning programmes.

Ineke Meulenberg-Buskens is Head of the Centre for Research Methodology in the Directorate for Research Capacity Building of the Human Sciences Research Council, Pretoria, South Africa. She is involved in research education with groups varying from voluntary health workers to academics, focusing mainly on qualitative and participatory research.

Stanley Okurut obtained a B.Sc. (Hons) degree in Zoology at Makerere University, Uganda. He worked for the Church of Uganda from which he resigned in order to work with the Pallisa Community Development Trust, a project concerned with issues of primary health care and environmental matters.

H. M. Oranga has a doctorate in biostatistics and is a biostatistician/ health information specialist with the African Medical and Research Foundation. His most recent publication is 'The Delphi panel method for generating health information', *Health Policy and Planning* 8(4), pp.405-12.

Eleanor Preston-Whyte is Deputy Vice-Chancellor (Research and Development) and Professor of Anthropology, University of Natal. Her doctorate examined the position of African women migrants in the Durban region. Her research and development interests include: issues of family and domestic structure, gender interaction, sexuality and the empowerment of women. She has been actively involved in developing AIDS intervention strategies.

Jan Ritchie is a lecturer in health promotion at the University of New South Wales, Sydney, Australia. Prior to this she gained qualifications and experience in physiotherapy and health education. Her research and teaching interests are focused on improving the practice of promoting health through innovation where challenges exist, such as in the Western Pacific areas with peoples from other cultures.

Rajesh Tandon is executive director of the Society for Participatory Research in Asia, New Delhi; chairperson of Voluntary Action Network India; president of the Asian-South Pacific Bureau of Adult Education and founder board member of CIVICUS, the World Alliance for Citizen Participation. Formerly he was vice-president for Asia of the International Council for Adult Education. Dr Tandon has provided participatory research, training, evaluation and consultation support to non-governmental organizations (NGOs) in India and other developing countries and has written extensively on participatory research.

SEWA – The team includes young professionals, mostly from the fields of health and the social sciences. Research conducted by SEWA-Rural supports its health-service and training programmes, involving mainly operational research to help health services become more effective within the context of primary health care. The chief contributors to this study are Gayatri Giri, S. Sridhar, Pankaj Shah, Ashok Patel, and Lata Desai, Society for Education, Welfare and Action-Rural (SEWA-Rural), India.

Betsy Tolley lived in Bombay, India from 1991 to 1994, where she worked as a consultant for the project on qualitative methods for research into women's reproductive health conducted by Johns Hopkins University. In addition, she provided assistance to Apnalaya, an Indian non-governmental organization that works with communities in several Bombay slums. She is a Research Associate for Family Health International in Chapel Hill, North Carolina.

Preface

Participatory research has gained considerable importance both as a research strategy and as an educational process. This has been especially true in the field of agriculture and rural development, and is increasingly so in the health sector.

This book presents experiences and reflections of first- and third-world academics and practitioners in participatory research (PR) in health. Contributors place participatory research within its historical and theoretical contexts, and examine its diversity, looking at the practice of and training for PR in various settings and cultures, at international, national and grassroots levels. The book offers an international perspective with contributions from a variety of countries in Africa, Asia, Latin America, the USA and Europe.

The case studies and accounts of PR practice examine the complexities, contradictions and common experiences that practitioners confront when facing diverse cultural, political and economic situations. The issue of equity as reflected for example in gender, race, class and sexuality is a major concern of contributors.

Several contributors analyse critically the research process and the changing power relationships between researchers and respondents, providing valuable insights into the complexities of the process and the qualities, skills and attitudes required from practitioners working in different situations.

Participatory rural appraisal (PRA) methods are described in a number of the case studies. The strengths of these methods are highlighted. The studies are examined critically, with ethical considerations and issues such as validity and reliability being addressed, and suggestions for integrating PRA methods into a participatory research process being made.

The first steps towards the development of this book happened at the International Symposium on Participatory Research in Health Promotion which was held in Liverpool from 17 to 21 September 1993 and was hosted by the Liverpool School of Tropical Medicine in collaboration with the African Medical and Research Foundation, Nairobi, Kenya. The contributions presented in this book are extended versions of a selection of papers presented during the symposium.

We would like to thank Paula Waugh for producing the camera-ready copy and for the efficient and approachable manner in which she organized the communication between editors and contributors.

We would also like to thank our colleagues in the Liverpool School of Tropical Medicine and the University of Manchester for their support. Thanks to Robert Cole for his ongoing comments on the text.

1 Participatory research in health: setting the context[1]

Korrie de Koning and Marion Martin

Many contributors to this book assume some familiarity with concepts which may not be familiar to all health professionals. Our aim in this introduction is to set into context those issues and theoretical concepts which are frequently referred to in the text. These include educational processes based on Freire's critical pedagogy (Freire 1972), issues around difference, for example in gender, and contemporary notions of knowledge production.

Why use the PR approach in health?

Participatory research (PR) and associated methodologies such as participatory rural appraisal (PRA), and the more extractive approaches such as rapid rural appraisal (RRA) and rapid assessment procedures (RAP), are considered increasingly important in the field of health. There are different reasons for the growing popularity of these methodologies. First there is an increasing recognition of the gap between the concepts and models professionals use to understand and interpret reality and the concepts and perspectives of different groups in the community (Grandstaff et al. 1987; WHO 1973). The biomedical interpretation and understanding of diseases, supported by studies carried out in laboratories, is in many cases different from the understanding embedded in a local culture and history. For example, a study in Tunisia shows that causes of diarrhoea similar to a biomedical explanation of diarrhoea are seen as only one possible cause among many others by the people involved in the study (Aubel & Mansour 1989). The implication is that communication about diarrhoea is much less straightforward than many health workers thought. Second, many factors, cultural, historical, socio-economic and political, which are difficult to measure have a crucial influence on the outcomes of interventions and efforts to improve the health of people: '[Development work] cannot ignore these factors and pretend that the world outside the laboratory is the same as inside' (Lammerink & Wolffers 1994:7).

Small-scale qualitative and rapid appraisal procedures aim to generate knowledge and information which represent the perceptions, concepts and practices of different groups and communities in a relatively short time. The emphasis is on generating knowledge from the perspective not only of the researchers but also of the researched. Qualitative research and rapid appraisals help to identify local needs and priorities, place issues in the context of people's lives and give direction to programme development and service provision. These methods are used increasingly in the development of specific disease control (Vlassoff & Tanner 1992), in health education interventions, such as diarrhoea (Bentley et al. 1988), nutrition (Scrimshaw & Hurtado 1987; Varkevisser et al. 1993) and more generally (Aubel 1990–91; Ramakrishna & Brieger 1987), and in assessing community health needs (Annett & Rifkin 1988).

The development of *participatory* rural appraisal, which evolved in reaction to the more extractive approach that characterizes *rapid* rural appraisal (Chambers 1990), is of importance. Within PRA there is a clear emphasis on learning with and from groups in the community in a relaxed and flexible way. PRA methods work through a powerful visualization of situations and knowledge generated in dialogue with local people, and have expanded the ability of many grassroots organizations to trigger discussion and to document and acknowledge local knowledge. Alice Welbourn (1992) shows how the applications of these methods in the field of health help to document differences between groups and their potential for initiating dialogue on health needs and priorities. Marindo-Ranganai (chapter 16), Oranga and Nordberg (chapter 17) and the SEWA team (chapter 12) describe, in this volume, how PRA methods were useful for involving community groups in documenting health information and demographic data.

Many workers in the field of health have been exposed mainly to quantitative research methods and, frequently, one of the first questions asked is: how valid and reliable are the PR methods?

The validity and reliability of qualitative data collected by PR methods

The debate about validity and reliability of qualitative data and participatory appraisal has developed substantially over the last decades. Few people who are in touch with the debate will question the possibility of obtaining valid and reliable data through qualitative and participatory methodologies. Maxwell draws our attention to the fact that validity always relates to data or interpretation of data. Methods are appropriately or inappropriately used to obtain data. An inappropriate choice of methods or the misuse of methods can be a threat to obtaining valid data (Maxwell 1992). In the literature about validity and reliability in qualitative research a variety of terms is used. While some authors refer to validity and reliability, others, such as Patton (1990) and Pretty (1993), use words like 'trustworthiness' and 'credibility' to address the concept of validity in qualitative research. They argue that the threats to validity and the ways we try to ensure validity are different when using qualitative from when using quantitative methods. To avoid confusion they suggest the use of a different terminology. The validity of research findings can be assessed in various ways. This may be done for example, by those responsible for data collection checking with participants in the research that the information collected from them accurately reflects the meanings respondents have sought to convey. In the course of data collection interpretation of data and conclusions drawn by researchers can be confirmed or disputed by the respondents. If the findings are confirmed as accurate then the credibility of the findings is increased greatly. Another way of enhancing credibility would be to hold occasional meetings with peer groups from the same community but otherwise not involved in the study. This helps researchers become aware of possible gaps, bias or error that they might otherwise have not been aware of without careful searching and probing for accuracy in meanings. PR, like qualitative research, seeks to examine and reflect the full context as far as possible by providing detailed information about the research community and offering precise quotations that validate statements on which findings are based (Pretty 1993). Tolley and Bentley, in chapter 5 in this volume, emphasize the need to offer trainees in PR the possibility of learning to cross-check information by using a mix of methods and of discussing an issue with different groups in the community.

Different interpretations of PR

Different interpretations are given to PR. These range from the researcher and research community designing the research together, researchers designing the study and then collecting data with the help of the community, to the community working closely with the assistance of a non-governmental organization (NGO). For some, PR means involving field-level health workers in the research in order to sensitize them to the needs of the community; for others it means research which is an integrated part of a process towards empowerment and emancipation. We think it is important to avoid adopting a purist attitude towards participatory research. At the same time it should be recognized that participation should genuinely be empowering and not just a situation where local people work with a researcher for the latter's convenience.

The quality of participation in PR can be evaluated by addressing a series of questions to the research process. For example, does community participation occur at all stages of the research (initiation, design, data collection and analysis, interpretation of data, discussion, presentation and dissemination of findings) and, just as important, which groups in the community are represented in which of these processes? There may be several reasons why representative participation of the research community has not occurred at all these stages. The research may not have focused sufficiently on local needs, or particular technical skills may be required which at the time the research community members may not possess, or the research community may have more pressing priorities, such as care of dependants, or ensuring a daily income to the household (Pratt &

Loizos 1992). On the other hand, lack of participation may occur because the researchers want to maintain their control over the research process. Some of these issues can be usefully addressed to the PR process in order to evaluate the quality or lack of quality of participation and to identify reasons for this. One of the unique qualities of PR is that of serving the shared interests of both researchers and researched. This may come about through a complex and often long-term process of negotiation. In her contribution to this volume, Marion Martin in chapter 8 examines aspects of this complex process of negotiation, with a particular focus on the movement of power between researcher and researched community. She does so in the light of her experiences working with a well-woman group in the United Kingdom.

Participatory research goes beyond documenting local people's needs and perspectives. PR emphasizes the *process* of knowledge production. First, it helps especially marginalized and deprived people to gain self-confidence and pride in being able to provide a useful contribution to community life. Second, it builds respect and empathy in professional groups for the insights and knowledge people have and the problems they face. Third, listening to local people helps to avoid mistakes and to develop programmes that take into account the specific situation and conditions which will influence the outcome of programmes (Chambers 1983). It helps to explain why interventions are not or are only partly successful. For example, visualization methods such as body mapping combined with individual and group interviews have emerged as useful in documenting and understanding local people's concepts of their body, providing a starting-point for improved communication about sexual practices between health professionals and the women in the communities involved in the research (MacCormack 1985).

Whilst the use of qualitative research in health and the concept of community participation have been discussed at length in a variety of professional journals, practices in, and concepts of, PR are much less shared and discussed. The aim of this volume is to present an overview of the historical and more recent development of PR and to share experiences and reflections on practice in a variety of settings in the field of health.

History of participatory research

The initial development of PR or participatory action research (PAR), as it is also called, originated in countries in Latin America, Africa and Asia. The common ground in the push towards this practice was the concern with persistent inequalities in the distribution of power and resources, and the processes which help to keep in place dependency and domination in the relationships between privileged dominant and marginalized groups of people. There was a growing awareness that to fight oppression and alleviate poverty one needed to address the feeling of helplessness that is associated with it. Pioneers in PR such as Fernandes and Tandon, Fals-Borda and Rahman, and Hall emphasize the need to link research with empowering education and action (Fals-Borda & Rahman 1991; Fernandes & Tandon 1981; Hall 1981). Budd Hall was one of the first writers also to emphasize PR's importance in the development of health programmes (Hall 1981). The emphasis in primary health care (PHC) on community participation has encouraged health professionals to look at the implications and relationships between that and research. Many of the initial applications centred around involvement of communities and health professionals at field level in needs assessment, planning and evaluation of programmes (Feuerstein 1988, MacDonald 1986, Nichter 1984). Since then other influences have contributed to further development of participatory research. In the last twenty years it has become more familiar in a diversity of disciplines and settings such as rural development and agriculture, community development, health and education.[2]

A more in-depth discussion of historical and contemporary influences on PR is presented by Rajesh Tandon in Chapter 2.

Educational processes and PR

Education has played an important role in the development of the concept of PR. The educational aspects involved in a participatory research process were a central element in the practice of adult educators in the South. They were the first to articulate the phrase 'participatory research' and promoted PR through the International Council for Adult Education. Adult educators in their education practice genuinely believed in education that helped the learners to establish control over their own learning process. Based on this experience and the realization that their research practice contradicted their education practice they started to reformulate their approach to research (Tandon 1988). Many contributors to this volume restate the emancipatory, transformative character of PR. Maguire, for example, states that:

> PR can be utilized to create knowledge and take collective action, short and long term, for potentially emancipatory, transformative structural and personal change.

Action for social change requires an educational process in which researcher and participants develop a critical awareness of circumstances influencing their lives, reflect on what this means in their individual and communal situation and decide what action would be most important and feasible to take.

Linking the process of knowing to learning and action

Paulo Freire had an important input in linking the process of knowing and learning. Linking knowing and learning through an ongoing cycle of action and reflection, leads to the development of a critical awareness about the world participants live in (Freire 1972). Freire's critical pedagogy has had a significant influence on the work of adult educators and others involved in education for liberation. An example of an application of his work in the field of health is found in the three volumes of *Training for Transformation* (Hope & Timmel 1984). These are based on projects implemented in Kenya and Zimbabwe.

It is not possible within the limited space available to discuss Freire's work comprehensively. His widespread influence on the development of participatory research, however, also shown by the range of contributors to this book who refer to his pedagogy, warrants a more in-depth discussion of some aspects. Facets which have a direct bearing on the PR process include his ideas about the different aims educational processes can pursue and the reasons for linking knowing, learning and action. Freire critiques general practices in education and asserts that most educational activities do not challenge inequalities in the learners' lives but keep them passive and uncritical. This 'domesticating' approach to education fails to help people break through apathy and question the situation they are forced to live in. People who have lived their lives in marginalized and deprived positions need to develop a critical insight into the structures, ideas and practices in society and themselves that place and maintain them in positions of inequality. They can then develop initiatives to change this situation. An example of this in the field of health would be teaching people in a didactic fashion about matters of hygiene and nutritious foods. Such an approach fails to enable them critically to question and come to recognize the reasons why, for example, water supplies are inadequate and food is short, and look at ways in which political, social and personal action can change this situation.

Freire's alternative 'education for liberation' has as its main goal the dynamic development towards a 'critical consciousness'. The advancement towards a critical consciousness evolves through a dynamic process which is informed by critical thought and action. The dynamic nature of this process is captured in the term 'critical transitivity of the group' and a 'critical transitive' individual: 'A critical transitive thinker feels empowered to think and to act on the conditions around her or him, and relates those conditions to the larger contexts of power in society' (Shor 1993:32). Research practices which take away information and knowledge, no matter how valuable in other respects, miss the opportunity to contribute to a process of thinking, reflecting and acting, and deny groups in the community the chance to fight inequalities.

The implication for research that wants to address inequalities is that it must become a continuing process of learning which integrates research, reflection and action. The consequences, opportunities and difficulties encountered in implementing such an ongoing learning process for research in health and especially health promotion are illustrated by some case studies which are expanded in this volume.

Annie George in chapter 11 draws our attention to the problems encountered when research is carried out by academics whose institutions and funding agencies have expectations, which make an ongoing process problematic. She illustrates the need for an ongoing process after the academics have completed their research. While exploring the meaning of sexuality during focus group discussions, poor women in Bombay shared painful experiences in their lives, established a bond with the other women in the group and discussed the opportunity for collective actions for change. The effects of participating in the research for the women involved differed, depending on the possibilities women had to integrate this experience into continuing action. In groups which were called together by NGOs, whose service did not provide the opportunity to absorb the experiences of women into their ongoing work, the research process reinforced a woman's lack of choices to make immediate changes in her life situation. This experience is contrasted with the experience of working with an existing group of women. As George says: 'For this group of women, the focus-group meetings were a means in their ongoing process of analysing the various forces which were bottlenecks in their search for greater autonomy'.

The implications of the above case study are not necessarily that research should not be carried out by professional researchers. The study merely reinforces the point that researchers need: to seek alliances with groups already in existence; to evaluate carefully the opportunity for groups initiated by the research to continue; to examine how the outcomes of the study can be integrated into existing services; and to look at how community action and lobbying for change can be supported. Furthermore, although there is a need to develop clarity in what it is we aim for in participatory research, there is also a danger in promoting a purist form of PR. A significant value of the contributions and case studies presented in this volume lies in their reflection on the experiences they relate and the descriptions of problems and constraints. Entry points can be identified. As Maguire presents it in chapter 3, we need to: 'look for ways to move deliberately along the participatory continuum'.

To ensure that research can be integrated into further action, different options are suggested. One is the involvement of NGOs, and possibly government agencies, and participants in the early stages of the research. A participatory planning framework used in a training with health professionals working in the NHS in Britain is presented by Grindl Dockery (chapter 15). Mavalankar et al. (chapter 19) and Dockery highlight the difficulties encountered when introducing such an initiative in government and in strongly service-oriented organizations.

Bloem et al. (chapter 13) and Okurut et al. (chapter 7) illustrate the opportunity for an ongoing process into which research is integrated. They present case studies of implementing research, education and development initiatives in projects in Bangladesh and Uganda which have a strong community involvement. Renu Khanna (chapter 6) shows in her case study of a women's health programme how initiatives to improve health from a biomedical perspective can be integrated into the overall aim of women's empowerment. The programme started with the training of traditional birth attendants which emphasized a learning process aimed at women's empowerment as well as teaching how to perform an aseptic delivery. This project illustrates how ongoing work with women went through a long process of shared learning which led to changes in ideas, insights and knowledge, increased self-confidence, and changes in the perceptions of the women both of themselves and of their bodies. This influenced and changed relationships with others such as husbands and health workers and culminated at community level in women organizing themselves for collective action around their own issues. Khanna presents a model for the development from intra- and interpersonal development to group- and community-level action and changes. This model can be seen as a cyclical spiralling movement where group and community action lead to further intra- and interpersonal development and vice versa.

Personal, interpersonal and collective development and action

Viewing intra- and interpersonal change and community action as interwoven aspects of development towards a critical consciousness is a powerful aspect in Freire's pedagogy and in feminist theory and practice (Freire 1972; Weiler 1991). Ira Shor indicates that critical consciousness can be described as having four qualities: power awareness, critical literacy, desocialization, and self-organization/self-education. Critical literacy means: analytical habits of thinking which go beneath surface impressions, mere opinions and clichés; understanding of social contexts; and discovering the deeper meaning of any subject matter, text, process and situation. Desocialization means recognizing and challenging the myths, values and language learned, and critically examining values operating in society (Shor 1993:32). Internalized images are an important and often insufficiently recognized concept in health education and link up with the potential of badly thought-out educational activities which blame the victim. To give messages to people without investigating what people already know and what are the reasons for health problems is potentially harmful. Freire has pointed out how formal education and a lifelong experience of being named and described by others leads to the internalization of images of oneself based on the perceptions of others. In keeping with his theory, educational activities can have the effect of strengthening negative images people have of themselves. For example:

A play is shown to a group of mothers during a mother and child health (MCH) clinic which aims to show the value of good nutrition. In the play there are two mothers. One feeds her child three times a day and has a happy healthy child. The other feeds her child only maize twice a day and has a malnourished child. The health worker then explains to the mothers how they should feed the child using locally available foods. The mother who watches the play and feeds her child only maize twice a day might be made to feel a failure, who does not look after her child well. She might already feel 'good for nothing' because no matter what she tries it will not help. The landlord has just told her not to come back so she will not be able to take the left-over cobs; her husband has not sent money for a while now and the goat from the neighbour has just eaten the young vegetables she planted in her kitchen garden. She might think: 'The play is right, I am good for nothing'. (de Koning 1995)

Freire's theory has implications for the strong focus on individual behaviour change in most health education practice and raises questions around the concept of 'informed choice'. How much choice has the mother in the above example to put the knowledge about nutritious foods into practice? Henriette Moore draws our attention to the debate about the suitability of the terms 'choice' and 'resistance' for analysing processes that are not always conscious or strategic:

Oppressed groups frequently develop their own discourses that work in contra-distinction to dominant ones, but the questions are, can people actively recognize and choose the subject positions they take up, and to what degree are they able to resist the terms of the dominant discourses? (Moore 1994:4)

Moore debates this issue in relation to the discussions of gender identity and gendered subjectivity, and the relationship of the individual to the social and vice versa. Theories about subject positions and individual and collective identities are not only relevant to issues related to gender, class and race but have implications also for theory and practice in health education.

One implication is that we need to question how the description of the ways in which behaviour affects the occurrence of disease is helpful in influencing and enabling individual and social change. One question that can be asked is related to the generalized description of at-risk groups, at-risk behaviour and identification as being-at-risk, when subsequent interventions do not enable individuals and groups in giving meaning to and reflecting on the implications of these descriptions.[3] For example, how helpful is it for a young woman to be informed that having sex can put her at risk of HIV/AIDS without giving her the space to reflect and analyse what the decision to have or not have sex entails. She needs to become conscious, in as far as this is possible, of the factors which influence her decision before we can start calling it a decision. How far does she desire to have sex, what are her fantasies about the type of girl she would like to be or she thinks others would like her to be? Where do these fantasies come from? What is the meaning to her of conflicting ideas about what is acceptable behaviour held, for example, by parents on the one hand and important peers on the other, and what are the consequences of taking up a certain position? PR that aims for empowerment and self-determination needs seriously to provide the space for analysis, and reflection on what are the series of congruent and conflicting ideas, self-images, self-representations, fantasies and desires which underlie and make up, for example, an adolescent girl's or boy's position in relation to compliance with, or resistance to, discourses on sexual practices.

Issues around the relationship of the individual to the social also have implications for the way we look at unreflected experience. There is a danger in looking at experience and at information and knowledge as a static given. PRA methods with their emphasis on visualizations, working with groups and the use of drama offer valuable entry points for setting a process of reflection into motion. The requirement is that the methods are used as a trigger for discussion and reflection in addition to documenting the position, ideas and practices which formed the starting-point.

Implications for the role of the facilitator

A process of critical reflection and action is developed to enable us to become aware of where the images, ideas, positions and opinions we have of ourselves and others come from, and to gain the possibility of giving a different meaning to who we are and a different direction to our lives. The use of 'us' and 'we' is important in this context. It is not only the poor, illiterate, and other categories of people classified as marginalized and deprived who need to think about how, in what ways and why they experience themselves and the world as they do. It is equally important for more privileged groups such as health professionals, researchers and activists to do the same. Meulenberg-Buskens in chapter 4, among others, stresses the importance of congruence, which means acting in accordance with the principles in PR when facilitating a training, conducting research and living our lives. In reflection on what was learned in relation to the role of facilitators, planners and researchers, Khanna states in chapter 6 that:

PAR requires an attitude of mutuality, an openness and a commitment to learning on the part of all those involved. These words have acquired a different meaning for us, as programme planners: we have really learnt how difficult it is to open ourselves as recipients of traditional knowledge. And how difficult it is to leave the position of those who have all the answers.

Desocialization relates to 'recognizing and challenging the myths, values, behaviours and language learned in mass culture; critically examining the regressive values operating in society, which are internalized into consciousness' (Shor 1993:32). To facilitate a PR process which enables people to become conscious of their internalized images, and norm and value systems which are taken for granted, requires a long-term process and workers who have the insight and skills to facilitate such a process. One of the problems in implementing PR in health is the emphasis in health worker training on a biomedical model of health as the only valid framework to explain disease, while communication skills are limited frequently to didactic teaching of groups and giving advice to individuals. Health systems often maintain a strict working hierarchy, leaving field-workers with a similar feeling of helplessness and dependency in their work situation as disempowered groups in the community feel in theirs. Given, however, that it is the health workers at health centre, sub-health centre and aid-post level who need to sustain a long-term communication with communities, it is as important to look at the empowerment and training of health workers in PR as it is for groups in the community.

Verbal and non-verbal communication

Critical reflection and co-learning, verbal and written communication are not the only, nor perhaps the most powerful, forms of communication. The use of visualization methods, such as drawings, charts, maps and drama, can be a powerful strategy to come to a shared analysis of, and critical reflection on a situation. Andrea Cornwall (Chapter 9) draws our attention to the many things that cannot be shared verbally. Sensitive or emotional issues, styles of interaction involved in persuasion, material and body expressions of domination, resistance and bargaining cannot easily be described. She provides an overview of the benefits of visualizations, including the use of drama. One of the editor's own experiences in conducting drama workshops with students from different countries in the UK, and groups of adolescents in Papua New Guinea, shows the potential of drama for acting out and searching for different ways of behaving, triggering a discussion on reasons for individual behaviour and relating these to a wider social and cultural context. The production of a play offers the space to share insights, knowledge and experiences. The observation and analysis of symbolic meaning expressed in body language and the use of space help to describe, reflect on and place in context emotions and attitudes. In the development of

'Theatre of the Oppressed' Boal goes beyond the use of drama which separates actors and spectators. Theatre is based on the observation of how people act in their daily lives and therefore everybody can be an actor. In what he calls forum theatre, discussion and dialogue are replaced by drawing the spectators onto the stage to act and through their acting to give a new direction to what happens in the play (Boal 1992).

The use of drama in the field of health is illustrated in this volume by the contributions of Preston-Whyte and Dalrymple (Chapter 10), and Howard-Grabman (Chapter 14). Preston-Whyte and Dalrymple found that workshops which followed the style of a formal talk did not elicit much response on issues around HIV/AIDS and sexuality. They then developed a drama workshop for teachers, who were encouraged to use this method with their pupils. The development of the plays in which school children, for example, 'graphically portray the scene in bars in which older men persuade young girls to have sex with them' shows the potential of drama to trigger an in-depth discussion about the reasons for girls consenting to sex, and an acting-out of different interactions. Although the plays at the moment are very much aimed at disseminating messages without discussion or critical reflection, the potential for addressing issues around gender roles, sexuality, reasons for resistance and consent are recognized, and ways to introduce this are sought. Howard-Grabman describes the use of drama for eliciting women's views on issues and problems related to maternal health.

The issue of difference in PR: gender and other factors

An important influence on the debate and development of PR is the feminist movement. Feminist researchers and action groups in different countries have emphasized the differing experience of women and men and the need to enable groups of women to pose problems, and to subvert private and public decision-making processes and relationships. PR aims to work with the poor to enable them to take more control over their lives. But who are these poor people? There is a danger in the use of categories such as 'the poor' which implies that communities of poor people are homogeneous entities. Feminist theory and practice have highlighted the need to look at the differing experiences of women and men to question all seemingly homogeneous categories. Several aspects play a role in the study of difference. One of the issues is who is actually given a voice by being included as participants, and whose ideas are informing the results. Maguire has documented how the specific context of PR, as it emerged in the 1970s, centred around male power, perceptions, problems and experiences. This male-centred view failed to recognize women's differing experience, and gender issues were not on the agenda. The feminist movement has started to re-address the male bias of many research projects other than all-women PR projects, where knowledge is both provided and produced by men, and women are largely excluded and invisible (Maguire 1987).

The use of abstract categories such as 'the oppressed' or 'the poor' raises further questions about difference, both in terms of the development of theory and in practice. Paulo Freire, like many other men writing about human experience in the sixties, failed to address differences between and among groups of oppressed people. By treating the poor as a single category, Freire suggested that the meaning of oppression and paths of action towards liberation were the same for all oppressed people. His examples include bosses oppressing workers, and men oppressing other men (Freire 1972), but he failed to look at situations where, for example, men who are oppressed in the workplace return home to become oppressors of their wives or daughters and sons (Weiler 1991).[4]

The use of 'women' as a unified category has been challenged by feminists in developing countries. They show us that the meaning of being a woman differs, depending on the specific place, situation and time. Many feminist and all-women PR projects have started to address the issue of difference. Alice Welbourn shows how the use of different PRA methods enabled her and the participants to document and raise awareness about the different experiences, insights and ideas of individual women and groups of women (Welbourn 1992).

It is one thing to identify differences but another to deal with the conflicting interests that emerge. Reports on the use of PRA/RAP and other qualitative research methods have emphasized the following: insights provided by these methods into what different groups of people know, think and feel; the enhanced confidence of participants in their capability to produce valuable knowledge and insights; and the effect that sharing experiences and knowledge has on the ability of communities to recognize different and in-common perspectives. Generally very little insight is given into the negotiating of different interests within the larger community. Obviously it is much more difficult for less influential groups to have their interests taken on board if these are in conflict with the interests of others. Worse, action taken by a group which has not thought through the potential backlash (and if and how it can cope with that) can be a disempowering experience. This can lead to lack of hope and confidence in the possibility of change. Strategic planning of action should include, therefore, the anticipation of possible reactions and how they will influence the development of a particular group. It is an essential part of enabling less powerful groups to act in their own interest.[5]

The question of how to negotiate the needs and priorities of different interest groups has direct implications for policy makers and planners in health and development. One possible practice is advocacy and lobbying to get interests taken on board by special interest groups. There is a need to look at the role of governments, donor agencies and their workers in providing a space for the least powerful groups to have a voice and to give them the possibility to influence decision-making.

Influences on ways knowledge production is perceived

Tandon highlights the influence of critical social theory and phenomenology (a philosophy which recognizes bodily experience as an important source of knowledge) on what are seen as legitimate ways of knowing. Insights derived from these perspectives emphasize that knowledge is conditioned by the historical context in which it develops, and that lived experience is implicated, albeit in a problematic way, in the creation of knowledge. Tandon and Maguire draw our attention to the implications of the notion that knowledge is historically produced, mediated and legitimized from the perspectives of the dominant classes. PR, as an alternative to research determined by the dominant groups, aims to produce knowledge from the perspectives of marginalized, deprived and oppressed groups of people and classes, and in so doing so aims to transform social realities.

Foucault's theory of how knowledge is produced and how power operates provides a useful framework for looking at the process of changing social realities. Arguably his greatest contribution to PR is his position on power relations. In Foucault's opinion, knowledge production is not the result of simple bipolar relations of power and powerlessness. Relations of power take specific forms in particular societies, and are organized through, for example, relations of class, race, gender, religion, sexual preference and age. In Foucauldian theory there is a direct relationship between the production of knowledge, social practices, and ways of being. Dominant knowledge systems can be resisted, consciously or subconsciously, by alternative perceptions and forms of knowledge. Alternative forms of knowledge exist and/or are produced at individual and group levels and their social power is increased through sharing and a winning over of others to accept these forms of knowledge (Weedon 1987).

Andrea Cornwall shows in her work with local women and health workers how the conceptual framework, introduced by health workers, of what contraceptives do to women's bodies did not fit the knowledge local women had about their bodies. Because of this, both health workers and women were left with a feeling of being inadequate. Cornwall then describes how individual drawings of the body and its functions, by local women and researchers, helped both groups to visualize, discuss and understand the different frameworks. Subsequent drawings in small groups and discussions about what was an acceptable framework to explain women's bodies and the working of the Pill produced a new commonly accepted framework. As Cornwall (1994) puts it:

> The idea of giving people information implies that knowledge is a thing that can be acquired or lost, rather than a process which is always in the making. We know our bodies in many different ways; our knowledge is dynamic, changing with new experiences; they too are in flux.

Different interpretations of what constitutes reality potentially have the power to influence services provided and action taken. The model emphasized depends on the power relationships between the different agents involved. Susan Rifkin makes clear how in the field of health, the bio-medical model and medical practitioners have a powerful influence on what is seen as health, and on what services should be provided and what policies developed (Rifkin 1994). The commonly accepted view is that the health worker holds power and that the local women are powerless. From a Foucauldian point of view we need to look at how each has the potential to accept, challenge or ignore the perspective of the other. Even if one ignores the view of the other, the other's perspective still exists to influence what types of information are acceptable, as in the example of working with women in body mapping. Where health workers ignored or could not understand local knowledge and perceptions of women's bodies, and presented a framework from a Western medical point of view, they had the power to decide what is taught and how but, nonetheless, this did not mean that the perspective of local women had disappeared. The role of PR, then, can be to acknowledge and help differing perspectives to emerge and to strengthen participants' confidence to explore their own views.

The practical implications of the issues addressed above can be summarized as the need to search for ways in which PR can be part of an ongoing process, a process which integrates the following aspects:

- acknowledging that the power relationship between the researcher and the researched is problematic;
- identifying training needs for practitioners in PR;
- confirming knowledge produced by 'common people';
- developing a process of critical reflection on reality;
- placing the production of knowledge and action within a specific context;
- an emphasis on community action; and
- developing ways in which different interests can be negotiated by less powerful groups.

At the same time as trying to put these processes into practice it is necessary to remain aware of the problems and constraints involved. It is, therefore, more helpful continuously to look for entry points to develop a next step, rather than to demand that the ideal be put into practice tomorrow.

Notes

1. We would like to acknowledge Beth Humphries and Margrit Shildrick for their helpful comments on this chapter.
2. The latest book of Orlando Fals-Borda and M.A. Rahman (1991) provides a useful overview of the widespread geographical and disciplinary applications of PAR and related initiatives.
3. In addition, there is a need to look at the hazardous implications of describing stereotyped at-risk groups rather than at-risk behaviour as if these groups have a collective identity. For the debate on the hazardous nature of the description of at-risk groups, see Frankenberg (1994) and Schiller et al. (1994).
4. Paulo Freire does acknowledge the feminist critique of his work in later publications. He also expressed the wish to place the critique of his earlier writings in the historical context in which they were written (Freire, in McLaren & Leonard 1993).
5. A helpful theoretical framework for examining issues around who determines need is provided by Fraser (1989). Janet Price (1992) explores the relevance of Fraser's model to Women in Development in the context of women's empowerment.

References

Annett, H. & Rifkin, S. (1988) *Guidelines for Rapid Appraisal to Assess Community Health Needs: A Focus on Health Improvements for Low-income Urban Areas,* WHO (Division of Strengthening of Health Services), Geneva.

Aubel, J. (1990–1) 'From qualitative community data collection to programme design: health education planning in Niger', *International Quarterly of Community Health Education,* Vol.1(4), pp.345-69.

Aubel, J. & Mansour, M. (1989) 'Qualitative community health research: a Tunisian example', *Health Policy and Planning,* Vol.4(3), pp.244-56.

Bentley, M. et al. (1988) 'Rapid ethnographic assessment: applications in a diarrhoea management programme', *Social Science and Medicine,* Vol.27(1), pp.107-16.

Boal, A. (1992) *Games for Actors and Non-actors,* Routledge.

Chambers, R. (1990) 'Rapid and participatory appraisal for health and nutrition', *Paper for the Silver Jubilee Celebrations of the Nutrition Society of India,* Administrative Staff College of India.

Chambers, R. (1983) *Rural Development: Putting the Last First,* Longman Group (FE) Ltd, England.

Cornwall, A. (1994) 'Sharing ideas: bridging the gap between medical messages and local understandings', in de Koning, K. (ed.) (1994), pp.109-12.

Fals-Borda, O. & Rahman, M.A. (1991) *Action and Knowledge: Breaking the Monopoly with Participatory Action-research,* Apex Press, New York.

Fernandes, W. & Tandon, R. (1981) *Participatory Research and Evaluation: Experiments in Research as a Process of Liberation*, Indian Social Institute, New Delhi.

Feuerstein, M.T. (1988) 'Finding the methods to fit the people: training for participatory research', *Community Development Journal*, Vol.23(1), pp.16-25.

Frankenberg, R.J. (1994) 'The impact of HIV/AIDS on concepts relating to risk and culture within British community epidemiology: candidates or targets for prevention', *Social Science and Medicine*, Vol.38(10), pp.1325-35.

Fraser, N. (1989) 'Struggle over needs: outline of a socialist-feminist critical theory of late-capitalist political culture', *Unruly Practices: Power, Discourse and Gender in Contemporary Social Theory*, Policy Press, pp.161-90.

Freire, P. (1972) *Pedagogy of the Oppressed*, Penguin, Harmondsworth, England.

Grandstaff, S.W., Grandstaff, T.B. & Lovelace, G.W. (1987) 'Summary Report', *Proceedings from the 1985 International Conference on Rapid Rural Appraisal*, Khon Kaen, Thailand, Khon Kaen University, pp.5-8.

Hall, B. L. (1981) 'Participatory research, popular knowledge and power: a personal reflection', *Convergence*, Vol.XIV(3), pp.6-17.

Hope, A. & Timmel, S. (1984) *Training for Transformation*, 3 volumes, Mambo Press, Zimbabwe.

de Koning, K. (ed.) (1994) *Proceedings of the International Symposium on Participatory Research in Health Promotion*, Education Resource Group, Liverpool School of Tropical Medicine, UK.

de Koning, K. (1995) 'Creating confidence', *Health Action*, Issue 11, December 1994 - February 1995.

Lammerink, M, & Wolffers, I. (eds) (1994) *Some Selected Examples of Participatory Research*, Special Programme on Research (DGIS/DST/SO), Ministry of Foreign Affairs, PO Box 200061, 2500 EB The Hague, The Netherlands.

MacCormack, C. (1985) 'Lay perceptions affecting utilization of family-planning services in Jamaica', *Journal of Tropical Medicine and Hygiene*, Vol.88, pp.281-5.

MacDonald, J.J (1986) *Participatory Evaluation and Planning as an Essential Part of Community Development*, PhD thesis, University of Manchester.

McLaren, P. & Leonard, P. (1993) *Paulo Freire: A Critique Encounter*, Routledge, London.

Maguire, P. (1987) *Doing Participatory Research: A Feminist Approach*, Center for International Education, School of Education, University of Massachusetts, USA.

Maxwell, J.A. (1992) 'Understanding and validity in qualitative research', *Harvard Educational Review*, Vol.62(3).

Moore, H. (1994) *A Passion for Difference*, Indiana University Press.

Nichter, M. (1984) 'Project community diagnosis: participatory research as a first step toward community involvement in primary health care', *Social Science and Medicine*, Vol.19(3), pp.237-52.

Patton, M.Q. (1990, 2nd ed.) *Qualitative Evaluation and Research Methods*, SAGE Publications, USA.

Pratt, B. & Loizos, P. (1992)   *Choosing Research Methods: Data Collection for Development Workers*, Development Guidelines, No.7, Oxfam.

Pretty, J.N. (1993) *Criteria for Trustworthiness* (excerpts from a paper on participatory inquiry).

Price, J. (1992) 'Who determines need? A case study of a women's organization in North India', *Institute of Development Studies Bulletin*, Vol.23(1).

Ramakrishna, J. & Brieger, W.R. (1987) 'The value of qualitative research: health education in Nigeria', *Health Policy and Planning*, Vol.2(2), pp.171-5.

Rifkin, S.B.D. (1994) 'Participation and research in health', in de Koning, K. (ed.) (1994), pp.20-25.

Schiller, N.G. et al. (1994) 'Risky business: the cultural construction of AIDS risk groups', *Social Science and Medicine*, Vol.38(10), pp.1337-46.

Scrimshaw, S.C.M. & Hurtado, E. (1987) *Rapid Assessment Procedures for Nutrition and Primary Health Care. Anthropological Approaches to Improving Programme Effectiveness*, Tokyo, United Nations University, UCLA Latin American Center Publications, Los Angeles, University of California.

Shor, I. (1993) *Education is Politics*, in McLaren, P. & Leonard, P. (1993).

Tandon, R. (1988) 'Social transformation and participatory research', *Convergence*, Vol.XXI(2– 3).

Varkevisser, C., Alihonou, E. & Inoussa, S. (1993) *Rapid Appraisal of Health and Nutrition in a PHC Project in Pahou, Benin*, Centre Regional pour le Developpement et la Sante (CREDESA); Amsterdam: Royal Tropical Institute (KIT).

Vlassoff, C. & Tanner, M. (1992) 'The relevance of rapid assessment to health research and interventions', *Healthy Policy and Planning*, Vol.7(1), pp.1-9.

Weedon, C. (1987) *Feminist Practice and Post-structuralist Theory*, Basil Blackwell, Oxford.

Weiler, K. (1991) 'Freire and a feminist pedagogy of difference', *Harvard Educational Review*, Vol.61(4), pp.449-74.

Welbourn, A. (1992) 'Rapid rural appraisal, gender and health – alternative ways of listening to needs', *Institute of Development Studies Bulletin*, Vol.23(1), 8-18.

WHO (World Health Organization) (1973) *Organizational Study on Methods of Promoting the Development of Basic Health Services*, Geneva.

PART I AN HISTORICAL THEORETICAL PERSPECTIVE TO PR

2 The historical roots and contemporary tendencies in participatory research: implications for health care

Rajesh Tandon

Context

The history of human civilization is also the history of education and science. In fact, one of the most critical dimensions in which human species have distinguished themselves from other forms of life is their intellectual capacity. Both education and science are built on this foundation. Throughout human civilization, therefore, different forms, approaches, methodologies and outcomes of education have been evolved, practised and abandoned. Similarly, science, even in its modern conception, has existed throughout much of human history. It was science which allowed human civilization to live with nature; some of it became science which encouraged human beings to control nature.

Further examination of this theme could indicate also that models and paradigms of development of human civilization have also been influenced significantly by, as well as influencing, systems of education and science. It has become obvious that people-centred, participatory development as an alternative paradigm of development is not possible within the framework of modern science and modern education (Tandon 1991). In a sense, modern science is built on the premise of destroying the system of science and education which was labelled as 'traditional', 'indigenous' or 'popular'.

These issues have acquired further salience in the contemporary context. Significant changes are taking place throughout the world, and human civilization is poised for the next phase of its life, or death. Contemporary society can truly be called the knowledge society. A huge number of occupations and a large number of people are engaged in the information and information-processing industry, and in the knowledge generation, production and dissemination industry. Diverse forms of organizations, systems, networks and institutions have emerged within this knowledge society. Sophisticated specialization and evolution of methodology have taken place in the production and dissemination of knowledge. Global dimensions of the knowledge society are increasingly influencing the research agenda within countries, universities and other institutions. In fact, the pressure to establish a globally accepted intellectual property right will be the hallmark of the culmination of the knowledge society.

History

It is within this broader contemporary reality that a critical assessment of alternative conceptualizations of science and education needs to be posited. PR, evolved over the last twenty years, is one such alternative formulation. It became visible in the early to mid 1970s. In its early formulations, PR was seen as an alternative social science research method which challenged the very premises on which traditional social-science research methodology was based: the premises of neutrality, objectivity and value-free character. The distance between the researcher and the researched, the dichotomy of the subject and object, the reliance on statistical and quantifiable techniques all were subjected to a comprehensive critique (Hall et al. 1982). As part of its history, therefore, it is important to recognize six significant trends that seem to have converged to contribute to the evolution of the concept and the practice of PR.

The first and the foremost was a debate about the sociology of knowledge and its implications for epistemological formulation (forms of knowing) throughout human civilization. This debate continues to pose the question that knowledge of human civilization is conditioned by historical context (Habermas 1971). Therefore, with human history. It is within this framework that alternative views of history, of struggle and of social transformation were posited. The most famous of these collections came to be known as Subaltern Studies. These presented a view of society, human order and human history from the position of the marginalized, the poor and the deprived as opposed to the dominant form of knowledge produced and articulated throughout history from the point of view of the rulers, the kings, the brahmins.

The second historical trend which in fact stimulated the very first articulation of the phrase 'participatory research' came from the practice of adult educators in the countries of the South. As genuine believers in adult learning and in facilitating a horizontal dialogue between the teacher and the learner, adult educators evolved a methodology of learning and education which helped to establish the control of the learner over her or his own learning process. The same adult educators, trained as professionals and engaged in systematic research, particularly around the outcomes of their own interventions, began to face the contradiction that was rooted in their training as researchers. As professionally trained researchers they began to distance themselves from the learner, establish one-way control in their hands over the research process and pretend to carry out their research in a manner which had little or no impact on the learner him/herself. This contradiction began to result in the reformulation, both in theory and in practice, of a view of research which was sympathetic to, integrated and congruent with the premises on which the practice of adult education was rooted. It is here that, in 1974-75, the phrase 'participatory research' was first projected and disseminated through this group of adult educators and subsequently promoted through the International Council for Adult Education and its national and regional member organizations throughout the world (Tandon 1988).

The third parallel and interrelated support to the ideas and practice of PR came from the work of Paulo Freire and Ivan Illich. Illich's critique of schooling in modern societies and Freire's contribution to an alternative pedagogy became the basis for linking PR as an educational process within the framework of popular education. A number of contributions related to this theme emerged in the late 1960s and early 1970s which paved the way for strengthening the arguments in favour of PR (Freire 1982). In particular, the processes of knowing and of education were shown to be interlinked, thereby reaffirming the fundamental human faculty of knowing, learning and reflecting. This gave further reinforcement to the argument promoted by adult educators in support of participatory research.

Another trend in the history of PR which travelled in parallel for a number of decades was the contribution of action research. In particular, action research challenged the myth of a static notion of research and inquiry. It argued for 'acting' as a basis of learning and knowing. This formulation of action research, going back to the work of Kurt Lewin, was recaptured in Latin America and subsequently became the basis for participatory action research (Fals-Borda 1985). It emphasized the notion of action as a legitimate mode of knowing, thereby taking the realm of knowledge into the field of practice.

A further trend which made a significant epistemological contribution to PR came from the work of phenomenologists (Solomon 1987). These contributions legitimated experience as a basis of knowing. This gave the impetus to human emotions and feelings as valid modes of knowing, along with action and cognition. The contribution of phenomenologists thereby expanded the basis of knowing beyond mere intellectual cognition. At the same time, experiential learning was recognized as a legitimate form of knowledge that could influence practice (Kolb 1984).

Finally, in the mid and late 1970s the debate on the development paradigm raised the question of participation – people's participation, women's participation, community participation, participation of those whose development is being attempted as central actors in their own development – as a critical variable. This received significant support from the emerging failures of top-down, expert-designed development projects and programmes. A fundamental tenet in the promotion of participation as a central concept in development is the requirement to use the knowledge and skills of those who are critical participants and central actors in the development process (Chambers 1983; Oakley 1991).

These historical trends in the evolution of PR are worth recalling because they represent the complexity in the evolution of the theory and practice of participatory research over the last two decades. Each trend has made its own unique and important contribution, both in the concrete practice of PR throughout the world as well as in elaborating its theoretical principles, methodology and epistemology.

Contemporary tendencies

Some significant tendencies have further developed the contemporary practice of PR. Many of these derive their roots from the historical trends and many are later developments.

The first important trend which has been re-articulated in the last few years is the new politics of science. It shows clearly that science based on instrumental rationality, based on the logic of manipulation and control of nature (both material and human nature) has been the basic tool of continued hegemony (power to rule) of the ruling classes (Dickson 1988). It is this science which has also been the basis of the expert-led, top-down, centralized model of development.

The second contemporary development is part of the long-standing historical trend of a linkage between ideology and education. It has been revised in the contemporary context where a large number of people in the South are beginning to be integrated into a global education order. In this situation, education is seen as a necessary part of their ideological preparation (Seminar 1992). Two contrasting streams of education have become visible once again. A system of education which perpetuates the status quo and socializes people into acceptance of the dominant order is based on the positivistic notions of modern science and knowledge enterprise. An alternative system of education which links education to social transformation is based on the traditions of popular knowledge and popular education. In a world at present divided into conflicting frameworks of a desirable future for humanity, the role of education and its links to ideology have become once again crucial instruments of regulation and control.

A third and significant contemporary development which has enriched the theory and practice of PR has its roots in feminist perspectives, struggles and contributions. On the one hand, feminist researchers have made a significant critique of the male bias and patriarchal roots of dominant science (Hubbard et al. 1982). They have challenged formulations about human endeavour and modes and forms of knowing (Bellenky et al. 1986; Cook & Fonow 1988). Highly revealing contributions from feminist ways of knowing and changing reality have strengthened the work of PR in the contemporary context (Maguire 1987).

The fourth contemporary influence which has reinforced many premises of PR has arisen from the ecological movement. Research in sustainable human life, ecological balance, and harmony has demonstrated the relevance of indigenous knowledge systems. The framework of knowledge acquired over centuries of struggle and survival by tribals and other indigenous communities throughout the world has found new support in the light of a growing critique of ecological degradation and destruction in modern societies (Colorado 1988; Heeralal 1993; Sen 1992).

A fifth contemporary tendency which has expanded the scope of original formulations of PR is demonstrated in many new methodological labels that have emerged in recent times. There is a growing body of literature available on participatory rural appraisal. This approach to analysing rural reality has evolved innovative techniques and tools which make the process of village-based investigations far more accessible and practical (Chambers 1992; SEARCH 1992). Similarly, new strength has been given to the forms of action research and its practice in diverse settings (Fals-Borda & Rahman 1991). Some of the most interesting forms of this have emerged in the work that has come from aboriginal educational systems, institutional development and community organizations (Human Relations 1993).

Another stream of work has been labelled 'new paradigm research' and has brought together a number of trends of PR in its practice of human social service, counselling, therapy and learning for slow learners.

Finally a number of practical applications of PR have emerged in the last decade. These have focused on evolving examples of people-centred development in organizing and mobilizing women, youth, tribals, workers and the marginalized. Applications of PR in training programmes and in systems of monitoring and evaluation have also grown immensely and further enriched PR's original formulations (Participatory Research in Asia 1987 and 1990). A number of examples have their origins in recent literature which described these applications and thereby contribute to further clarifying this vast alternative that was originally labelled PR.

PR and health care

What are the implications of the above dimensions of PR in health care? One of the important issues in the area of health care facing humanity at this juncture is the very definition of health and the location of respon-sibility in maintaining and improving the same. As in many other fields, the rise of expertise, specialization, technology and commercialization in the area of health care has also resulted in the very narrow definition of health as an issue only in situations where disease or ill-health occurs. Therefore, medicines, doctors, hospitals, surgery and treatment become important in any programme of health care far more than the people whose health is the purpose of any effort. It is similar to the question of trainers, training institutions and training technology acquiring far more significance than the learners and their learning in an educational enter-prise. In that framework, one of the first implications of the above dimensions of PR in the context of health care is a redefinition of health as part of life and as a dimension of lifstyle. Human health is not something independent of human life and human lifestyle. Therefore, meeting the essential prerequisites of life and living and ensuring a sustainable lifestyle become key variables affecting the status of health in any community. Highly consumptive, over-exploitative lifestyles are bound to be associated with numerous dimensions of ill-health. As PR has made amply clear, education, knowledge and learning are part of life and lifestyle. Health as part of a human variable is, therefore, no different.

The second implication of PR in health care is to find the value of relevant indigenous practices and knowledge systems. It is of great interest to participatory researchers that traditional health care practices and indigenous knowledge in child-bearing, the treatment of diseases and maintenance of harmony in the human body have been eroded and destroyed with the rise of modern medicine immediately after the Second World War. But in the last ten years, fresh interest in and the relevance of indigenous knowledge and practices have emerged. This renewed interest clearly testifies to the validity and appropriateness of indigenous knowledge in the area of health care. The most telling example of this, of course, is the return of breastfeeding, despite the attack from the 'bottle'.

A third significant implication for practitioners and promoters of health care in the light of the framework of PR is the need for demystification of, for example, modern knowledge, technology and medicine which are making the human being a dependent patient as opposed to an active agent in pursuit of her/his own health. To the extent that people themselves can be responsible for their health care, they must not be afraid of or confused by the rise of modern science and knowledge. Demystification of that modern science and knowledge and its easy, popular access become necessary factors in ensuring their ability to take responsibility for their health.

In the light of the above, the need to struggle to demand and acquire the right to know on the part of human beings and communities becomes evident. As applied to health care, this means the right to know about such things as health status, the causes of ill-health, the nature and type of treatment and resources available to improve health. This can then become a part of the larger societal struggle of human beings' right to know about themselves, their communities and events and factors that affect their life.

The implications of PR in improvements in the field of health care can only be amplified further when we look at the needs of people and communities for new knowledge with respect to health. It is true that health issues needs have become far more complex now than they were a few decades ago. As a result, people and communities need to acquire the capacities to understand issues related to health care. As has been demonstrated amply in the practice of participatory training, new knowledge and skills can only be accumulated and learned if they build on existing knowledge and skills. Acceptance of people's current state of knowledge and skills with respect to health and health care and recognition of its value in their life become prerequisite for creating conditions for new knowledge and skills to be acquired by them.

The fundamental question that PR has raised is the question of the political economy of knowledge, science and education. Whose interests do knowledge, research, science and education serve? It is a question that continues to be raised and debated because it is a perpetual enquiry in human endeavour. As has been demonstrated earlier, knowledge, science, research and education are not neutral human endeavours. Similarly health, health care and health care provision are not neutral human activities. A fundamental issue, therefore, is whose interests health sciences, research in health care, knowledge about health care and health practices serve? Who has control over health, health care, health science, health research? If in the final analysis, research in health and health sciences and practices only serves the interests of the medical profession, the pharmaceutical firms and other commercial networks associated with the same, then it will serve to perpetuate the current system of inequality and injustice related to health and health care. It is only when the issues of control over health and the political economy of research in health sciences are addressed, both in our practice and in our theory, that we will be able to make health a truly human endeavour, and not one that is limited to experts, scientists, laboratories and medicines.

References

Bellenky, Mary Field, Clinchy, Blythe M., Goldberger, Nancy R. & Jill Mattuck Tarule (1986) *Women's Ways of Knowing*, Basic Books, New York.

Chambers, Robert (1983) *Rural Development: Putting the Last First*, Longman Press, London, England.

Chambers, Robert (1992) 'Rural appraisal: rapid, relaxed and participatory', *Institute of Development Studies Discussion Paper 311*, Brighton, England.

Colorado, Pam (1988) 'Bridging native and Western science', *Convergence* XXI(2-3).

Cook, Judith & Mary M. Fonow (1988) 'Knowledge and women's interests: issues of epistemology and methodology in feminist sociological research', *Sociological Inquiry*, 56.

Dickson, David (1988) *The New Politics of Science*, University of Chicago Press, Chicago.

Fals-Borda, Orlando (1985) *Knowledge and People's Power*, Indian Social Institute, New Delhi.

Fals-Borda, Orlando & Ansar Rahman (1991) *Action and Knowledge*, Apex Press, New York.

Freire, Paul (1982) 'Creating alternative research methods', in Hall, Budd et al. (eds).

Habermas, Jurgen (1971) *Knowledge and Human Interests* (Translated by Jeremy J. Shapiro from original publication in Germany in 1968), Beacon, Boston.

Hall, Budd A., Gillette & Rajesh Tandon (eds) (1982) *Creating Knowledge: A Monopoly?*, PRIA, New Delhi.

Heeralal, Mohanbhai (1993) *People and Forests: A Participatory Study*, PRIA, New Delhi.

Hubbard, Ruth, Mary Sue Henifin & Barbara Fried (1982) *Biological Woman: The Convenient Myth*, Schenkman Books, VT.

Human Relations (1993) *Action Research*, 46(2) (special issue).

Kolb, David A. (1984) *Experiential Learning*, Prentice Hall, Englewood Cliffs, NJ.

Maguire, Patricia (1987) *Doing Participatory Research: A Feminist Approach*, Centre for International Education, Amherst, MA.

Oakley, Peter (1991) *Projects with People*, ILO, Geneva.

Participatory Research in Asia (PRIA) (1987) *Training of Trainers* (A manual of participatory training methodology in development), PRIA, New Delhi.

Participatory Research in Asia (PRIA) (1990) *Participatory Evaluation: (Issues and Concerns)*, PRIA, New Delhi.

SEARCH (1992) 'PRA', *Search News* 7(1) (special issue).

Seminar (1992) *Education and Ideology*, December (special issue).

Sen, Geeti (ed.) (1992) *Indigenous Vision*, Sage Publications, New Delhi.

Solomon, Robert C. (1987) *From Hegel to Existentialism*, Oxford University Press, New York.

Tandon, Rajesh (1988) 'Social transformation and participatory research', overview article in special issue of *Convergence* Vol.XXI(2-3).

Tandon, Rajesh (1991) *Politics of Life: Knowledge, Science and Education in the Contemporary World*, Mimeo, PRIA, New Delhi.

3 Proposing a more feminist participatory research: knowing and being embraced openly[1]

Patricia Maguire

For years I have been nibbling around the edges of the question of what more could the many feminisms contribute to participatory research (PR) practices, theories and debates. Put another way, how might PR and its advocates be any different if feminism was incorporated more intentionally? This is to move beyond exposing the androcentric or male-centred filter of published accounts, if not some of the work itself, of participatory research's ground-breaking work (Maguire 1987). It is a shift from the question 'how PR might be human-centred, not man-centred?' (Hall 1981:17), for there is contention that the centre has been decentred. I want to promote dialogue on how feminist theories, practices, research and activism might influence PR, not merely PR by or about women but by and about all of us. It is time to explore feminisms' potential contributions to PR that are so much more expansive than the contribution of 'interactive knowledge' (Park 1993).

A similar shift is already taking place in rethinking or reframing development. This shift moves us from the early Women in Development (WID) questions, such as how to make development assistance more responsive to and inclusive of women's issues, to a total rethinking of development itself from feminist perspectives, particularly those of feminists of the South. I am referring to alternative visions for development proposed by groups such as DAWN – Development Alternatives with Women for a New Era (Sen & Grown 1987).

Totally reframing PR is beyond this chapter's scope. Nonetheless, a more feminist PR adds consciously the ontological[2] to the methodological and theoretical perspectives when discussing 'what is PR?' (Park 1993:6).

Any consideration of a more feminist PR invariably starts with a definition of feminism. For me this includes a recognition that there is not one monolithic feminist perspective, but rather many feminisms. A definition of feminism is followed by a brief review of my earlier critique of PR (Maguire 1987). Finally, after an overview of PR, I raise questions for future exploration so we might consider what an intentionally more feminist participatory research brings to table. Can there truly be emancipatory PR or PR advocates without incorporation of feminisms' perspectives and issues?

Feminism/s

While any attempt to define feminism immediately puts one on contro-versial ground, I start with the belief that there are many feminisms, many feminist standpoints (Lather 1991; Mohanty 1991a; Stanley & Wise 1990). Given our 'common differences' (Joseph & Lewis 1981; Mohanty et al. 1991), there are some identifiable threads in the feminist quilt. I use feminism/s to mean the following:

- Feminisms arise from an understanding that women, in all our diversity, face some form of oppression and exploitation. Yet, aware of Mohanty, Russo and Torres's (1991) cautions, I am not suggesting any feminism which equates all oppression, struggles, and experiences, thereby pretending to flatten hierarchy or to ignore power dimensions (1991:x). While there may be the commonality of struggle, all struggles and their agendas take place in a specific historical, cultural context in response to specific, complex realities (Mohanty 1991b). Feminisms, while acknowl-edging the diversity of oppressions experienced, acknowledge also, and celebrate, our diversity of strengths and resistance strategies.
- As women, we experience our oppressions, struggles and strengths differently, based on a complex multiplicity of identities, includ-ing race, class, culture, religion, sexual preference, age, physical abilities, and our nation's place in the international order.
- Feminisms involve a commitment to uncover and understand the complex and interwoven forces that cause and sustain all forms of oppression.
- Finally, feminisms seek a commitment from each of us to work individually and collectively in everyday life to end all forms of oppression, to challenge and transform the systems, structures, and relationships that sustain oppression in its many forms. This commitment includes a willingness, in our diversity, conflicts and disagreements, to build alliances, bridges and networks without minimizing or surrendering our differences. Feminist activism includes but is not limited to an agenda of struggling against gender oppression, for gender oppression is not experienced or structured in isolation from other oppressions. Feminist activism goes be-yond attempting to dismantle oppressive structures and relation-ships to trying to create new structures and relationships or, in essence, a new way of being in relationship in the world.

Feminisms are about attempting to bring together, out of the margins, many voices and visions of a more just, loving, non-violent world. In that sense, feminism/s and PR share emancipatory, transformative intentions. Yet in practice and theory, PR has often ignored the gender factor in oppression.

The androcentric filter

When I first became curious about PR in the early 1980s, I had been active in the US women's movement, working locally on reproductive rights and efforts to influence legislation. I had been involved in development work in Jamaica, the USA, and West Africa, and in exploring feminist critiques of development (Maguire 1984). Eventually I got deeply involved in working against violence against women through direct involvement with Native American, Hispanic and Anglo battered women in rural northwest New Mexico. Although a feminist, I was not much of a feminist theorist; likewise I came to development work as a practitioner not as a theorist or academician. In fact, my own struggles with and sense of inadequacies in grasping the theoretical debates and underpinnings of development assistance and adult education led me to the Center for International Education, University of Massachusetts, Amherst.

The Center for International Education, an international community of learners, is a place for practitioners to take time for critical reflection, heated theoretical debate, and continued skill-building for more action, or praxis. Among other things, the centre is known in the international development community for promoting non-formal education for empowerment (Kindervatter 1979). The centre remains an amazing place which openly struggles with the internal practice of the participatory and emancipatory approaches it promotes externally. In the early 1980s the centre saw a regular flow of male guest speakers such as Rajesh Tandon, Paulo Freire, Miles Horton and Ira Shor. In that context, many of us grappled with the contradictions of doing traditional, non-participatory doctoral research or actual project evaluation when the centre's approach to education and development was premised on participatory philosophies and practices. This struggle to find congruency among our education, development and research practices brought many of us to the door of PR.

When I moved to Gallup, New Mexico in 1984 to live and work, I was determined to attempt PR. In classic research tradition, I had things back to front. I had a research approach in search of a problem rather than a problem in search of the most appropriate research method. Working in the community with the local battered women's shelter, I eventually attempted a PR project with a small, multicultural group of former battered women. As we worked together, I began noticing and questioning seriously what seemed to be male or androcentric bias in the PR literature, perhaps in the work itself.

At first I felt just a vague annoyance as I devoured accounts of the early PR work. I kept wondering, where are the women? In many case studies, the voices of women were silent or invisible. Gender was hidden in seemingly inclusive terms: 'the people', 'the oppressed', 'the campesinos', or simply 'the community'. It was only when comparing separate descriptions of some projects that it became clear that 'the community' was all too often the male community. In instances where projects dealt only with women, they were usually more clearly identified: 'women villagers', for example. The written PR accounts clearly had a male bias as did, in some cases, the work itself. My understanding of feminism, which grew first out of my daily life and activism, was like a dry cloth on a foggy window. Feminism helped me to *see* things differently.

I believe that in many instances the exclusion of women and gender from much of the early PR literature and work was more than a semantic or logistical oversight (Hall 1993). If women, in all our diversity, were being excluded or marginalized from question-posing, problem-posing community forums of some PR projects, then women's diverse voices, visions and hopes were also excluded. Exactly whose problems and questions was PR addressing? If women had unequal access to project participation, then women no doubt had unequal access to any project benefits. How can you share in the supposed empowerment from a project which continues your silence and marginalization?   I found myself wondering, was this potentially emancipatory research approach intended only for the male oppressed? Exactly which systems and structures of oppression would PR attempt to dismantle or replicate? Would men engaged in PR ever seek to dismantle patriarchy?

At issue was and still is more than the exclusion of women as women. It is the exclusion of, or minimal attention to and understanding of, gender relations, as context-bound as they are, and subsequent efforts intentionally to shape more just gender relations.

I also delved into PR's theoretical debates and critiques of positivist social science. Feminist theories, critiques, and the growing body of feminist research were largely absent. Would they have us think that only men create emancipatory approaches to knowledge creation? Was PR to become yet another male monopoly?

As both the work represented in this volume and others testify, women in all our diversity have not allowed PR to be monopolized by and for men. PR acknowledges the centrality of power in the social construction of knowledge. But it is feminist research which alerts us to the centrality of male power in that construction, a power which PR too often ignores. Likewise there is a peculiar silence on exploring how male power still manifests itself behind the scenes in the world of PR advocates. While PR builds on the Freirian notion of man's alienation in the world, it still too often minimizes or ignores women's alienation from a man-made world (Westkott 1979).

Feminism has taught me to pay attention to my vague annoyances. What is PR proposing we emancipate ourselves from and transform ourselves and structures into? Without an intentional space for a multi-plicity of voices and visions explicitly including feminism/s, just what kind of worlds would PR have us create? Put another way, can any PR effort and its advocates, real human beings, be considered emancipatory if leaving unchallenged and intact oppressive gender relations and the host of systems and structures which sustain them? There is no way to challenge power relationships within the research process, for example power between the researcher and the researched, without also being intentionally self-conscious of our own behaviour in all our social relationships, each of which have power dimensions. Self-reflection is not only for 'those people, out there', it is for all of us, in here, in the world of advocating for, conferencing about, practising, training others, writing and reading about PR. And it is for us, in here, when out there in our institutions, agencies, networks, friendships, families and love relation-ships.

Feminisms' challenge to me continues to be to hold myself account-able for congruency between my avowed philosophies and my actual daily behaviours, to recognize the interconnections between the private and public, the personal and the professional. In essence, feminism challenges me to fight fragmentation not only in the knowledge creation process but within myself. Of course I often fall short. I am not suggesting in any way that feminists and feminisms have no flaws or inconsistencies.

PR may recognize that seeing and knowing grow out of our specific experiences, situationally complex and shaped by our many multifaceted identities. Yet the profound challenge of knowing differently is then to act and be differently in the world, in our many contexts and relation-ships. What might it mean for PR advocates and practices if we link being with knowing more explicitly, if we demand greater congruency of ourselves in all our relationships, not merely relationships within our research efforts?

I understand now that one of feminisms' gifts is more than a way of seeing, a way of knowing. It is more than interactive knowledge. It is attention to concrete ways of being in the world of relationships. It is not merely that knowing differently requires acting differently on and with that knowledge (praxis). Seeing and knowing differently pushes us to be differently at our very core, who and how we choose to be daily in all our circles of relationships. And therein lies the ontological challenge. Can we embrace that challenge?

Participatory research – back to the background

PR attempts uniquely to combine the traditionally isolated practices of research, education and action (Hall 1993). PR proposes that its advocates join in solidarity with oppressed peoples who are not already conducting and utilizing research for empowerment and social transformation. Together they can utilize PR to create knowledge and take collective action, short- and long-term, for potentially emancipatory and transformative structural and personal change.

PR advocates boldly declare an intention of collectively investigating reality or, as the postmodernists would remind us, investigating realities in order to transform them. PR attempts explicitly to link theory and practice, knowing and doing and, in profoundly new and different ways, the doers and those historically done to.

PR attempts to provide one avenue for those whose voices have been ignored to raise their voices in naming problems and questions worthy of investigation. Ultimately, PR attempts to provide a means and, when necessary, more confidence-building whereby those marginalized can be heard in the decision-making centres where resources, opportunities and privileges are divided (Khanna 1994). Perhaps more important, each PR endeavour attempts, at however micro a level, to transform not only the particular problem-posing process but also decision-making, resource-allocating institutions and processes. PR challenges the oppression of silence and isolation (Freire 1970) and the many institutional structures, processes and relationships which maintain or foster silence and isolation. So how can PR challenge the silencing of women and the ignoring of gender relations within projects, institutions, relationships and communities?

PR advocates propose that because knowledge is one basis for power and control, PR has power-sharing, power-shifting potential. While knowledge may be one form of power, knowledge in and of itself is not sufficient for structural, institutional or personal transformation. Clearly, power has material, institutional and ideological bases. We are then challenged to consider how any PR endeavour actually redistributes, consolidates or reconfigures power and privileges that have material and institutional bases. Ultimately, a more feminist PR challenges us actually to live and work in ways that go beyond facilitating redistribution ultimately to modelling new configurations for relationships and definitions of power. More feminist PR challenges us to be differently in relationship with others.

The transformative intentions of PR are of sobering proportion. Its proposed combination of research, education and action can be overwhelming and exhausting. One might wonder, how can we take on all this with one project, one endeavour? In fact, why take it on with so-called research? It has helped me to recognize that PR is but one approach, one player if you will, in the long-haul struggle for a just, loving, nonviolent world.

PR advocates are not alone in this struggle. We are part of the many loose alliances working in a multiplicity of settings, in a multiplicity of ways, on a multiplicity of issues for transformation. Thus PR may be one but not the only tool with empowering, emancipatory intentions and potential. In some instances it may not even be the best tool. Perhaps we can free ourselves of some unspoken proposal that all research be 'pure' or ideal PR. Instead we might look for ways to move deliberately along the participatory continuum. Tandon (1985) proposed that we ask of our projects: is people's control increasing over time? Are we moving in that direction or 'still nibbling at the same place'? Are PR advocates decreasing our control in collaborative work? Does participation in others' empowerment require to some degree the disempowering of ourselves, if power has come from control and expertness (Campos 1994)?

PR, then, is one of many ways to challenge oppressive structures, relationships and practices which stifle participation and voice-raising. As a feminist PR advocate, whose views have grown out of experience, I am not seeking nor proposing some pure and perfect PR for all research needs. I am much more an advocate of participation for transformation, as a power-shifting means and end, whether it be more participatory and emancipatory education, evaluation, organizing, managing or research. The process of engaging in collective investigation, education and action is as potentially empowering as any of the actual knowledge produced. It is also not only the oppressed who may find themselves empowered, transformed or more critically aware of injustices. As advocates of PR, we may find ourselves changed and challenged in profound and unsettling ways. I certainly am challenged and often found lacking in the daily struggles waged within the circles of relationships in my life. This is the ontological convergence of feminism and PR.

To embrace a more feminist PR is to acknowledge implications for how we work and live, love and play, even when we are not engaged in PR, indeed, even if we never actually use or attempt full-scale PR in our work. More feminist PR is not merely some set of techniques, however unique its combination of research, education and action. More feminist PR is broader than techniques. It is grounded in a multiplicity of critiques of *what is*. It is firmly situated within the larger alternative paradigm approaches to human inquiry which are challenging the positivist research paradigm and its often dehumanizing assumptions, methods and implicit messages. PR advocates are not alone as researchers questioning domination and dominating research structures and relationships. PR is part of a family of emancipatory approaches to human inquiry that push us to act boldly and unapologetically with instead of on or for the less powerful and voiceless. How, then, can PR not intentionally incorporate feminisms' attention to the multiplicity and interconnectedness of oppressions which include gender? While the alternative research paradigm in which

PR is situated promotes alternative ways of seeing the world, it has never adequately alerted us to the dangers and limitations of seeing the world through male eyes only. Feminism has done this (Duelli Klein 1983; Smith 1974; Spender 1983).

As part of the broader search for alternatives to traditional social science research, feminist and PR advocates join with those exposing the myth and safety of value-free knowledge creation. From the instant a research question is framed, values are apparent. Who frames the question? Is this framing a solitary act or done in collaboration with those closest to the problem? What is worth investigating? The questions we pose are as telling as the questions we avoid. For example, for years in the field of domestic violence or woman-battering, researchers framed a major question: why do women stay in violent relationships? This not only framed a research focus, it implied subtly that something was wrong with these women. Even more subtly, this took the focus and responsibility off violent men for their abusive behaviour and beliefs. With the help of feminists, but even more significantly at the urging of battered women themselves, many of whom would not identify themselves as feminists, the question was reframed. 'Why do men brutalize women in so-called love relationships?' (Schechter 1982). Other questions have been added. What are the systemic bases and props for male power which allow, perpetuate and even promote degradation and violence in love relationships? Clearly, the knowledge creation process, from the moment questions are posed, is not value-free, despite the many orthodox social science devices which attempt to assure us that research can not only be value-free, but that it should be value-free. PR questions both assertions, because action for a just, loving, non-violent world requires that we take sides. Feminist research adds attention to gender relations in their specific, historical, cultural context and within the research production itself (Stanley & Wise 1990).

If PR taught me the need to be explicit about personal values and how those values impact on the research process, then it is feminism, in all its diversity, that taught me to recognize that the personal is highly political. Now, third-world feminisms highlight a recognition that the politics of the public affects the personal (Hurtado 1989; Mohanty 1991b; Johnson-Odim 1991).

Any transformation 'out there' must start with people's self-identified agendas in which, as third-world feminists suggest, the struggles against gender oppression cannot be disconnected from the struggles for liberation and autonomy (Mohanty 1991a). Likewise, struggles for liberation and autonomy cannot ignore struggles against gender oppression. A more feminist PR pushes us, relentlessly, to examine then increase congruency between our personal politics and public practices, research and otherwise. A more feminist PR pushes us to examine our own institutions, organizations and agencies, and our practices and relationships within them. Transformation is not only for 'out there'.

Issues for further dialogue

While exploring a more feminist PR, I have found myself wondering about many issues over the past few years. You, no, doubt have your own wonderings.

1. *Does PR, as currently conceived, require something fundamentally different of and from men and women, participants and advocates?*

One of the greatest requirements of engaging in PR is simply *time*. Just as building meaningful, reciprocal, caring relationships take time, over the course of time, so too actual participation in all phases of a PR endeavour takes time pure and simple. What are the implications of the sexual division of labour for doing PR? What are the implications of many women's double day, which adds on the responsibilities for care of children, the sick and elderly, responsibilities often not equitably shared by the men in our lives?

Participants' time in project participation, often unpaid or uncompensated, is time taken away from life's other obligations. Whatever the context, do women face different constraints then men on involvement in participatory processes, the very participatory processes essential to meaningful input, control, benefits and, ultimately, empowerment? Are we proposing a set of participatory processes or project phases which requires something essentially different of women and men, based on differing realities of daily life constructed in part by gender? Even among PR advocates, who is it that is raising our sons and daughters or caring for the sick among us? Who has to arrange or purchase child care to participate in all this?

2. *PR promotes profound changes in the relationship between the researcher and those traditionally researched. What other relationship changes might a more feminist PR suggest? What about changes among and between researchers and participants?*

Development, true human development, requires at its core human interaction, the building and nurturing of relationships. A more feminist PR causes us to examine more closely how our actual organizational structures, processes and practices shape and influence how people of unequal power and privilege are in relationship with each other. Human relationships take time (over the course of time), space, purpose and reciprocity to grow and flourish. Human trust and concern cannot be hot housed. What does this imply for the training of, practice of, and alliance-building of participatory researchers?

In some ways, the motives for even attempting PR, feminist or not, come from a place in the heart where we dare not only to *believe* that change is possible but where we know that through collective work, it will happen. This belief sustains us as we witness or experience daily degradation and violence in its many forms. If we are to consider that a more feminist PR requires that we choose to *be* differently in the world and to be more self-reflective in all our relationships, what does this mean for the training of participatory researchers? As Ineke Meulenberg-Buskens declares: 'There is no dance without a dancer' (1994:44). We cannot merely train technicians who know the steps but cannot feel the music, its rhythm and beauty.

3. *Since PR openly promotes redistribution of power, how might a more feminist PR reconceptualize the very notion of power?* Hartsock (1974; Harding 1986:14) argued that instead of conceiving of power as domination over others and resources, feminists have been redefining power. Power is conceptualized as sharing and providing energy and access to resource mobilization to others as well as to self. What would this look like in PR projects? How is power-sharing taking place within the PR advocates' world? Who sets the agendas for debate among PR advocates? What kinds of power dynamics exist in the relationships PR advocates are working and living within?

4. *Could a more feminist PR help us rethink the organization and community building aspects of PR? If a goal of PR is to mobilize oppressed people to act on their own behalf, is then a popular people's organization a necessary prerequisite or a hoped-for outcome of PR?* Park (1993:18) proposed that, where there is little shared life, PR must first create a community base before it can do collective investigation. What conditions are necessary to create such communities and organizations, particularly ones inclusive of the multiplicity of women who are often excluded through many arrangements, overt and covert, from problem-posing, decision-making, and allocating resources and opportunities? What need we consider not only to expand women's meaningful inclusion in historically male bastions, but also to transform those bastions in meaningful ways that speak to issues of human relationships, community, and shifting power-definitions and realities?

What do PR advocates need to consider in working within our own organizations and agencies to push them to be not only more inclusive of women's and children's diverse issues 'out there' but also actually to create internal organizational structures and processes which themselves model and promote new power-sharing and power-shifting within these very organizations? I am not interested in advocating a truncated PR which pushes us to work in solidarity with the so-called powerless and voiceless while leaving intact and unexamined oppressive practices and relationships within our own organizations, situations and lives. I am not proposing that PR advocates be held to some abstract, pure standard, only that in the concrete organizations and relationships in which we live out our daily lives we try, however imperfectly, to live what we advocate for 'out there'. It is all connected, different edges of the same fabric.

5. *PR often starts with some kind of problem naming or posing.* Yet based on lives in which gender partially shapes different experiences, do men and women sometimes name and pose different problems for investigation and action? The instances seem rare in which men name their oppression of the women in their lives as a problem to be investigated and solved. Have PR projects and advocates colluded, unintentionally or strategically, with oppressive gender relations? How might a more feminist PR interface with the many localized actions of women's groups challenging specific oppressive practices and beliefs rooted deep in culture and religion?

6. *How might a more feminist PR help women utilize the technical, instrumental knowledge generated by the traditional social sciences, even medical sciences?* Many consciousness-raising and mobilization efforts by and for women have utilized information produced by traditional social science. For example women have been able to utilize statistical, descriptive data from large-scale studies in areas as diverse as sexual harassment, rape, wage disparity, and even the use of amniocentesis for sex selection. How can advocates of PR, which is usually not large-scale, utilize technical or descriptive knowledge which can be powerful for mobilizing, consciousness-raising education?

7. *How might a more feminist PR account for the conditions of its own production?* Stanley & Wise (1990), when analysing feminist research, call for a concrete account of the process of the research's production and the social relations which give rise to it. What might this look like in a more feminist PR? How can we make more visible and open to analysis the ways PR is being produced?

8. *Finally, how might a more feminist PR influence which endeavours and outcomes we allow ourselves to celebrate?* PR proposes an extensive, at times overwhelming, agenda and process. It can be near-paralysing to compare one's faltering beginnings and exhausting middles to the neatly documented endings of others' PR efforts. No such effort lacks critics. Yet it is in the sharing of the flaws and shortcomings that we free ourselves from the paralysing need for perfection.

When I tried to use a Freirian problem-posing format with former battered women, I began by asking, 'What problems do you see in your lives and communities?' Their answers began some place else. Almost to a woman, they started by describing and acknowledging the strengths and successes in their lives. In the sharing of successes, however small and micro, we gain courage and encouragement to learn by doing. Feminism includes joyful affirmation and celebration of our strengths and successes, even redefining success in an increasingly isolating and alienating world. In closing, as we ponder what feminism/s might bring to PR, let us consider carefully what exactly it is that we are each trying to liberate ourselves from and transform ourselves, relationships, communities and structures into. How are we willing and hoping to be in the world?

Notes

1. An early version of this chapter was presented as a keynote address at the International Symposium on Participatory Research in Health Promotion, Liverpool, 17-21 September 1993. I would like to acknowledge Korrie de Koning for encouraging and then arranging my participation in the symposium.
2. I am grateful to the work of Liz Stanley and Sue Wise (1990) for articulation of the ontological–epistemological connection regarding feminist research. For extensive discussion and definition of feminist research, see Harding (1986); Lather (1991); Harding, (1986); Stanley & Wise (1990).

References

Bowles, G. & Duelli Klein R. (eds) (1983) *Theories of Women's Studies.* Routledge & Kegan Paul, Boston.

Campos, J. (1994, 30 September) Personal telephone conversation.

Duelli Klein, R. (1983) 'How to do what we want to do: thoughts about feminist methodology', in Bowles, G. & Duelli Klein, R. (eds) (1983).

Freire, P. (1970) *Pedagogy of the Oppressed*, Seabury Press, New York.

Hall, B. (1981) 'Participatory research, popular knowledge and power: a personal reflection', *Convergence*, Vol.14(3), pp.6-19.

Hall, B. (1993) 'Introduction', in Park P. et al. (eds) (1993).

Harding, S. (1986) *The Science Question in Feminism*, Open University Press, Milton Keynes.

Hartsock, N. (1974) 'Political change: two perspectives on power', *Quest: A Feminist Quarterly* (1)1, reprinted in Charlotte Bunch (ed.) (1981) *Building Feminist Theory: Essays From Quest*, Longman, New York.

Hurtado, A. (1989) 'Relating to privilege: seduction and rejection in the subordination of white women and women of color', *Signs* 14(4), pp.833-55.

Johnson-Odim, C. (1991) 'Common themes, different contexts: third-world women and feminism', in Mohanty, C.T. et al. (eds) (1991).

Joseph, G. & Lewis, J. (1981) *Common Differences: Conflicts in Black and White Feminist Perspectives*, Doubleday, New York.

Khanna, R. (1994) 'Participatory action research (PAR) in women's health', in de Koning, K. (ed.) (1994), pp.25-32.

Kindervatter, S. (1979) *Non-formal Education as an Empowering Process*, Center for International Education, University of Massachusetts, Amherst, Massachusetts.

de Koning, K. (ed.) (1994) *Proceedings of the International Symposium on Participatory*

Research in Health Promotion, Education Resource Group, Liverpool School of Tropical Medicine, UK.

Lather, P. (1991) *Getting Smart: Feminist Research and Pedagogy within the Post-modern*, Routledge, New York.

Maguire, P. (1984) *Women in Development: An Alternative Analysis*, Center for International Education, University of Massachusetts, Amherst, Massachusetts.

Maguire, P. (1987) *Doing Participatory Research: A Feminist Approach*, Center for International Education, University of Massachusetts, Amherst, Massachusetts.

Maguire, P. (1994) 'Participatory research from one feminist perspective. Moving from exposing androcentricism to embracing possible contributions of feminisms to participatory research and practice. Voices and visions', in de Koning, K. (ed.) (1994), pp.5-14.

Meulenberg-Buskens, I. (1994) 'The participatory researcher as educator in research: some notes', in de Koning, K. (ed.) (1994), pp.42-5.

Mohanty, C.T. (1991a) 'Introduction: cartographies of struggle: third-world women and the politics of feminism', in Mohanty, C.T. et al. (eds) (1991) pp.1-47.

Mohanty, C.T. (1991b) 'Under western eyes: feminist scholarship and colonial discourses', in Mohanty, C.T. et al. (eds) (1991) pp.51-80.

Mohanty, C.T., Russo, A., & Torres, L. (eds) (1991) 'Preface', *Third-world Women and the Politics of Feminism*, Indiana University Press, Bloomington.

Park, P. (1993) 'What is participatory research? A theoretical and methodological perspective', in Park, P. et al. (eds) (1993).

Park, P., Brydon-Miller, M., Hall, B. & Jackson, T. (eds) (1993) *Voices of Change: Participatory Research in the United States and Canada*, Bergin and Garvey, Westport, Connecticut.

Schechter, S. (1982) *Women and Male Violence*, South End Press, Boston.

Sen, G. & Grown, C. (1987) *Development, Crises, and Alternative Visions: Third-world Women's Perspectives*, Monthly Review Press, New York.

Smith, D. (1974) 'Women's perspective as a radical critique of sociology', *Sociological Inquiry*, 44, pp.7-13.

Spender, D. (1983) *Women of Ideas (and What Men Have Done to Them)*, ARK, Boston.

Stanley, L. & Wise, S. (1990) 'Feminist praxis and the academic mode in feminist research process', in Stanley, L. (ed.) *Feminist Praxis: Research, Theory and Epistemology in Feminist Sociology*, Routledge, London, pp.20-62.

Tandon, R. (1985, 28 April) *Participatory Research and Social Action*, speech at the Center for International Education, University of Massachusetts, Amherst.

Westkott, M. (1979) 'Feminist criticism of the social sciences', *Harvard Educational Review*, 49(3), pp.422-430.

PART II TRAINING IN PARTICIPATORY RESEARCH

4 Critical awareness in participatory research: an approach towards teaching and learning

Ineke Meulenberg-Buskens

This chapter sketches an approach towards teaching-and-learning[1] in participatory research (PR) in which the striving towards critical awareness plays an important role. The very nature of PR implies often that the participatory research practitioner has to take up the role of educator in research (O'Connor et al. 1987). As is the case in any teaching situation, three questions can be asked: what is the learning for? what to teach? and how to teach? These questions (and their answers) have of course a bearing on one another, especially in PR. In this chapter, some answers are sought, and the concepts of participatory research education are examined.

What is the learning for: participatory research and education

In order to make statements about research education in PR, it will be necessary at least to state what participatory research is about. Hall seems to present the most common description of what is entailed in practice, namely: the integration of social investigation, educational work and action in an inter-related process (Hall 1981), Participatory research is geared ideologically towards structural change and social transformation (Rahman 1993).

As an approach to research, participatory research seems to be able to accommodate a mixture of pragmatic and political points of departure (Mulenga 1994), for example obtaining information for decision-making, and enhancing the involvement of the participants in the research in the decision-making process. PR draws on various disciplines: adult education (Hall 1981), education (McTaggart 1989), development studies and cultural anthropology (Brunt 1992; Welter 1984), feminist studies (Maguire 1987, 1994) to name but a few. Participatory research also stimulates interdisciplinary approaches to research and programme development.[2] Some practitioners stress the element of action, others the importance of a shared process of knowledge construction. Some feel that it is important that practitioners see a total participatory research process through, while others regard their degree of dispensability as an indicator of their success.

What is research?

The concept of research used in the context of participatory research should allow for the insight that PR might entail a different experience for everybody involved. Any research practice is a multi-faceted, complex issue. In a participatory research project the reality has become even more complex because of the intentional interplay of research, education and action. The same research project can simultaneously mean many things to many people, for example: a policy prerequisite, a marketing strategy, a professional career opportunity, a teaching device, an educational opportunity, a time-consuming nuisance, an organizing mechanism, a tool for control and manipulation, or a strategy for mobilization.

While acknowledging the existence and validity of many different perspectives, in my view, for the purposes of teaching and learning about the research aspect in participatory research, three perspectives are particularly useful: research as a process of knowledge construction, as a process of disciplined enquiry, and as an area of human capacity and skill. These perspectives are inter-related. Striving towards participation of research participants would, then, imply a striving towards:

- *the sharing of and participation in* the process of knowledge construction, for example, consensus regarding the problem statement and the research approach to be followed, and the collective ownership of the research results;
- *the sharing of and participation in* the development or acceptance of the norms, methods and techniques which guide the process of inquiry; and
- *the sharing of and participation in* the processes of developing research capacity and skills.

Research education

Conventional social science research education practices cannot be transferred uncritically to the area of participatory research. This type of education tends to focus mainly on research as 'a process of disciplined enquiry', functioning almost completely separated from everyday life.

Research practice and theory, research methodology, research methods, research techniques, and research terminology are presented to novices as areas where they have to conform to rules and conventions. More often than not, it is left to the novices themselves to find their own relationship with research. This objectified image of research has left many aspiring researchers too much in awe of research actually to become practitioners.[3] Scientists who created dominant ideas about research are presented as historical figures, not as social actors with specific research interests and values. What is being taught is what these people have contributed, not the contexts in which or the means by which they have come to their specific contributions.

Conventional social science research education reflects and reinforces the objectified and mystified image of social science research. The reflective and creative research processes have been made invisible in the conventional presentation of research practice and so the capacity to reflect, decide and choose will not function as an important feature in the conventional curricula. Learning and teaching in research will focus rather on the mastery of procedures, the application of techniques and the command of a body (or disconnected bodies) of knowledge.[4]

I think that it is important to approach research as a process of disciplined enquiry. It is important to know about various research approaches, norms, methods and techniques and about various contexts relevant to processes of enquiry. Research is, however, also an area of human experience, capacity and skill and a process of knowledge construction. These aspects should also receive attention from research educators, especially at a novice level and especially in participatory research. Teaching and learning in participatory research should demystify the research practice.[5] I strongly believe that this can be done, not so much by simplifying the practice, but by making the research process recognizable and transparent and by developing research capacity and 'research literacy'. Research can be re-owned. Research education can start where the students are. While this approach to research education would be preferable for novices in all social science research approaches, in PR it is an imperative.

What does the participatory researcher have to know, be, do?

There are, of course, various insights and strategies participatory researchers have in common. One of the commonalities is the striving towards empowerment of the research participants and concern about processes which disempower them. Another common aspect is the intent and commitment of participatory researchers to start where the people are. Participatory researchers have to be able to respond to situations and interactions, rather than instigate and control them. Participatory researchers are therefore committed to grow in sensitivity and flexibility. Anyanwu (1988:15) mentions 'a willingness to learn from and with the people, sensitivity, adaptability, patience, empathy and a flexibility of attitude' as necessary skills (in human relationships) for participatory research. Rahman speaks of the 'stimulation of self-reflected critical awareness on the part of the oppressed people of their social reality' (Rahman 1993:81).

I would like to add to this list *an attitude of and a capacity for critical reflection on the participatory-research process*. This would imply *the commitment to stimulate that attitude and capacity in others who are involved in the research*. Critical reflection is not only an inherently empowering activity, viable as an end in itself. Critical reflection on the research process can have a specific significance for that process, for academic or professional participatory researchers as well as for community participants. Given the people-orientedness of PR, the research process will most probably be open-ended and may even be unpredictable. It is, therefore, of crucial importance that participatory researchers are flexible and do not have to rely on procedures. Flexibility in the research process can prevent a mechanical (blueprint) use of research strategies and can provide the space for a response which respects the specific situation in which the research takes place. Critical reflection will enable the researchers to act flexibly and creatively, to make choices, reflect on them, justify and communicate them. Community research participants who are able to reflect critically on the research process can truly take part in the decision-making, and in designing parts of the research process. They will feel empowered because they will see themselves as decision-makers, as creators and choosers instead of people who apply techniques and follow rules. Community participation in a PR process can then mean more than collaboration in action. Critical reflection also opens up the path towards congruence: congruence between 'the being' and 'the doing', between words and actions, behaviour and intent, between the message of PR and the way the message is conveyed and worked out in the research (and education) process.[6] Congruence is crucial given the normative and emancipatory claims of PR. Incongruencies in self and others can be detected and faced.

What to teach?

In order to be able to reflect critically on the research process, a certain research literacy is needed, as well as an effective research attitude. This research literacy implies an insight into research processes as well as knowledge of research terms, principles and techniques. Just as theoretical concepts can open up reality, research terms can provide insight into the research process.

Research attitude

In an open research approach such as PR, where even the objectives set out at the beginning of the project may change, some questions must be brought up continuously during the research process: What do we want with this specific research project (now)? Why do we want what we want? Where are we at this moment in the research effort? Where do we want to go? How are we going about that? Who are we? And why do we want to go about that in this particular fashion? With all our good intentions are we still going in the right direction?[7] Critical reflection could be formulated as the art of raising relevant questions as well as the commitment to raising those questions. Critical reflection also refers to the need critically to assess oneself and every situation of personal involvement. As the researcher is the main agent in the processes of research and knowledge construction, as well as in the processes of social transformation and change, it is important to stimulate an attitude of 'self-reflected critical awareness' in oneself and others.[8]

Research literacy

Research is a process of knowledge construction. This process does not take place in a vacuum but is the result of raising and trying to answer questions. A research question is a creation in itself. A specific question will lead to a specific answer and will result in specific knowledge. The research question will reflect a certain perspective on reality, and by raising this question that perspective will be reinforced. Which question is chosen to address or translate a certain problem will depend on who is in the position to make that choice. As Pat Maguire says so clearly: 'Who controls the question controls a lot' (Maguire & Mulenga 1994).

The translation of a problem into a research question will be influenced by the approach which is chosen for the research project. A variation on Pat Maguire's saying might read: 'Who controls the research approach, controls a lot'. How answers to questions are sought and what criteria are used to guide the process of investigation depends on the model of research that is used. Different models exist and each has its own sets of norms to guide the research process. The most well-known of these are: objectivity, intersubjectivity, generalizability, validity and reliability. These norms have been constructed in a specific place, during a specific time, for a specific purpose, out of a specific perspective and in a specific way. Within the dominant research model they acquired a specific meaning. They are, however, generally perceived as rather absolute standards to guarantee the quality of any research action and result. It is obvious that this situation creates a lot of tension: how can the norms based on one model be the basis for judging the quality of research which is based on a different research model? On the other hand, how can quality in research be guaranteed without using quality standards?

The debate, which is relevant for the practice of participatory research, focuses on the issue of whether these traditional norms can be used in alternative research approaches (such as participatory research) or whether new norms have to be created. Rahman suggests that research can be objective 'in the sense of the methodology and product having passed a process of *social* verification. ... Objectivity in this sense requires transition from the individual to a collective' (Rahman 1993:90). The norms which will be accepted as guiding principles for a certain research process will obviously influence the research process. Who controls the research norms, controls a lot. Rahman describes an immediate objective of participatory action research (PAR): 'to return to the people the legitimacy of the knowledge they are capable of producing ... through the verification systems *they may decide to establish themselves*, as fully scientific' (Rahman 1993:91). Rahman seems to adhere to a conceptualization of the 'scientific' which is argumentative and based on consensus.

Research methods and research techniques

I find it helpful to distinguish between method and technique. Methods can be created and designed in response to the needs of a certain research context and are made up of techniques. Techniques are practical applications and have a place within methods. Skill is needed to apply a certain technique. Knowledge about techniques is necessary in order to make appropriate choices and design methods. But 'knowledge about' remains impotent knowledge when it is not accompanied by the necessary 'know-how'. There are various participatory techniques. These techniques are and will be used in various non-participatory methods. The application of participatory techniques will not automatically make research participatory in my view.[9] Participatory techniques are used in market and policy research, where the research results and interpretations are not shared with the research participants, who may not even be aware of the implementation.

The dominant Western-developed research techniques have found their origin in the world of the Western intellectual. They might not be appropriate in every research situation. They play, however, an important role in various research (funding) contexts. The challenge is to come up with the most appropriate response to a certain situation, taking everything (as much as you can) into consideration. Apart from these more conventional research techniques, in a process of dialogue with the group respecting their (prevailing) mode of communication and education, other modes of knowledge construction can be explored. Experiences such as sitting silently together, mind-webbing or mind-mapping, story-telling, exchanging pet theories, drawing and dancing together, can play just as important a role.

Objectives of the learning

The objectives of the learning relate both to the content of teaching and how to teach. The objectives are:

- to stimulate the participants' reflection on their situation and their confidence in their own research capacities;
- to create the opportunity for participants to develop the skills needed to utilize the necessary techniques; so that, aware of their situation, confident and skilled, they are able
- to choose their own research path, reflect on it and justify it. In this

process they will be able to develop their own methods in a responsible and congruent fashion, in response to their own specific contexts.

How to teach?

Participatory research requires from the (professional) participatory researcher the capacity to help develop the research capacity in others. In the process of teaching and learning, I am working at the moment with four sets of concepts (or norms) to guide me. I try to create an appropriate balance between safety and risk-taking. The learning process is as participatory and experiential as possible and I try to establish respect for the process. I also strive towards congruence between the content of the learning and its process by emphasizing an atmosphere of *critical reflection* and *confidence building*.[10] These sets of norms are inter-related with each other and various exercises and activities can fulfil several objectives.

For the participants to *take the risks* which are unavoidable in this learning process, the facilitator has to *create a safe environment* and draw the participants into a continuous process of expanding themselves. A facilitator who lives to learn and who loves to share personal learning processes with the participants can be very effective as a role model and in creating a safe environment by showing her/his own vulnerability. Invisibility of the facilitator as a person may reinforce the power imbalance in the relationship with the participants.

The main learning mode is *experiential and participatory*, involving the participants as the total human beings they are, with everything they bring into the process. The skills to be acquired will be decided on in a negotiation process. The format of the learning process will depend on the specific needs of the participants and the trainer's interpretation of these needs. The skills to be acquired can vary from the skill to work with the community's database in the community's resource centre to the skill to facilitate group discussions. These didactic moments have to be defined clearly and ritually distinguished from the experiential moments, especially in the beginning. When the participants have seen the research educator learning from them in the process, when the roles of teacher and student have appeared to be complementary and interchangeable, the distinction need not be so severely protected anymore. From the start the facilitator has to guard the process in such a way that the participants can make informed decisions about what they want to learn and when.

Careful focus on the research process can provide a tool to detect power abuse quickly. Despite its empowering potential, this specific learning approach with its emphasis on critical reflection has not prevented me from falling into the traps participatory research has laid for its (academic) practitioners (Rahman 1993: Chapter 6). The conscious choice for and specialization in PR as a viable, alternative research approach already indicates a certain stance on science, on society and on human beings. Regardless of whether a specific research project has been initiated by a group/community or by a researcher/research team, the traps for participatory researcher(s) to become patronizing and manipulating have already been laid. The implicit, perhaps unconscious attitude of knowing better and wanting to do good seem to be in contradiction with the feelings of respect and equivalence one should have towards the research participants.[11] In the teaching process, a similar threat presents itself. The researcher's skills seem to be greater than those of the participants. It is therefore very important to create the conditions for an atmosphere of mutual trust where constant reflection can take place. This reflection will also take form in various exercises of self-evaluation, in evaluation of learning experiences and in the final evaluation of the total learning process.

Confidence refers to the confidence one has not only in what everybody involved knows but also in what can be made, but may not yet be known. It implies a belief in a human capacity for learning and sharing. Confidence is needed to nurture an attitude of critical reflection. The combination of confidence and critical reflection functions in the learning process as the brief that the participants, facilitator included, should treat themselves as well as each other as the confident and critically reflective human beings they are (becoming). These concepts are interwoven, they support and reflect each other. They also create a particular atmosphere: an awareness of 'self acting in relationship to others'.[12]

I believe that most aspiring researchers participating in research learning have already mastered the basic research skills the moment they start their more formal learning. The capacities to gather information, identify problems, formulate questions, test hypotheses, draw conclusions, implement research findings and evaluate the implementations are part and parcel of what it means to be a human being.[13] Exactly this capacity has enabled the participants to survive their various contexts and to create more or less successful coping mechanisms in their own lives. The participants have probably also made use of this research capacity when they had to decide whether to join a process of learning in participatory research. Reflection on these decision-making processes could become an appropriate starting-point in the total learning experience.

A final word

This chapter reflects a moment in an ongoing process of struggle and growth. In the process of writing it I experienced over and over again how interwoven so many aspects of participatory research are with each other. The writing about my experiences became a process in a process. It may well be that the immense scope for personal growth in participatory research is one of its greatest attractions. In this chapter I have been working with the questions what is the learning for?, what to teach? and how to teach? Next time around, I might be working with totally different questions. The fascination is that, right now, I do not know what they will be.

Notes

1. Reflecting on the practice of education in participatory research, the term 'training' strikes me as absolutely inadequate in this context. It even degrades the actual experience by evoking associations of a technical, instrumentalist nature. I would rather speak of teaching and learning in PR. Margot Ely shared this insight with me some years ago. It has become my own experience only recently.

2. Problems as experienced by the community or knowledge deemed necessary by this community to solve these problems are seldom defined in terms of disciplinary distinctions.

3. I am speaking here 'as a competent member of the community of learners in social-science research' (a term of Harold Garfinkel).

4. In such an environment it will be difficult to (re)introduce individual responsibility and accountability of the researcher as integral dimensions of the research attitude.

5. I have more affinity with the concept of demystification of research than with the concept of deprofessionalization of research, as for instance used by Nichter (1984).

6. In South Africa where, for instance, language has been used for long to disguise real intent by indicating exactly what is not meant, congruence has taken on a very special significance.

7. I owe this last phrase to Tsietsie Molebatse, training coordinator of SANTA (South African Tuberculosis Association).

8. Self-reflected critical awareness (a term I borrowed from Rahman [1993:81]) reflects in my view a process rather than a state. I also think that in order to stimulate that process in other people, one must live it oneself. Hence the importance of a growth in 'self-reflected critical awareness' in participatory research learning, by *all* participants, the facilitator included.

9. See for instance, Srinivasan (1990:15ff) who contextualizes consistently participatory techniques and their use.

10. Lack of confidence might be the biggest stumbling block. If you do not trust your experiences, how can you really engage in experiential learning? Confidence is also indicated by most participants in the participatory learning processes I facilitated as the most important quality to be gained.

11. The term equivalence is used by Harry Coenen (*An Action Research Reader*, publication forthcoming 1995).

12. A word of thanks to my colleague Phambili ka Ntloko who put words to this experience: 'You must be aware that you act in the presence of others.'

13. Research has been done ever since there were people with inquisitive minds who wondered about reality and/or wanted to improve their environment.

See Tandon, this volume, for a similar vision on research and knowledge construction. Research took place, before there were research institutions, research councils, universities and professional researchers who now seem to claim the monopoly to do research.

References

Anyanwu, C. N. (1988) 'The technique of participatory research in community health', *Community Development Journal*, Vol.23(1), pp.11-15.

Brunt, D. (1992) *Mastering the Struggle*, doctoral thesis, University of Wageningen.

Coenen, H. (1996 forthcoming) *An Action Research Reader*.

Hall, B. L. (1981) 'Participatory research, popular knowledge and power: a personal reflection', *Convergence*, Vol.XIV(3), pp.6-17.

de Koning, K. (ed.) (1994) *Proceedings of the International Symposium on Participatory Research in Health Promotion*, Education Resource Group, Liverpool School of Tropical Medicine, UK..

McTaggart, Robin (1989) 'Principles for participatory action research'. Paper presented at The Third World Encounter on Participatory Research, Managua, Nicaragua, 3-9 September.

Maguire, Patricia (1987) *Doing Participatory Research: A Feminist Approach*, Center for International Education, University of Massachusetts, Amherst. Massachusetts.

Maguire, P. (1994) 'Participatory research: from one feminist perspective. Moving from exposing androcentricism to embracing possible contributions of feminisms to participatory research theory and practice. Voices and visions', in de Koning, K. (ed.) (1994), pp.5-14.

Maguire, P. & Mulenga, D. (1994) 'Participatory research-knowing, being and social transformation presentation', Participatory Research Summer School, Umtata, 12-16 December.

Mulenga, D. (1994) 'Participatory research in Africa: a critical appraisal', in de Koning, K. (ed.) (1994), pp.33-37.

Nichter, M. (1984) 'Project community diagnosis: participatory research as a first step towards community involvement in primary health care', *Social Science and Medicine*, Vol.19(3), pp.237-52.

O'Connor, P., Franklin, R. R. & Behrhorst, C. (1987) 'Hospital record studies as a tool for staff education: a participatory research project in Guatemala', *Journal of Community Health*, Vol.12(2,3), Summer Fall, pp.92-107.

Rahman, M.D.A. (1993) *People's Self-Development*, Zed Books, London.

Srinivasan, L. (1990) *Tools for Community Participation*, PROWWESS/UNDP, New York.

Welter, B. (1984) *Participatief Onderzoek*, doctoraal thesis, Rijks Universiteit, Utrecht.

5 Training issues for the use of participatory research methods in health

Elizabeth E. Tolley and Margaret E. Bentley

A wide range of organizations and researchers has begun using participatory rapid appraisal (PRA) and participatory research (PR) techniques in health, as in other fields. The demand for training in PRA and the need for documentation are high. This chapter discusses several issues that are related to training different categories of individuals and organizations in PR methods.

Throughout the chapter we draw upon our experiences in training a variety of individuals and organizations in PRA methods in India. One experience has been working with a group of NGOs and academic organizations which belong to a women's reproductive health network. Johns Hopkins University, funded by the Ford Foundation/India, has been training individuals in this network for the past three years in applied social science research, particularly qualitative research (Bentley et al. 1992). As part of the training, a workshop on PRA was conducted in H.D. Kote, in Karnataka and hosted by MYRADA, one of the pioneer PRA-training organizations in India. In addition, one of the authors has been working on an informal and continuous basis with a community development NGO in Bombay. The NGO's social workers have been trained in the fundamental concepts of PR to investigate issues that affect their work.

We begin the chapter by defining PRA, following on the work of Chambers (1992) and others. We then discuss why we believe PRA is particularly suited for research into health in developing countries. We propose three categories of users of PRA in health and discuss six issues that are shared to some degree by each category. Distinctions between user groups are indicated. Finally, we make several recommendations for training in participatory research techniques and raise some questions for further discussion.

What is participatory research?

Perhaps the most important distinction between participatory research methods and other qualitative techniques is a philosophical one, pertaining to the roles played by researcher and informants. In traditional research, both quantitative and qualitative, these two roles are distinct.

The researcher defines the questions for investigation and the data-collection process. To varying degrees, definition of the research problem and the methodological tools are predetermined. Informants provide information but are seldom involved in collecting or analysing data. In PR, however, 'outside' researchers and 'inside' respondents are partners, exploring topics of mutual interest together. As Robert Chambers points out, in PRA 'outsiders are conveners, catalysts and facilitators to enable people to undertake and share their own investigations and analysis' (Chambers 1992:12).

The objective of participatory research is exemplified in a concept introduced by MYRADA at the workshop on PRA in Karnataka. Johari's Window, or the Four Squares of Knowledge[1] illustrates the conceptual movement necessary for conducting authentic participatory research.

Figure 5.1: The Four Squares of Knowledge

I We know They know	II We don't know They know
III We know They don't know	IV We don't know They don't know

Too often the third quadrant of this diagram characterizes the attitude of outside experts. The local community, impressed or more often intimidated by the neat pens and notepads of researchers, place themselves in quadrant II. The lines are drawn. In PR, knowledge is pooled and a shift in attitude pushes out the boundaries of quadrant I and reduces those of II and III.

Use of visual and diagrammatic methods in participatory research helps shift the ownership of data from proprietary to shared. Maps, diagrams, charts, graphs and pictures are constructed by local participants using available materials in order to explain their concepts. Stories and role plays can also be used. Most techniques are grasped easily by literate as well as non-literate participants, and, therefore 'level the playing field'. 'Information is visible, semi-permanent, and public, and is checked, verified, amended, added to, and owned, by the participants' (Chambers 1992:23). Visual materials have another advantage. By helping focus all group members' eyes and attention on the topic in question, they lead to greater in-depth discussion. For example, during a PR session with a family in rural Maharashtra we were able to discuss household dietary composition in great detail, including the total quantities of food consumed by all family members, relative costs of food items, intra-household consumption patterns, changes in seasonal diet and more, in under two hours. Throughout the session, household members remained interested and responsive. This would have been difficult to achieve in an interview format.

Categories of users

We have identified three different types of individuals and groups that may require training in PRA. The categories are not inclusive and may, in practice, overlap at times. To ease discussion of the different training approaches possible, our categories are based on two criteria: the purpose of the group in undertaking participatory research; and the possibility of continuing interaction between researchers and participants. The categories are:

- academic;
- NGOs and action-oriented groups; and
- programme and policy makers, government-level workers.

The first group of trainees includes people in academic settings. Researchers and teachers take up research to contribute to the general body of knowledge on a particular subject. They are concerned with issues of validity and reliability. Important outcomes of their research are papers and seminars to disseminate their findings, and the development of materials for further education and training. Academic researchers may or may not have a permanent set of communities in which to work, and even when they are involved in intervention work, the time is often finite.

When NGOs take up research it is for pragmatic reasons, such as the identification of needs for service delivery or to understand why a specific programme is not having the anticipated impact. The relationships that NGOs build with local communities, and their relatively decentralized or autonomous nature, allow them to respond in a timely way to new or changing community needs. The outcome of such research may be shared with the community, but it is rarely shared with other organizations or the general public.

Programme and policy makers seldom conduct their own research, but could benefit greatly from training in participatory research. Plans and programmes implemented at a state or national level often have unimagined impacts on people at a local level. Government workers operating at the latter level may not feel free to make operational or programme changes without a mandate from the central office. By bringing policy makers face to face with local communities and providing decision makers with tools for talking with and understanding programme beneficiaries, public policy can be more effective and focused.

Issues in participatory research

Understanding the value of local knowledge

Most trainers will agree that the methods must be learned by doing. Some concepts, however, are fundamental to PRA and warrant discussion before practice. Without understanding of the value of local knowledge, PRA techniques lose their power (Mascarenhas 1990a). Most PRA methods encourage and enable villagers and slum dwellers to share their knowledge, beliefs and behaviours with us, but there is no guarantee. The researcher's attitude and skills are vital for enabling the real picture to emerge (Mascarenhas 1990b).

During our March 1992 workshop, Jimmy Mascarenhas spoke of the delight and utter surprise one government agricultural official had during fieldwork, as he talked with local farmers about cropping patterns and other things. For some, the realization that the rural and urban poor are intelligent, rational people who can provide important insights into how programmes and policies affect them changes their whole perspective on how to do development work.

Of course, not all officials find an introduction to participatory research easy. Heaver suggests that government functionaries, more prone to inspection of development programmes than interaction with local staff and clients, have the hardest time learning and adopting the correct attitude (Heaver 1991). On the other hand, the physical proximity of NGO staff to local communities may lead them to believe they understand local priorities without ever asking directly. Attitudes are not always changed easily, but direct experience is often many times more powerful than words in changing behaviour.

Researchers must learn to ask the right questions and not insist on the correct answers. That means asking relevant open-ended questions, ones that give local participants freedom to answer as they wish, not as they feel they should. In a physical sense, it means 'handing over the stick' to local participants (Chambers 1992:15). They draw the map and measure out the beans. The outside facilitator watches, listens and learns, asking questions or probing for more information only after local participants have had a chance to modify, complete and explain their work.

This doesn't mean that a researcher should accept at face value all information that emerges from a participatory research session. Local knowledge is a complex social construct. The composition of the participant group in terms of gender, economic and political power, as well as its members, expectations of the researcher, may influence the information members provide. Therefore, trainees of participatory research techniques must learn to recognize the quality of the data being provided. Action Aid includes interactive exercises in their PRA training to learn how to distinguish between fact, opinion, hearsay, assumptions and inferences (Joseph 1991). Trainees can learn to cross-check information by using a mix of methods to discuss an issue and by actively seeking out and speaking to different groups within the community. In anthropology, this type of cross-checking through use of a mix of methods is called triangulation and is an important research strategy (Jick 1979).

Interactive versus extractive approach

An important question for academic researchers is whether the key philosophical premises of empowerment and joint ownership of the research are in conflict with their roles. PRA tools and techniques, often adapted or borrowed from classical and applied anthropology, are respectful and highly effective means of collecting data. As such, researchers may want to add them to their methodological toolbox to extract information that is taken away to be analysed, packaged and published. In this process the informants do not benefit directly. Unless there is joint ownership of the process and outcome, this is not PRA, and it is important to acknowledge this difference in training (Chambers 1992).

Another related issue has to do with what happens to the data. Most academic researchers have to publish in referred journals in order to remain in their academic institutions. However, in PRA, if the data and research process are shared, how can it be published? Can this be negotiated as part of the research process with the community?

Action-oriented groups would seem predisposed to participatory research, but NGOs with participatory intentions may still give priority to their own agendas. They see the services they provide as inherently good, even essential for the well-being of those they serve. One could argue that it is because services are provided at little cost to clients that they are used. Client use of services becomes the justification for continuing them with little modification over time. In some cases, when participatory research is undertaken it provides further endorsement of an agency's programmes. On the other hand, this research might reveal that the community has a very different set of priorities from the NGO. If the organization is unwilling or unable to respond to needs expressed during the research, it loses credibility in the community. Effective training of NGOs must address this.

Academic researchers, policy makers and even NGOs often share the view that the poor are incapable of actively collecting and analysing information to improve their lives. Moreover, the illiterate poor will usually support them in this view. In a sense, they have learned their lessons well.

Quantitative versus qualitative research

Academics seem particularly absorbed by this dichotomy that defines and devalues 'soft' science versus 'hard'. Qualitative data are often considered not scientific enough because they are not amenable to statistical testing, inference, reliability and validity testing. Among the toolbox of qualitative methods, PRA techniques may be considered the softest by those who make such distinctions. Susan Rifkin attributes the perception that participatory research data is soft to its emphasis on:

> the value of internal changes as well as results, specific application of findings rather than global views and the recognition that the researcher is an active participant not an objective observer in the study (Rifkin 1993:5)

This ability to describe and analyse processes is, in fact, one of the strengths of qualitative data (Bernard 1994:136).

Findings reported from PRA in one community may not be valid for another. However, because participatory research recommends using a mix of methods to triangulate data, internal validity can be much greater than in data gathered through surveys. If the design requires a more systematic approach, the researcher can standardize the techniques and types of data collected through PR. Thought needs to be given as to how this affects the power balance between researchers and local community members, however.

Even small community NGOs are affected by this debate. In India, such organizations are compelled periodically by government agencies to carry out population surveys or other quantitative studies. They often act as data collectors without being involved in critical aspects of the survey design. And, while NGOs may find the work time-consuming and disruptive to their own activities, they can be left with the notion that research is synonymous with surveys and quantitative analysis. Due to the scientific nature of research, NGOs may consider it beyond their capabilities, and yet disqualify participatory or other qualitative research as too soft.

Just do it. Then talk about it!

Conceptually, participatory research methods are simple. Methodological strengths, as well as difficulties, must be experienced. Therefore, training programmes must be oriented towards practice, not theory.

In the five-day training hosted by MYRADA a series of slides provided a visual depiction of various PRA techniques (Tolley & Bentley 1992). The session lasted about one hour. Participants were divided into five groups to go in the field. Fieldwork was over ten hours, depending on the needs of each training group. All groups were asked to conduct a village mapping exercise in their training village so that participants would have a common basis for discussion of their first PRA experiences. After this point, however, trainees were encouraged to develop their own research topics and approaches. By doing so, they had the opportunity to practise techniques in context and draw upon their own creativity.

Once trainees have conducted participatory research activities in a real-life situation, plenty of time should be allocated for training participants to share their experiences with one another. They learn from each other. In the MYRADA training, approximately eight hours were allocated for group presentations and discussion. Trainees and trainers were asked to look critically at the way they conducted activities. Were they listening? Did they allow local participants to teach them, or were they dominating the process? What kind of information came out during the exercise? Was it cross-checked by other participants or using other methods?

How much training and by whom? When and where?

Many of the documented training experiences are from formal workshops, lasting from just a few days to a few weeks. In the March 1992 workshop, a mix of participants came from NGOs, academic environments and research institutes for a five-day introduction to PRA. The group included medical doctors and social workers, people with experience in training or in computers. All stayed in a MYRADA training campus surrounded by a number of villages within a 30km radius. This mela (festival) atmosphere has many advantages.

Bringing participants together from different backgrounds and away from the normal strains and stresses of their jobs encourages lively discussion. It allows them to concentrate fully on learning and critiquing the methods. For an intensive workshop of short duration it is possible to bring in a team of trainers from various backgrounds. A PRA training manual by the Save the Children Fund suggests that awithin the training team experience in adult non-formal education techniques and practical experience in PRA or RRA should be present. Assistants should have experience in data collection and analysis, journalistic interviewing techniques or ethnographic methods (Theis & Grady 1991).

Participants did raise some concerns about this kind of training, however. For example, there are some problems with practising techniques in 'someone else's field'. If communities have been used numerous times for training purposes, local people may themselves become experts at PRA. Researchers or participants from NGOs, trying out these techniques for the first time, wonder whether it will be so easy when they return to their own villages or urban communities. In addition, there were language problems. Very few of the participants actually spoke the local language and so translators worked with each group. Because the staff acting as translators already had a relationship with villagers, they introduced participatory research activities, asked the questions and translated local responses, smoothing over many of the training teams' awkward questions or ill-timed probes. Working through translators reduces the learning experience, as participants are not able to make their own mistakes and correct them.

Whenever possible, it is recommended to practise and learn the techniques purposively. It is best to select a training location where on-going activities are possible, and to allow trainees to select research topics and methods that match their organization's needs. The above and what follows present a strong case for learning participatory research techniques on one's own turf. During the initial session of an on-going training with an NGO in Bombay, the trainer presented some of the fundamental concepts of participatory research. Thereafter, the participants themselves determined the time and place for the next session, what the topic of inquiry would be and which method(s) would be used. Methods can be learned and practised as the need arises for information in the organization's daily work. Furthermore, participants are familiar with the local community and language and are highly motivated to learn and use the techniques.

Documentation

There are actually two levels on which to discuss documentation. At a micro level, individuals and organizations need to determine how to record the data that results from participatory research activities, and what kind of emerging information is actually useful to them. The exuberance, and at times chaos, in which some participatory research activities are conducted make them difficult to record. During one very lively body- mapping session on women's health problems several women began at once to discuss their experiences of 'the operation' and subsequent complications. What emerged was a sort of composite picture of how women view sterilization and its ensuing problems. Individual voices were lost in the rapid to-and-fro of the session. NGOs that conduct participatory research should pay attention to and document the process in which they learn information as well as the content. While reviewing notes from PR sessions, they can then decide whether they have obtained a complete picture of a topic under research with a community and what information needs to be cross-checked for individual or group variations. Community needs must be considered as well when documenting PR sessions. Some methods lend themselves well to recording information to be shared with local participants. Whenever maps or diagrams are drawn on the ground, a copy should be made on paper, so that research participants can refer back to it, review and revise it.

On a macro level, users of participatory research techniques need to share honest and thorough accounts of such efforts with the wider research community. In this regard, attention to process – what worked and especially what didn't work – is as important as content. In our March 1992 workshop each group was responsible for writing up detailed field notes on the process, content and problems encountered during each of their field exercises (Tolley & Bentley 1992).

Questions for discussion and training recommendations

This chapter raises several questions that call for further discussion:
- To what degree does the local community need to be involved, and how should it be involved, for research to be participatory?

Chambers and others have suggested that we look at participation as a continuum and not as a factor that is either present or absent (Chambers 1992). The various users of PR face different challenges from within the local community in moving towards fuller participation. Susan Rifkin suggests that the key to this issue is power and control. If, by taking part in the process of research, local community members gain more control over their health, participation is present. Rifkin states that this control concerns issues like resource allocation, decentralization of power and of decision making, and can, therefore, be threatening (Rifkin 1993). Below we discuss some of obstacles to increasing local participation.

In analysing the potential applications of PRA in Indian health and family planning programmes, Heaver recognizes the inherent challenges to the local government structure. Increased community participation may cause tension between different economic or caste groups within a village. It may increase the pressure on local government staff to perform. Local people may themselves resist giving more or continuous time to PRA activities. For these reasons, he suggests introducing greater participation into the existing system in stages. By introducing local-level fieldworkers to simple PRA techniques such as community mapping, conversational interviewing on local perceptions of health, and verbal autopsies, government workers will become more sensitive and responsive to local needs. Once these simple techniques are well-established and a measure of cooperation has developed, the community can be brought into health-monitoring activities and eventually the development of services tailored to the local situation. He emphasizes, however, that until government programmes operate in a more decentralized environment where local fieldworkers have the scope to make the decisions based on the local situation, only simple applications of PRA should be used (Heaver 1991).

The pressure to delegate more responsibility and decision-making power to the middle and lower levels may bring resistance from higher-level government planners. Mavalankar and Satia feel that the work culture within the Indian bureaucracy must change before participation from local communities is possible. Lower-level supervisors and other staff must be empowered to function with a degree of independence and become accountable on the basis of performance. Performance criteria, however, must not be judged on the basis of service targets set at the central level. They should instead be linked to 'ground-level realities' and community feedback (Mavalankar & Satia 1993:9).

Within Indian governmental organizations a dual process of training should take place. Programme and policy makers should be introduced to the power of participatory research. Training for these groups need not be long and intensive, but must emphasize the importance of role reversal for PR and include face-to-face encounters with people from the local community. Chambers suggests that it is necessary but not sufficient, however, to win the directors of organizations over to PRA; PRA must be supported actively and used by lower field-level staff. Programme and policy directors can support the use of PR methods by providing training opportunities to field staff and demanding data gathered through these techniques to design or revise programmes. They can support the use of participatory research in day-to-day monitoring and evaluation of programme activities (Chambers 1992).

NGOs in India have a wide range of working styles. Some, but certainly not all community development organizations initiate their programmes only after consulting and involving local people. The use of participatory research in this process of problem prioritization and the identification or evaluation of resources helps the NGO ensure it is remaining true to organizational goals. Initial training may be through formal workshops or informally at home. In addition to learning about and experimenting with basic techniques, such organizations should think about and discuss how they will deal with unexpected situations arising out of collaborative research with local communities.

One such challenge appears when the community's expressed needs do not match the organization's capabilities or interests. The Bombay NGO, interested in improving its health services for women in a Bombay slum, undertook participatory research only to find out that the women in that community ranked health care well behind other concerns, namely obtaining a reliable supply of water and electricity, and addressing problems related to government-subsidized rations. The NGO's dilemma was either to take up more important issues first, ignore the women's requests and risk damaging its reputation, or put the women in contact with other individuals or organizations that could work with them on primary concerns. While this last choice seems an efficient and economical choice, it is often avoided. When NGOs rely on external funding that is tied to specific project activities and target populations, there is a disincentive to liaise with competing NGOs for fear of losing their clients or their funding.

- How can these techniques be used in research that is not directly linked to action? How do we ensure that follow-up does take place when research is conducted by traditional researchers?

PRA and participatory research are tied inextricably to action. This would seem to put traditional researchers at a disadvantage. Le Boterf recommends that those promoting PR should work in close collaboration with local organizations that represent the population. These organizations may be formally established: associations, trade unions or religious groups, for instance; or they can be set up as the research is undertaken (Le Boterf 1983:173). Collaborating agencies should, however, be selected carefully. Consideration should be given to whose interest the group represents, and how capable it is of following up on initiatives raised during the research.

Mark Nichter provides one novel example of how an academic researcher attempted to ensure that action followed from participatory research. In a study in southern Karnataka state, India, Nichter explored whether local community members could be trained in social science research methodology. After training, these indigenous social scientists became members of community diagnostic teams. The teams provided much valuable information on locally felt health needs and the context in which the community meets these needs, as well as appropriate means for communicating health information. Nichter questions whether such participatory research teams can function independently with periodic support and supervision from trained social scientists (Nichter 1984). With practice, these local researchers may become important representatives of their communities, with useful problem-solving skills.

Le Boterf suggests an important way to involve the local community in research:

> Placing the emphasis on participation in identifying resources means mobilizing energy for positive research, restoring confidence, and promoting natural or cultural elements which have been rejected or suppressed by the dominant ideology. Developing people's ability to mobilize such resources is as important as identifying problems. (Le Boterf 1983:181)

The process of identifying and mobilizing local resources, however, can be very long. NGOs working in local communities may find this time well spent. Academic researchers with time constraints and a less permanent presence in the community will have to rely on their local partners to take up such work.

A question remains: Yes, but do these methods work better than more traditional ones, especially in terms of impact?

This question can be raised and debated during training, but it will be answered only after careful practice and documentation. The question will be asked especially by programme and policy makers who fund intervention research and community development. We believe there will be a real need to demonstrate that PRA techniques and research do deliver. Applied research comparing PRA with other intervention approaches could be an important activity for those interested in PRA research.

Note

1. The Four Squares of Knowledge is adapted by MYRADA (an Indian NGO involved in rural development) from the four squares of self-knowledge published in Luft (1963).

References

Bentley, M. et al. (1992) 'Use of qualitative research methodologies for women's reproductive-health data in India', *Rapid Assessment Procedures: Qualitative Methodologies for Planning and Evaluation of Health Related Programmes*, International Nutrition Foundation for Developing Countries, Boston, MA.

Bernard, R. (1994) *Research Methods in Cultural Anthropology*, Second Edition, Sage Publications, London.

Chambers, R. (1992) 'Rural appraisal: rapid, relaxed and participatory', Institute of Development Studies Discussion Paper 311, October.

Heaver, R. (1991) 'Participative rural appraisal: potential applications to family planning, health and nutrition', Asia Technical Department of the World Bank, Departmental Papers Series, No.3, September.

Jick, T.D. (1979) 'Multiplying qualitative and quantitative methods: triangulation in action', *Administrative Science Quarterly*, Vol.24, pp.59-68.

Joseph, S. (1991) *Tagore Society of Rural Development: Participatory Rural Appraisal Training Notes*, unpublished document, ActionAid.

Le Boterf, G. (1983) 'Reformulating participatory research', *Assignment Children*, Vol.63/4, pp.167-92.

Luft, J. (1963) 'Group processes: an introduction to group dynamics', National Press Books, p.70.

Mascarenhas, J. (1990a) 'Enhancing Participation in PRAs', unpublished document, MYRADA Palm Series No.IVC.

Mascarenhas, J. (1990b) 'Interviewing in PRA', unpublished document, MYRADA Palm Series No.IVB.

Mavalankar, D.V. and Satia, J.K. (1993) 'Experiences and issues in institutional participatory research approaches in government health programme', paper presented at the *International Symposium on Participatory Research in Health Promotion*, Liverpool School of Tropical Medicine, UK, September.

Nichter, M. (1984) 'Project community diagnosis: participatory research as a first step toward community involvement in primary health-care', *Social Science and Medicine*, Vol.19(3), pp.237-52.

Rifkin, S. (1993) 'Participation and research in health', paper presented at the *International Symposium on Participatory Research in Health Promotion*, Liverpool School of Tropical Medicine, UK, September.

Theis, J. and Grady, H. (1991) *Participatory Rapid Appraisal for Community Development*, International Institute for Environment and Development and Save the Children Fund, London.

Tolley, E. and Bentley, M. (1992) 'Participatory methods for research on women's reproductive health', *Rapid Rural Appraisal Notes*, Vol.16.

PART III PR PROCESSES AND EMPOWERMENT

6 Participatory action research (PAR) in women's health: SARTHI, India

Renu Khanna

I would like to place these reflections in the context of my own experiences, both personal and work-related. I do this because I believe that I am typical of my kind, an activist and a practitioner working on women's issues.

My educational background and training have contributed to the way I see myself. I have been a practitioner concerned with pragmatic action to bring about social change. I understood research as something lofty and abstract, concerned with a world of ideas. I have had, in fact, a mortal fear of research, resulting in a tendency to distance myself mentally from anything which was even remotely research-like. Second, somewhere quite early in my working life, I began seeing myself as an enabler, a facilitator for empowerment. This commitment to empowerment grew and gradually I began recognizing this, and around nine years ago I made some very conscious choices about my future work which I decided was to be in the area of women's empowerment. It is against this background that I shall examine the topic of PAR in women's health. What implications and meaning does PAR have for practitioners and for women's empowerment?

In order to arrive at a conceptual understanding of PR for women's-health action, I shall draw upon the last nine years' experiences that I have had working with Social Action for Rural and Tribal Inhabitants of India (SARTHI).

Background to the Social Action for Rural and Tribal Inhabitants of India (SARTHI) case study

SARTHI is a voluntary organization which started its operations in 1980 in the Panchmahals District of Gujarat in western India. This district is classified as backward and as a drought-prone area. It is resource-poor and, has a higher population density and a far lower literacy rate than the rest of India. Originally SARTHI started as a branch of the Social Work and Research Centre (SWRC, Tilonia). In 1985, it was registered as an independent entity. Its initial work consisted of conventional development projects like installing hand pumps, deepening wells and setting up income-generating projects.

The status of the women in Panchmahals, as elsewhere in the country, is quite discouraging. Their workload is heavy. In addition to all the housework, many women work on daily wages either in the fields of big landowners or in public works. Women of landowning families also perform substantial agricultural tasks. While men do the ploughing and marketing of the produce, women shoulder the major responsibilities of hoeing, weeding, irrigating, harvesting and processing the produce. Women's work also consists of collecting fuel, fetching water and cattle care.

Desertion, domestic violence, alcoholism among men (despite prohibition in Gujarat) and husbands bringing in second wives to beget sons are common problems facing women in the area. On top of that, during drought years they have also to shoulder the responsibility of men's work if men migrate in search of wages. Many women also migrate with men to labour in more prosperous areas.

The F:M sex ratio in the Panchmahals has changed from 959:1,000 in 1981 to 953:1,000 in 1991; female literacy in the district is 22.66 percent as compared to 41.18 percent for Gujarat state (figures from 1991 Census).

Also, as elsewhere, women own little land or property. Whether at her parental home or that of her in-laws, although she labours hard in a subsistence economy, the woman's economic status is like that of an unpaid domestic labourer. Decision making concerning land is almost exclusively a preserve of men.

My involvement in SARTHI began in 1984. Our team was invited to help the voluntary organization start its first programme with women. This was the improved cookstoves (*chulhas*) programme. My colleague, Madhu Sarin, had devised a system and a methodology to improve cookstoves. The philosophy underlying our approach was empowerment of women by helping them gain control over a technology which was, until then, controlled by men. And the main goals of this programme were to help reduce the drudgery of women related to fuel collection, cleaning of cooking pots and the house, as well as to reduce the health hazards for women by reducing the smoke within the house. By 1987, we had succeeded in creating a cadre of about thirty local women, the *chulha mistries* (technicians), who were in constant touch with SARTHI. The year 1987 was a period of dialogue and reflection. Through leadership-and-awareness *shibirs* (camps) and village meetings with the local women and the *chulha mistries*, SARTHI tried to find out what direction its women's programme could take. This was also the time of an acute drought in this area. The women reported high morbidity due to weakened physical states resulting from malnutrition, anxiety and work overload. They suggested that SARTHI start a health programme for them. Thus, in 1988 a women's health programme was launched.

The women's health programme

The years 1988 to 1992 can be considered the pilot phase of the women's health programme. The perspective with which this programme was launched is summarized below.

Women exist within a social framework where they are defined primarily through their bodies. Their physique is assessed for the ability to work or to bear children, their appearances are judged within the framework of traditional beauty and their bodies are restricted to satisfy the claims of ownership by men. Surrounded by and immersed in the stereotypical images of women, as mother, woman as sacrificing wife, woman as burden, there is little space for women to value their experiences and ways of being in the world, and through this, to take control over their bodies and lives.

Woman's subjectivity, her experiences of existence, are negated and rendered invisible, her body is used as a battleground by the forces both of tradition and of progress. Women continually face both external and internal, physical and emotional violence. This violence against women, their lack of control over and identification with their bodies, become visible through the statistics reflecting women's poor health status, through deaths in infancy and at childbirth and through invisible but high levels of morbidity such as anaemia and gynaecological problems. Alongside the health problems women themselves face is the role of women as carers of the sick. Within the family context, a large amount of a woman's time, energy and resources is spent on tending those who have fallen ill, particularly children and old people. Yet again she receives little recognition for her input of physical, emotional and economic energy. In approaching women's health, it becomes vital, therefore, to move away from the paradigm of issue-based health care inputs that focus primarily on maternal and child health (MCH) and family planning (FP), developing instead a fresh conceptual framework. Working with women's health involves exploring and understanding woman's experience of herself within society, her relationship to and control over her body. The layers of negation and devaluation need to be peeled off, so that women are empowered, their experiences are validated and they are enabled to develop their self-image within a context where they can exert control over their bodies and recognize their intrinsic strengths, both individually and collectively.

From this will emerge a space in which women are then freer to define and work with what they perceive as health problems, definitions that may well include the components of MCH and FP but have the potential to expand to issues of water and sanitation, physical work burdens, liquor and much else. The possibilities become enormous as the stereotypical, pre-defined barriers are broken down and women come to value themselves and to recognize and value their contribution to society.

In this context, development is seen as a process which begins with the validation of the individual and encompasses the changing relationships of that individual and other individuals within that community, rather than being simply a set of targets to be achieved.[1]

The women's health programme in the pilot phase had three distinct, chronological parts:

- the maternal and child health component;
- action research on traditional medicines; and
- training for gynaecology through the self-help approach.

Today the women's health programme is being implemented through a group of fifteen trained and experienced *arogya sakhis* (barefoot gynaecologists). They treat the common gynaecological problems of women in their villages with validated herbal medicines. They also work as counsellors and as organizers, mobilizing women for collective action on common problems. In May 1993, in response to increasing demands from other women in the community, SARTHI initiated training for a second group of thirty women health workers. Four of the original *arogya sakhis* were helped to develop their skills as trainers and undertook the training of the new group.

SARTHI has decided to focus on sexually transmitted diseases (STDs) in the next phase of their women's health programme. STDs seem to be a significant problem in the area. The causes may perhaps be the seasonal migration patterns of the local people, and cultural mores influencing sexual behaviour in the community. In the second phase of the programme, the voluntary agency has decided that it is necessary to include men, too, in its work on women's health issues.

Participatory action research in SARTHI's women's health programme

On reflection it appears as though PAR was built into the women's health programme in three ways. Although not originally planned to be a PAR, the entire programme actually emerged as this: the problem was identified by the local women, SARTHI decided to respond to it and with the participation of the women as well as a lot of external support succeeded in creating an alternative model of woman-centred, holistic health care at the primary level.

An essential part of the introductory work had to do with creating space for the local women to start sharing their stories. In workshop sessions, as well as out of them, women were encouraged to talk about their experiences of their bodies, for instance their experiences of menstruation and childbirth. This sharing helped the women to recognize how their bodies had been used to keep them in a subordinate position. The aim of this kind of sharing was also to shed their sense of *sharam* (embarrassment) and help them revalue and claim an essential part of themselves.

Second, the action research on traditional remedies for women's health was PAR. Through workshops with traditional healers, village meetings with elders, participatory field exercises with school-children and field visits with local women into the forests, identification of flora traditionally used for common health problems, especially women's gynaecological problems, was carried out. This process was strongly empowering; once we started putting it together, the local women began to realize the wealth of knowledge that they have. Validation by the SHODHINI (a feminist network in India, doing action research on alternative healing practices based on traditional remedies) botanist revealed that almost 80 percent of their remedies had a sound phytochemical/botanical basis. This was further reinforcing. The result of this PAR is that the village people are now making conscious efforts to propagate medicinal plants and revitalize the systems of traditional medicines for their primary health care needs.

Third, the self-help workshops for training in social and gender-sensitive gynaecology were also a PAR. Eleven of us (eight *arogya sakhis*, two programme planners and the facilitator) met regularly each month for three days from December 1990 to February 1992. The purpose of these meetings was to learn the basics of gynaecology by examining our own selves. We also started dealing with our own common health problems with the use of validated traditional remedies and other non-drug therapies. As we started equipping ourselves with these skills and knowledge, many of us could begin working in the community as barefoot gynaecologists. The self-help effort was, to my mind, a classic example of PAR.

- There was no distinction between the researcher and the researched. The group of eleven women, eight of whom were local, came together as equal members of the self-help groups. The research question, how to treat common problems of women, was defined jointly. The data were generated by using each of our own bodies and relating these to our life experiences. The analysis and the planning for follow-up action was done collectively.
- This process had the effect of transforming each and all of us. Our ways of perceiving reality were changed radically, as were our responses to situations which faced us.
- We started becoming actively conscious of imbalances due to gender relations in our own lives and the society at large. We also became aware of our own rights in relation to the state, particularly the government health structure. In short, this PAR resulted in the politicization of us all.
- The politicization and transformation processes resulted in many

of us initiating concrete action to change the situation that we saw around us.[2]

PAR and the difficulties faced

The major initial difficulty that we faced was related to breaking mental barriers. As mentioned earlier, I myself resisted anything to do with research. The aura surrounding research activities as they are typically carried out was not appealing to me. Treating people like objects, limiting interaction with them to the extraction of information, not leaving behind anything that they could use in a reciprocal process, were elements of research with which I disagreed.

With the women, the major barrier that had to be broken was one of participation. For generations, women were used to contributing only their labour to society and not their conscious thoughts. The women that we were working with had tremendous difficulty in seeing themselves as anything other than passive recipients of handed-down knowledge. Through a gradual process, which was painful and slow, the women first began formulating their own opinions and then moved on to analysis and formulating conclusions.

It was because of these mental barriers that we saw the initial stages of our women's health work as pure action for empowerment rather than as participatory research. Once we overcame our resistances, we realized that with our commitment to empowerment and participation, any grassroots action addressing people's own issues could be termed PAR.

The second difficulty (if it can be called such) that we faced in the PAR in women's health was devising suitable methods. The methods of data collection and, of analysis had to be based on women's own reality, reality in terms of their abilities, their belief systems, their metaphors. For instance, we learned that to ask the traditional healers to name the plants that they used in their practice would not get any results. There was a belief that uttering the name of the plant, which was considered sacred in its healing power, was paramount to disrespect and would result in the plant losing that power. A more correct way of approaching the data-gathering for this purpose was to go on a field visit with a group of women, including the traditional healer, who would then point out the plant whose local name the other women would then speak. In this way the PAR became a true partnership, facilitating mutual exchange rather than just a one-way process of either extracting information for research purposes or imposing our own knowledge and beliefs in the interests of an efficient service-delivery programme and, with some of us who had received training of a different kind having to de-learn and re-learn.

The third difficulty, which remains unaddressed and unresolved even at this point in time is related to the issues of the recording, documenting, writing and dissemination of the PAR experiences. How can the women truly own the body of knowledge resulting from the PAR experience? How can they participate as equals in the production of the documented material and not just as notional members? How can they disseminate their experiences directly? These questions haunt us still.

PAR and the lessons learned

Some of our learning from SARTHI's PAR in women's health may be reflective of the collective wisdom of experienced participatory researchers. However, we do feel the need to list the lessons here, because they are a part of our own personal discovery. We learned that :

- PAR requires an attitude of mutuality, an openness and a commitment to learning on the part of all those involved. These words have acquired a different meaning for us, as programme planners: we have really learned how difficult it is to open up ourselves as recipients of traditional knowledge, and how difficult it is to leave the position of those who have all the answers.

- Truly participatory action research results in all the actors going through a process which transforms them at a very personal level and politicizes them with respect to relationships at another level. The transformation of Rasiben was amazing. In the first few self-help workshops, she could not even come near a woman doing a self-examination because, as she stated, 'It is dirty, the odours make me vomit.' By the sixth workshop, she was the keenest learner, the first one to see the cervical erosion or the infections! The transformation really had to do with different ways of perceiving things.

- PAR calls for a form of organization which not only allows space for this kind of transformation but which can also respond to it by changing itself. SARTHI, for instance, has had to respond to the growth in the women by allowing them more space. The organizational structure, the programmes, the processes have all undergone some degree of change. The women's health programme is used as an illustration of sustainable development, an example that has to be emulated in the other programmes that the organization takes up. Had the organization remained rigid and not kept pace with the women, an unmanageable tension would have been created, perhaps resulting in many of the women health workers leaving.

- Further, PAR can succeed in or through organizations whose ultimate objective is empowerment. The chances for success are less in organizations whose ultimate goal is efficient service delivery. This is because the values which govern the two kinds of organization are different.

- PAR, to be truly successful in relation to women's issues and women's empowerment, has to challenge patriarchal structures and modes of thinking. For instance, conventional methods have created a divide between the researcher and the researched. In this division, the researcher is ascribed a greater value on the basis of a more cerebral function. A corollary of this is the notion that only professional researchers can generate knowledge for meaningful social reform.
- PAR has greater chances of success where some feminist values and modes of functioning already exist, for example, a more equitable division of labour based on gender analysis and revalued gender roles, an holistic perception of reality, principles of mutual support, 'personal is political', non-hierarchical or fluid and adaptive structures.
- There is a difference between PAR and PR methods. The assumption that the use of participatory research methods is actually participatory research leads to serious problems. Participatory research is much more than the application of PR methods. It is an entire process which includes education, pain and struggle and results in empowerment.

Conclusion

I would like to examine some of the concepts contained in the title of this chapter. I will begin with the concept of participation. In recent years, participation, and especially 'community participation', has become a slogan to be adopted by community health programmes before they can be evaluated as successful. The questions 'participation by whom?' and 'participation in what?' are seldom asked. It is accepted that community participation at its simplest level occurs when local people contribute in cash or kind to the implementing agency's programmes. A high level of community participation is thought to occur when the community is involved in identifying a problem and managing a programme. But the programme is still that of the implementing agency. In my mind, it is becoming clearer that we need to put the horse before the cart. We need to understand that it is the people's (or community's) needs and programmes that we, the action groups or implementing agencies, need to participate in. This calls for a fundamental shift in our perception of our work. Our agenda in the community thus becomes one of helping the community to recognize and focus on its needs and helping it increase its capacities to meet these needs, rather than to implement health care delivery programmes for it and solicit its participation in these.

As mentioned earlier, the participatory research process would have greater chances of success if the action component of the PAR has as its goal empowerment of women and not just efficient service delivery for women. Empowerment of women with respect to women's health programmes would need to be defined clearly so that all those who are involved in action know in unambiguous terms what they are striving for. One possible way of conceptualizing manifestations of empowerment related to women's-health action could be as follows:

Figure 6.1: Manifestations of women's empowerment

Building confidence in self, shedding off sharam (shame), owning one's body, beginning to talk about what affects the body and health.	Awareness and increasing control over relationships through which the body is affected.	Appropriating health services that rightfully belong to the group.	Organizing for collective action - demanding and getting quality health care; health rights - dealing with issues which are health issues of women, eg. violence.
Intra-personal	Inter-personal	Group	Community

The above diagram indicates that empowerment of women could be manifested along a continuum. At an intra-personal level, empowerment begins with individual women having a changed perception of themselves. What they thought earlier was dirty and a cause of *sharam* (shame, embarrassment) they now begin to claim and own. The physical problems which earlier went undiscussed now begin to come out of the shrouds. At the inter-personal level, women begin to realize how certain relationships and their subordinate role in these directly affect their bodies. An example of this is the relationship with their husbands. In small ways they also begin to negotiate relationships in the environment. For instance, a small group of women may decide to accompany their neighbour to the health centre to make sure that she gets the service that she requires. At the community level, women organize themselves for collective action around their own issues, for example, to pressurize the state to have their health rights met, or to draw attention to issues which affect their bodies and health directly, issues like rape and violence, which were till recently left unaddressed.

My present understanding of research leads me to believe that any grassroots action which is interspersed with serious reflection to bring out learning is research. This research may or may not contribute anything new to a larger body of existing knowledge. However, at a micro level, it becomes research because it contributes to an increase in local people's understanding about existing problems. This kind of participatory, grassroots-level action research does not in any way lessen the value of research done by academicians and researchers. The two, to my mind, can feed into and strengthen each other, but this strengthening can occur only if there is an appreciation of the strengths and limitations of each mode of research by both the action researchers and the academic researchers. Patronizing attitudes of academic researchers or the short-sighted self-righteousness of activists can both be damaging to the agenda of large-scale social change.

How then can PAR contribute to the traditional paradigm of 'good' research? First, PAR, by not separating the subject from the object, can identify research agendas which matter to people, especially poor people. This is important in a country like India where research priorities (and paradigms) are still copied from the West, making our research institutions lifeless and, by and large, irrelevant. Second, PAR would (re)introduce feelings and human considerations into research by teaching us to respect people's concerns and feelings as opposed to the objective and often amoral stance traditional science and research tends to take. Third, PAR reaffirms by its inherent relevance that knowledge building and the frameworks of knowledge are not neutral. They have to be circumscribed by the morality of the people they purport to serve. Thus planning and policy frameworks and social programmes emerging from such research will learn not to marginalize poor people but truly serve them.

Women's health as a concept also needs to be examined. The definition of women's health needs to be made broader than maternal health which views women in only their reproductive roles. Women as persons, having health needs other than just antenatal and postnatal care, must become the focus of women's health programmes. Further, women-centred health programmes need to acknowledge that women's health status is a product not just of their condition but also of their position in society. Health programmes for women need to be based on an analysis of the gender issues. Women's health is not just a physical issue, it is also a psychological, social and political issue.[3]

Notes

1. Excerpted from 'Working note on SARTHI's women's health programme', April 16 1988 by Janet Price and Renu Khanna.
2. For other details of the self-help approach, see Chapter 4 ('Becoming *aroygya sakhis*'), *Taking Charge: Women's Health as Empowerment; the SARTHI Experience*, SAHAJ/SARTHI, Baroda, India, 1992.
3. This chapter is dedicated to the women of Santrampur Taluka who have been partners in this PAR. I also acknowledge the contributions of the following: Nirmalben, my colleague at SARTHI, Janet Price, who gave us the courage to take the first step, and the SHODHINI network which continues to sustain our efforts, especially Vd. Bajpai and Rina Nissim.

7 Participatory research processes and empowerment: the PACODET community, Uganda

Stanley Okurut, Amos Odong, James Imalingat, Anne Okurut, Lawrence Oloit and Filder Oloit – PACODET[1]

Background

This chapter looks at the participatory process that has empowered the Pallisa Community Development Trust (PACODET) Community in Pallisa District, eastern Uganda. It highlights the strengths and weakness in the process and the ways local people have responded to challenges, as well as the lessons learned and the wisdom gained. The chapter recounts the evolution of a small development project that has benefited from growing community participation. Numerous voices from the youth, women and elders in the community have all contributed to the development both of the project and of this chapter.

PACODET is a locally generated and controlled trust to promote Primary Health Care(PHC)/Primary Environmental Care(PEC) for a population of about 60,000 people. Its general objective was to stimulate, promote and coordinate all the voluntary efforts of the communities for PHC/PEC in the district. The project is located in the 10 neighbouring parishes of the five subcounties of Kibale, Kameke, Agule, Putiputi and Butebo in Pallisa District. Two tribes, Iteso and Bagwere, live peacefully together in the area, a generally flat-wooded savanna plain interspersed by some low granite rocks with extensively encroached woodlands and swamps. A good number of species of insects, birds and some small animals are still found but are under threat of extinction due to human influence. Birds are most affected, through pesticide poisoning. The people are subsistence farmers growing cereals, and tubers. Rice is a major cash crop but sale of staple food crops also occurs.

The household income levels are low as a result of poverty and the narrow income base. Within the households, men plan and control the income. Women and children provide the bulk of unpaid farm labour. Women do all the household duties, handling water, gathering firewood, cooking, cleaning up and the laundry in addition to providing farm labour.

Education levels are low, school enrolment is poor and females are less favoured. There are 10 semi-permanent primary and four senior secondary schools constructed on a self-help basis in the catchment area; all of them are day schools. Most of the teachers are not qualified.

PHC/PEC project

Malaria, upper respiratory tract infections and diarrhoea are major health problems. Before the PACODET PHC/PEC project started, the nearest health care unit was at Pallisa Hospital, over 25km away. There was no transport and communication was generally poor.

The PACODET PHC/PEC project started with provision of essential drugs, followed by immunization; other elements have been added one at a time as needs required and resources allowed. Activities are identified, planned, managed and overseen in group process.

Current activities include provision of essential drugs, immunization, health education, nutrition education, water and sanitation education, family planning, training of community health workers (CHWs) and traditional birth attendants (TBAs), construction of community clinics, environmental education, a credit scheme, development of environmentally sensitive income-generating activities, training and community-based research. Women's participation is relatively high.

Current achievements to date include: an average immunization rate of 700 children a month, an average treatment rate of 4,000 patients a month and an average of 90 births a month assisted by TBAs. We have seen reduced infant mortality rates of 63/1,000 (the national average is 105/1,000). The community has developed environmentally sensitive income-generating projects like mosquito-net making and quilting. We have increased local capacity to carry out research and deliver health care. Five community clinics have been built on a self-help basis. All of this relies on strong project committees and highly sensitized community involvement.

Development of PACODET

Three categories of people – students, elders and the whole community in general – were involved in the evolution and development of PACODET.

Involvement of students In 1986, some university, secondary and primary-school students of Kapuwai came up with the idea of forming a village students' association. To us, forming a village students' body was both very exciting and challenging, since we did not know exactly what to do. We called a meeting to involve all interested students in the village to discuss a students' organization. A total of twenty students, five of whom were girls, turned up for this meeting. We agreed that the purpose of our student body should be relevant to both students and the village as a whole. We did not just want entertainment. On reflection we agreed on three topical areas to brainstorm:

- What are the most common and pressing problems that affect the students and village as whole?

- What activities are necessary to solve the problems and which ones are within available means?
- What resources are needed, what plans, management and organizations are crucial for implementation of activities?

These topical questions were handled one at a time. We brainstormed using a strategy based on the idea that 'every idea is good'. On final analysis, frequent deaths among expectant mothers and children of five years and under were recognized as a major problem. The goal therefore agreed upon was to work to improve the health and welfare of children and women. The activities involved in meeting this goal we identified as the provision of essential drugs and vaccination to prevent rampant immunizable diseases.

The student body named itself the Kapuwai Students Progressive Association (KSPA). We decided to raise money through payment of subscription fees and the students would serve as community health workers (CHWs). We elected a student executive board, answerable to the entire student body, to implement the decisions.

It was surprising and exciting to see how we managed to come up with some sense of direction. But soon we realized that we could not proceed because we, as students, were being supported by our parents and could not do anything without their support. We therefore resolved to hold another meeting to consult with elders.

Involvement of the elders Elders are both men and women who are usually above 50 years of age and are respected because of their ability to handle and resolve serious conflicts amongst community members.

At a meeting between elders and students everyone agreed that the intentions of the students were appropriate. Elders pledged total support to the students' proposal on the condition that they, the students, were serious and committed. The elders requested the association be opened to the whole community for continuity when the students were back at school. The elders warned of the consequences of raising people's expectations and then abandoning them. This had happened before and was dangerous. We finally resolved to hold a meeting for all interested community members. Elders were to extend the invitation to all the community since an invitation from the students would not be taken seriously.

The involvement of all members of the community A week later, the youth, women, men, elders and children of Kapuwai gathered under a mango tree to hear what their school brothers and sisters had to present. The atmosphere was charged with expectation. In an organized formal meeting of about 100 people the chairman of the KSPA announced its aim and purpose. KSPA requested that the community present their views on the decisions taken by their sons and daughters. Comments of approval and wishes that it had been initiated long ago came from all categories of people in attendance.

We decided to break the meeting into subgroups to work out the activities, resources, implementation plan, management and organization necessary to bring about the improvement of women's and children's health. There were groups of women, men, elders and youths. Two students were assigned to each group as mediators. Activities identified to address the health situation of women, children and the community as a whole included provision of medicines to cure the sick, immunization, building a community clinic and training CHWs. Immediate resources were to be generated by a contribution of 100 shillings per person as a membership fee. Youth, women's and elders' coordinating committees were needed for advice, education, mobilization and monitoring of resources. The name of the students' association (KSPA) was retained in honour of the project initiators. Having been empowered to do all that was within our means to get started, we saw it as necessary to inform the government about the birth of this new organization and to seek permission to carry out these activities in this part of Pallisa District. Formal authority was given by the Ministry of Women in Development, Youth and Culture. At this moment in time the foundations for the PACODET project were laid but it would take three years before it was actually called PACODET.

Organizational structure The general assembly is composed of all those people involved and is the supreme body of PACODET (see Figure 7.1). The PACODET executive is responsible for supervision, monitoring and evaluation of project activities and is answerable directly to the general assembly. Individual projects have management committees which are identified and monitored independently by youth, women's and elders' committees and are answerable to their respective parent committees and to the PACODET executive. The youth, women and elders play an advisory role to PACODET and vice versa. The chief advisor to the PACODET executive is a patron recognized by three committees.

Implementation of the PACODET PHC/PEC project

There was a break of three years between the drawing up of an action plan for the project and its implementation. Pallisa district was plunged into insecurity by rebel activities and Karamojong cattle rustling. Property and human lives were lost. Towards the end of 1989 the security situation started improving. By then, the health of women and children had worsened and community life in general had deteriorated drastically. As a result, the students' executive called a meeting of elders, women and youth for immediate action on resolutions made at the last meeting three years earlier.

Figure 7.1: PACODET structure

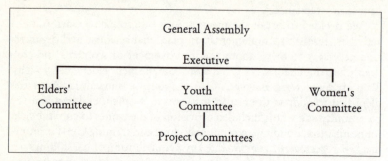

By this time the community was very poor but managed to come together for action. The elders gave the go-ahead and within one month, by December 1989, 40,000 shillings had been raised from membership fees. At a later stage, the community built the sixteen-room project house, with funding from the European Development Fund whose administrators were amazed by the achievements.

The students faced a big challenge since none had received any medical training. On the advice of friends, we decided to buy training manuals and literature on PHC and PEC from bookshops. The most useful reading resource proved to be David Werner's *Where There is No Doctor*. We studied it, reading carefully. We trained ourselves and then initiated training on the treatment and prevention of common diseases for other students. Soon essential drugs, mainly for malaria, worms and anaemia, were identified and bought from drug shops. A general meeting was called to decide on the distribution of the drugs; a user charge was introduced for sustainability.

This was the beginning of our PHC/PEC Project. CHWs, all volunteers, met once a week to review the activities of the past seven days and plan for the new week. The sick visited CHWs at their homes. CHWs moved around their area once a week to acquaint themselves with community problems and offer advice to families. The mango tree near the elementary school was chosen as the central location for the chief CHW to manage and coordinate the activities of other CHWs. General meetings were held fortnightly to review progress.

The trained CHWs started providing essential drugs and health education, both facilities being open to all community individuals both inside and outside Kapuwai village. Only user charges for essential drugs varied, depending on whether one was a subscribing member or not. Many people from neighbouring villages became interested and joined. In this way our activities expanded to cover neighbouring villages that needed a similar project. Five satellite clinics have been constructed by those communities. This precipitated a change of our name from KSPA to PACODET.

Involvement of the District Medical Officer's Office

For coordination and technical advice, the PACODET executive consulted the District Medical Officer's Office (DMO). This was responded to by a visit from the DMO himself to see what was happening on the ground. The gathering he found amazed him since he had never had such a crowd for his health education meetings. We informed the DMO about the existence of our community medicine kit and the reasons for it. We then requested training in immunization for eight CHWs, since lack of fuel and the poor condition of vehicles had hindered his team from reaching the area. The community pledged to motivate CHWs and to provide transport. We rejected an offer from the DMO to support a few of our CHWs with allowances on grounds of sustainability.

The CHW training was provided locally under the supervision of the district health visitor. By early 1990, the project was running its largely community-supported immunization programme. Through the DMO, more essential drugs were received from the Uganda Essential Drugs Management Programme. A room was rented from the school and coordination of the project shifted from under the mango tree.

Involvement of the Ministry of Health

A midwife and a medical assistant were contracted by the community to offer curative services, strengthen the capacity of CHWs and TBA training to improve traditional maternal care. The health providers worked very well for the first year but proved rather arrogant and tricky in subsequent years. First, they secretly accepted allowances that were opposed by local people on the grounds of sustainability. Second, they refused to train CHWs and TBAs, saying they did not deserve training and, third, many resources entrusted to them went missing.

Many management meetings tried to tackle these problems but did not yield fruit. The professional staff's attachment to some staff in the DMO's office gave them a feeling of superiority. The community realized it was better to suffer the absence of services from these people than to put up with the ongoing frustration. We resolved to discontinue these two workers' services. We also requested the DMO to honour the community initiative by supporting only those areas which we suggested. Since then our CHWs have continued to offer services from 2 to 8 hours a day.

Professional training to upgrade the skills of some capable CHWs was requested from the Ministry of Health in 1992. We were granted two vacancies to train a midwife and a nurse, which we filled. By the end of 1992, we will be joined by two CHWs who have completed their training. We hope, with continuing help from the Ministry of Health, to send more CHWs for training.

Involvement of the Child Health and Development Centre, Makerere University

The experience we had with the contracted workers demonstrated clearly that the success of the project was possible only because it had been carried out by local people. We decided to direct our attention to upgrading the local skills to gather data, synthesize and use them for the planning and implementation process. This prompted us to seek technical advice to help us in this area.

At the beginning of 1991, the Tororo District administration and the Child Health and Development Centre (CHDC) provided an opportunity when they organized an operational research-training workshop for the district administration. The workshop trained staff to use research skills in their departments. A number from PACODET attended this workshop. We met the CHDC technical advisor and requested a similar training at community level for our programmes.

In November 1992, the CHDC provided a four-day training to the PACODET executive and some CHWs. Our next activity was a general meeting when over two hundred people gathered to participate in a needs assessment. We used our newly learned skill of focus-group discussions to generate the community research agenda. During this meeting different issues came up in the form of community concerns, including nutrition, immunization, family planning, adolescents, water and sanitation, and many other environmental and social status considerations. After generating a broad agenda we sat down to prioritize. The nutrition and baseline data emerged as the immediate concerns of women and the PACODET executive respectively. We planned and conducted the two studies with the CHDC providing some technical advice throughout the process from design to dissemination of results. Community meetings remained a vital part of the data-gathering, analysis, interpretation and utilization processes.

The nutrition study[2]

The women expressed a need to assess the food practices in the community. The research-needs assessment indicated that food taboos existed and that intra-household preparation, food-serving and storage practices were poor. There was therefore need to explore community perceptions and behaviour in these areas.

Objectives

The objectives of the study were to:
- Describe local food patterns including food crop choices, preparation of ingredients, combinations served, food taboos and food storage/reservation.
- Develop local skills in qualitative discussion-group methods of

action research.
- Develop target-health education for improving local nutrition.

Methods

Since women are culturally responsible for household nutrition, they were the subjects of the study. Two age groups were considered, the mature to elderly (> 35 years) and the young (< 35 years), to identify any differences between the two. For each age group, six focus-group discussions of 10 women were conducted by a facilitator and notes were taken.

Results

The issues of greatest concern which affected nutrition were identified as destruction of nutrients during preparation, the cultural pattern of low consideration of women and children during food serving, periodic food shortages and poor storage practices.

The findings have been discussed with the community and a number of strategies are being adopted to address identified concerns. They include extensive sharing of nutrition information among women, development of labour-saving technologies, diversification in agriculture and provision of credit. Women are also planning a community nutrition centre.

Lessons learned

We have learned and continue to learn in the process of doing. The strength of participation and our visible successes motivate us to press on. Among the things we have discovered, the strongest is that the participatory process is self-generating: the more we do it, the more we are able to do it.

People relate more freely when they treat and value each other as equals. Genuine participatory processes release potential among participants to excel beyond expectations in tasks and challenges before them. The spontaneous generation of ideas helps all people to make good contributions.

When participatory processes are initiated by the community they promote self-reliance. Such processes cannot succeed where force is used to initiate them. The process builds rapport, confidence, unity and resistance to external exploitation and intimidation. To strengthen participatory processes, entry should be made through activities people have confidence in handling, and all the subgroups should be consulted as important entities in the process. The role of the expert should be confined to the identification of gaps and the building up of local capacity to fill them.

In initiating a PR process, a careful study of existing structures should be made, so as to adopt a neutral attitude towards conflicting interests. Terms of reference should be made clear. An explicit public presentation of goals, a realistic plan of action and mutual accountability are vital for theparticipatory process. PR is more likely to be sustainable than top-down forms of development activity. Early, even small success brings about confidence and willingness to participate more.

Some problems in PR processes

On the other hand, we are not falsely idealistic. There are, of course, difficulties in participation. We found that the development of PR is slow in the initial stages because the limited knowledge participants have about each other and their environment can delay the process, but the pace soon gains momentum. In addition, there are so many voices to be heard and considered. We have noticed also that some people want to participate by talking or supervising. However, this is not participation. What is needed is active on-the-ground involvement.

Success can create rivalry among some organizations which might not want poor people to realize their own potential for self-improvement. We have noted that external agents have a tendency to participate in PR by imposing their views and want to limit their involvement to exploitative concerns. Some external agencies may try to use their financial influence to direct the developments to their own agendas. This can undermine the participatory process. Money is most useful when requested for a direct community-identified need.

Conclusion

Participatory processes have served to build up the capacity of PACODET to respond meaningfully to its situation. This is because the community has retained control. Active participation has freed people from manipulation and exploitation through mutual learning, openness and respect of others' opinions. An atmosphere of free interaction and expression has promoted extensive learning and the adoption of beneficial practices leading to an optimistic outlook. Unity is preserved, while achievements are made and guarded jealously. Through group processes, leaders acceptable to the people are identified and sustainability is more assured.

PACODET serves to illustrate how the participatory process can develop the capacity of local people to formulate their own research and development agenda. The PR process has helped us develop a sense of direction for our involvement and an ability to guide the use of external resources when available.

Active participation has built great confidence in women who can now act on their own behalf more freely. In fact, of the eleven-person PACODET executive, seven are women. These women initiate projects which affect all women, such as the nutrition study. They are able to argue articulately among themselves and with men about the value of a proposed action. They freely take up leadership roles and speak for women's issues. During involvement in such activities as the nutrition study, the baseline study and the food security workshop, participating women came to realize the value of education. Information was portrayed through pictures, and women realized how much valuable information they had been missing because of limited education. This has led to a concern among the community, especially women, about the education of their children. 'When one can read, no one can deceive.'

Participatory research processes promote justice and love and develop local abilities to recognize and reject manipulation. Through participation, resourcefulness is developed and this strengthens the ability to act without instruction. The participatory process has, in the case of PACODET, created a hope for self-improvement with or without external help. The PACODET experience demonstrates the wisdom of local people and illustrates how they can recognize good intentions but can be moved to act fully only by good practice determined by good intentions.

Participation has helped us link a sustainable environment with the irreversible improvement of our community. It has helped us realize that it is not money we lack but rather information on the wise use and protection of the vast resources we have. We have learned that it is possible to acquire and construct that information.

Notes

1. This chapter is dedicated to our late patron, Mzee John Alfred Okodoi, for his wise counsel, involvement and perseverance in the initiation and development of PACODET. We would like to acknowledge the Child Health and Development Centre, Makerere, for research, training and support; Rosy Asera Barton for editing the text.

2. The detailed report of the nutrition study is contained in a paper entitled 'Pallisa Community Development Trust (PACODET) – nutrition study' by F. Oloit, S. Okurut, G. Wamai, J. Arube Wani, and T. Barton. It can be provided on request to Stanley Okurut, PACODET, P.O. Box 64, Pallisa, Uganda.

8 Issues of power in the participatory research process

Marion Martin

Power, empowerment and participation are central to a discourse on participatory research. These are broad and nebulous terms, attractive in their grandness yet often difficult to work with in practice. A clearer understanding of these concepts as applied to research can be revealed through reflection on and analysis of the research process.

The purpose of this chapter is to analyse the process of participation as it took place in a specific research context in the United Kingdom. I aim to illustrate something of the complexity of working towards participation in research by examining the fluid nature of power in researcher/research-community relationships and in so doing to identify some of the contradictions inherent in the participatory research (PR) process. The major concepts and activities of PR are outlined; the research context and relevant parts of the study are described and questions that arise from a reflection on process, especially as these relate to issues of power among those engaged in the research, are discussed.

The conceptual framework: PR and feminist research

The discussion of this case study is framed within both PR and feminist research (FR) paradigms. While both paradigms have much in common in that they are concerned with issues of equity and the creation of knowledge that results in empowering those participating in research, there are also differences that need to be highlighted.

Participatory research

PR is based on a strong commitment to social justice and a vision of a better world. The key concepts/activities of PR are inter-related and include 'participation', 'education' and 'collective action' (Hall 1981; Martin 1994). Some unpacking of these terms will help to clarify meaning. PR aims to be a learning experience for those engaged in the process. The aims of the research are centred around the interests of those participating in it with emphasis placed on individuals and community groups as active subjects of research as opposed to passive objects having research 'done on' them. That is to say, community groups or representatives of these groups take an active and informed part in establishing the directions of the research: what issues will the research address? from whom should information be collected and why? how will the information be collected and who should be involved in this, and why? how will the data be analysed, by whom and why? to whom should the findings be disseminated, and to whom should they not be disseminated and why?

how should this be done? A major objective of the PR process is to work towards reducing the power often held by researchers who come from outside the community to do research, and by élite groups within the community. The bias is towards marginalized groups in the community (Mulenga 1993). The researcher is a committed participant in the process and is actively involved as opposed to being impartial and detached.

The educational process in PR helps to facilitate the growth of critical awareness in the individual and group. In doing so it draws from the field of adult education and the influence of educational theorists, most notably the Brazilian educator Paulo Freire (Freire 1972). This educational process is sometimes referred to as transformative education (Mezirow 1995) and involves all engaged in the research process. An aspect of transformative education is 'conscientization'. This is a learning process that is empowering in that it leads towards the increasing ability of the learners to question relationships of dependency on those who consciously or unconsciously control and exploit them. Transformative learning can lead people towards taking action on their new understandings of the world. These actions are aimed towards increasing their liberation from oppressive forces (Mezirow 1995). Social action is thus the third concept, or key activity, of PR.

PR can employ a variety of research methods. Quantitative methods such as structured questionnaires may be used along with qualitative methods such as focus group discussions, unstructured interviews as well as increasingly innovative methods used within PRA, such as seasonal calendars (Welbourn 1992) and body mapping (Cornwall 1993).

PR may be initiated from and carried out entirely within a community such as a tenants' association concerned, for example, about damp housing that is affecting the health of the community. Alternatively, the idea for the research might come from the community who call in professional researchers to work with them in carrying out the research. Again, the research may be initiated by an outsider to the community who is concerned to work alongside the community in research that will benefit all engaged in the process. The research process itself may thus be initiated from either within or outside the community. The main question to address is: which individuals or groups are controlling the direction the research is taking? This is a crucial issue and one that easily gets neglected. It requires careful, ongoing reflection and analysis throughout the period of research.

Feminist research

The meaning of the term 'feminism' is much contested, not least by critical third-world feminists who hold that there are as yet no simple ways of representing the diverse struggles of women across historical, geographical, ideological and political boundaries (Mohanty et al. 1991).

Some women have argued, however, that this diversity has to some extent found common ground in the wider women's movements of the world (Mies & Shiva 1993). Within FR there remains considerable debate concerning issues of research methodology (Reinharz 1992).

The assumptions that inform the FR paradigm are broadly similar to those that inform PR (Humphries 1995). An important contribution of feminism to knowledge creation has been the way feminists have explored feeling and experience as sources of knowledge and as guides to analysis and social action. The sharing of women's experiences was and continues to be in many instances a central element in feminist research (Weiler 1991).

A feminist critique of PR developed in the mid-eighties identifies its patriarchal foundation and male bias. This results, it is argued, in male control of the research process, and in the experiences and perspectives of women being distorted, or excluded from PR activities (Maguire 1987). Many feminists hold that research focusing on women's lives is best carried out by and with other women rather than by men. An argument that supports this understanding holds that if women research with women the potential of the researcher exploiting the researched is decreased. This view assumes a position of commonality across women's experiences of oppression, ignoring differences of, for example, national identity, class, race, sexuality and disability. The discussion returns to the issue of difference later. It was with a view to combining PR and FR that I entered the research environment described below.

The research context

The research study took place in a small English town where most people had until recently been dependent either directly or indirectly on the mining industry. Not long before the study, the local mines, which were nationally owned, had been closed down by the government. As a result there were growing problems of unemployment, poverty and stress. This was placing almost intolerable pressure on relationships within families, between friends and between community groups. Much of this pressure landed ultimately on women in the community. In an attempt to deal with this pressure a small group of working-class women from the community came together to explore the possibility of some form of local support structure being established. This action was combined with an increasing dissatisfaction among these women with the local health services, particularly with the ways they felt problems like stress, anxiety, bereavement and depression were being dealt with at primary health-service level.

The group approached the community health council (CHC), a local government structure, one purpose of which is to identify community need in health care. The CHC took a supportive role and worked with the women to organize public meetings to establish if there was wider support for such an initiative. Eventually a Well Woman Centre (WWC) was established in a rented flat in the town centre. The centre evolved from a social rather than a medical model of health. Control was maintained by the women, while professionals were consulted about issues linked to health but had no control over the daily management of the centre, which was funded indirectly through a government grant and through money-raising activities carried out by local women. Emphasis was placed on the prevention of ill-health through self-help, information dissemination, group education and strategies of collective education, organization and action. Services provided included health studies courses, a small library and information centre, one-to-one counselling, self-help-group activities, occasional public meetings, money-raising activities and health days.

The centre had been running for three years when I first made contact with the Well Woman Group (WWG). At the time of this meeting I was considering embarking upon research in community health as part of a higher degree. Through negotiation with representatives of the WWG it was decided that both the WWG and I might benefit from the research taking place within their centre, provided that a main objective of the research was to evaluate the work of the centre. All being well the findings could be used to attract future funding support. It was broadly on this basis that research got under way. In the following discussion I refer to myself as the researcher, not because I was the sole person actively involved in the process of researching but as a means of distinguishing myself from the WWG, which I call the research community.

In the course of preparing for the research I came across the work of a feminist researcher, Reinharz, who had developed a participatory research model called 'experiential analysis' (Reinharz 1983). Reinharz identifies two qualities she maintains need to be present if cooperative and trusting relationships are to be established between researcher and researched:

- the research aims should be of genuine interest to both researched and researcher, as the success of participatory research is due partly to developing mutually dependent and cooperative relationships;
- the outcomes of the study should be relevant to the needs of all those involved in the research.

If researchers are to encourage growth in cooperative and trusting relationships they must be seen about the group with whom the research is taking place. Reinharz comments: 'one's trustworthiness is not confined to what one says ... but also to how one acts and who one is' (Reinharz 1983:177). Thus the power imbalance that exists in conventional research is in PR to some extent shared between the parties involved. While the 'outside' researcher observes, s/he is also being observed.

Given the preceding discussion regarding the development of an appropriate theoretical framework, the question arises as to how far research practice can meet theory? Where do the gaps between theory and practice emerge? Why have these gaps occurred? Such questions are useful in that they provide a framework from which to trace the patterns of power in the research process and in so doing evaluate the process of participation. Though this may be a rather crude evaluation it is still an important exercise.

The following research aims were negotiated (at length) and agreed by elected representatives of the WWG and myself:

1. Examine the ideology, aims, and objectives of the WWG.
2. Examine and clarify the nature of the educational processes employed in the health studies courses.
3. Enquire into WWG users' perceptions of their health education needs.
4. Enquire into users' perceptions of the purpose of the WWG.
5. Enquire into the extent to which the centre met users' health needs.
6. Enquire into the worker group's perceptions of the style of leadership in the centre.
7. Enquire into the health professionals' understandings of the purpose of the centre and their attitudes to it.

As can be seen from the above the major interest of the WWG was the evaluation of the work of their community. We were united in a concern that the research should result in public recognition of the work of the group, increased financial support and increased use of the centre by local women and health professionals in the form of appropriate referrals.

The research process: issues of power

Perhaps contrary to popular opinion PR can integrate both qualitative and quantitative methods of data collection. A crucial question other than the suitability of methods for a specific purpose is who decides which methods are appropriate? This issue is essentially about the locus of power. Does it lie with the researcher or with the community? Who in the community exercise this power? Do those representing the community represent adequately the various interests of different groups, particularly of those who are marginalized? The process is complex and difficult to evaluate in a sensitive manner.

In the case of this research the aims of the study were negotiated between elected representatives of the WWG working alongside the researcher. The selection of methods was, however, given over almost entirely to the researcher on the assumption that she possessed the necessary skills to carry out research. Many community members felt also that they did not have the time to take on additional responsibilities other than those they were already carrying, such as family care, jobs and, voluntary activities with the WWG. The idea of the research also held a certain mystique and most of the women did not feel confident enough to become very involved in the process. The issue of the time, energy and sometimes the financial implications of participation in PR by community members can be one of the major obstacles to sustaining active and representative participation. This may be the case particularly where the involvement of those from poor and marginalized communities is concerned, particularly women (Moser 1993). Anticipating such problems and planning strategies to tackle them, such as building the information, skill and confidence base of marginalized individuals and groups, so they are not excluded from participation should be an integral part of PR design.

Negotiating the focus
In the case of this study, the research aims were negotiated between WWG representatives and the researcher, so power seemed fairly well balanced. The locus of power changed significantly, however, in the selection and design of methods when there was minimal community participation and responsibility was given over largely to me during the period of data collection, analysis and writing of the initial report setting out the findings. The report was discussed at a meeting to which all members of the WWG were invited. Here discussion took place, the report was modified accordingly and a final copy was typed and made available to all members of the WWC. It is not possible, here to enter into a detailed discussion of research findings and social action taken as a result of the research. A more detailed discussion of this can be found elsewhere (Martin 1994).

As the primary concern here is with participatory processes a question that needs to be addressed is: when and how is power exercised by community members and/or the researcher at different points in the research process? This is an important exercise as it can offer a means of increasing the validity of the research while also increasing access to its benefits, provided it results in drawing greater representation from community groups. As this research was initiated by the outsider researcher and ultimately agreed by community representatives it could be said that the initiation stage, a crucial point in participatory processes, while first stimulated by the researcher was in the end largely a negotiated process. Community representatives could at any time have decided the research should not take place. This did not occur.

One reason why this may be the case, though it is conjecture, is that the collaborative approach helped community representatives to see clearly that the group would benefit from pursuing the research. The recognition by community representatives that they could control many aspects of the study and would directly benefit from it helped towards an element of trust emerging gradually at an early stage in the initial negotiations.

In discussing some of the qualities necessary to an environment that helps stimulate participatory processes and more open communication Mezirow (1995) identifies the following elements: that there should be a gradual growth in the feeling of trust (though this can be exploited at any time) and an:

> empathic solidarity with those participating in the process; information should be made available so decisions can be participatory and as democratic as possible. ... There should be freedom from coercion ... and equal opportunity to participate in discussion, to have ... voices heard and understood (Mezirow 1995:11).

The dominant values are equality, participatory democracy, caring and inclusiveness. The reality, however, is that ideal collaborative discourse and participation rarely if ever exist. They are at risk from:

> the devastating distortions created by inequalities in the distribution of power and influence associated with ethnicity, gender, class, that distort one's ability to participate under such idealized circumstances (Mezirow 1995:12).

While the ideal may be impossible to attain it offers, however, a vision and direction, a means by which to evaluate progress towards participation.

Sharing learning

The financing of the research was shared fairly equally between the WWG and the researcher and did not appear to be an area of contention. The actual study in terms of method selection and design, data collection, analysis and report writing was almost totally researcher-controlled and therefore not very different from traditional research activities where the vertical power relationship (researcher directing researched) is common. With regard to the learning that took place, some degree of learning appeared to be achieved to varying degrees by all those involved in the research process in that both official researcher and WWG increased their understanding of what this approach to research entailed and felt more confident as researchers. Where the WWG was concerned this confidence was expressed in various ways, one of the more obvious of which was the carrying out of an internal evaluation of the centre the following year using a similar process.

As a researcher I developed skills appropriate to PR, such as negotiating aims, communicating the use of different methods and learning how to use some of these methods myself. WWG members gained insight into the reasons why the centre had developed a certain style of leadership that contradicted their formal ideology of collective working, and they gathered information as to how the approach to leadership in the group might change in line with centre ideology. The research process gave a platform and voice to some of those who up till this time had little or no voice in the group. Group members learned how they might more usefully build relationships with one another and with those local health professionals who expressed interest in the activities of the centre and appeared to respect the philosophy on which it was based. Some members of the WWG and the researcher also developed greater insight and more critical awareness of issues linked to gender and class inequality and those with strong personal motivation learned more about the links across inequalities. In these ways, the educational impact of the research process was considerable. The more the community participated in the process the greater was the opportunity for learning and the higher the motivation for collective action. This measurement of participation provides a map to guide future research planning. As participation is complex it is necessary to reflect on and analyse the process in order to learn from mistakes and to build on strengths.

Power as a dynamic and fluid force

I turn now to a different aspect of the discussion. Power in research is not simply concentrated in either researcher or research community. It is, rather, a dynamic, moving force. Drawing on Sawicki's (1991) discussion of discourse theory Humphries (1994) discusses the basic elements of power as outlined by Foucault. Foucault (1980) holds that power is not possessed but is exercised; that it is productive rather than primarily repressive; that it emerges from the grassroots rather than coming from the top down. While power is exercised in vertical directions (e.g., researcher over researched), it is also exercised from the bottom up. Viewed in this light, power permeates all (Bhavnani 1991). While this makes sense of my experiences of research it is contrary to most accounts of conventional research I have read. Humphries (1994) notes that Foucault's view of power helps us understand power relations in the researcher–researched relationships as it:

> reveals not a simple hierarchical loading based on socially ascribed characteristics, but ... complex multifaceted power relations which have both structural dominance and structural subordination in play *on both sides*. (p.3)

Given this notion of power as a dynamic force, I now move towards a closer examination of power in the research process as it applies to *interactions between* researcher and members of the research community.

Some members of the research community perceived me as an expert in the initial stages of the research. They appeared to refer to me as such as far as research activities were concerned as no one else in the group had research experience in the formal sense. An effect of this labelling was to place me outside the norm of the group. In this way I was periodically excluded from participation. When I was drawn into decisions, it meant I was consulted as the expert who was seen to have the answer to whatever research problem there was at that time. When this occurred it both excluded and threatened me. Ironically, in the early stages of the research I dealt with this sense of alienation by playing on the expert role by, for example, using specialist research language as a conventional researcher might do. This gave me back some sense of control but at the risk of alienating others. The fluidity of power in this sense was constantly in play in the research process in a multitude of ways.

In order to look more closely at the fluidity of power and the tensions of both the productive and obstructive qualities of power at play in the researcher/research-community relationship, I have selected an example of my contact with an individual member. I will call her Alison. As the formal leader of the research community, Alison was in a position of structural power. She had an overview of information about particular aspects of the community, such as its history, organization and finances, and had established contacts with professionals or other significant organizations. Other members of the research community did not have the same power. Alison was in charge, therefore, of much information that was important to the research. She also had a special investment in the continuation of the WWG as she had been among its initiators and was the only person who received a salary for her community work, all the others being voluntary members. She had much to gain from the research yet at the same time the research itself was a potential threat to her, in that one of its agreed aims was the exploration of community views on appropriate leadership styles for the WWG. Alison had been, however, one of the strongest supporters of the research, and she particularly favoured the PR idea.

The research relationship between Alison and myself was fraught with contradictions and tensions combining elements of anxiety, fear, competition and admiration. We were of a similar age and other than both being women we appeared to have little else in common. We seemed to be separated by many differences, such as class, education and life experiences.

Alison came across as a powerful person. While power can be expressed and used in productive ways it can also be an obstacle to collaboratively working. Alison's power came across more frequently in the latter fashion, though both qualities were present at different times.

In the productive sense, as formal leader she facilitated participatory processes through offering practical support and active encouragement to other members of the research community. She also played an active part in the design of the research by investing considerable time and energy in discussing the development of questions for interview schedules and identifying organizations and professionals to whom questionnaires might be sent. These were important contributions to the PR process.

At the same time, Alison appeared to use her power in ways that were obstructive to participation. She had a strong physical presence with a loud voice and extrovert personality. She dressed in a manner that emphasized a certain formality and social respectability. She seemed to exert considerable influence over decisions made in the group and fought hard to maintain control over conversations and keep attention fixed on her. As researcher I was not without power and I became aware that when I felt particularly threatened personally or felt that the participatory process was being threatened I might bid for control through humour or by withdrawing to take notes, so building on the notion of expert researcher. Such behaviour tended to be an obstructive use of power in the PR process. A major problem in such a situation is that the research can become diverted from its formal aims in the sense that the back-and-forward movement of power becomes an end in itself and acts as a diversion from the research. The researcher needs to be aware of these issues and recognize that people in formal roles of structural power may have an investment in not sharing power and may find difficulty in working in collaborative ways as the process in itself threatens the power base on which their status may rest.

This example of the relationship between the researcher and one member of the research community might help to highlight the complexity of PR processes, complexities that are rarely referred to in any depth in accounts of PR. This relationship is not necessarily typical of others in this particular research context but it is useful in that it highlights the significance of structural position. The dynamic nature of power and some of the contradictions inherent in the researcher/research-community relationship are illustrated. It becomes clear that contradictions exist and that they create tension but it is unrealistic necessarily to expect to resolve these (Sawicki 1991). The example might also help illustrate that power is exercised and not possessed. Where power seeks to dominate it is met with resistance. The flow of power is influenced by structural factors which interact with personalities and ideologies.

The research relationship with Alison was difficult for us both. It is not easy to work in collaborative ways when there is mutual fear, suspicion and competition. Difference can be uncomfortable and can threaten a person's or a group's power base. It is also likely to create fear if those involved are not willing to recognize and acknowledge diversity. The African-American poet Audre Lorde (1984) writes of ways in which difference can threaten, and how poorly equipped many of us are in coping with it in others as well as in ourselves:

> We have no patterns for relating across human differences as equals ... (so) ... differences have been ... misused in the service of separation and confusion. ... Much of our energy that could be put into exploring our differences is put into pretending the differences do not exist or making them insurmountable barriers to working creatively together. (p.115)

In the context of PR, the question arises as to whether the differences between those involved in the process present a threat to effective political action on an individual and group basis. These examples help, I hope, to illustrate the dynamic nature of power and the complexity of facilitating participatory processes. Power pervades all and has potential, in virtually every situation, for domination and resistance and while difference can be a source of division and conflict it can also be a source of learning and change. In practice PR processes are neither easy to understand nor are they easy to achieve. One of the reasons for this is that the universalized goals of liberation processes do not address the specific contexts of people's lives (Weiler 1991), nor do they examine the contradictions that exist between different oppressed groups or the ways individuals can experience oppression in one situation while acting as oppressors in another.

In this chapter I have examined issues of power in the PR process from the conception of research to negotiating with the community to individual research relationships drawing on a notion of power as a fluid, multi-faceted force that permeates all research activity. Accounts of research often present researcher/research-community relationships in unproblematic, unanalysed ways. There is a need for attention to the detail of process and the complexities and contradictions inherent in it. I have found Foucault's analysis of power a helpful framework for making sense of some of these complexities.

References

Bhavnani, K.K. (1991) 'What's power got to do with it? Empowerment and social research', in Parker, I. & Shotter, J. (eds) (1991).

Bowles, G. & Klein, R. (eds) (1983) *Theories of Women's Studies*, RKP, London.

Cornwall, A. (1993) 'Sharing ideas: bridging the gap between medical messages and local understandings', in de Koning, K. (ed.) (1994), pp.109-112.

Foucault, M. (1980) *Power/Knowledge: Selected Interviews and Other Writings*, Pantheon, New York.

Freire, P. (1972) *Pedagogy of the Oppressed*, Penguin, London, New York.

Hall, B.L. (1981) 'Participatory research, popular knowledge and power: a personal reflection', *Convergence*, Vol.14(3), pp.6-19.

Humphries, B. (1994) 'Empowerment and social research: elements for an analytic framework', in Humphries, B. & Truman, C. (eds) ((1994).

Humphries, B. (1995) *Understanding Research: An Open Learning Pack*, Whiting & Birch.

Humphries, B. & Truman, C. (eds) (1994) *Re-Thinking Social Research*, Avebury.

de Koning, K. (ed.) (1994) *Proceedings of the International Symposium on Participatory Research in Health Promotion*, Education Resource Group, Liverpool School of Tropical Medicine, UK.

Lorde, A. (1984) *Sister Outsider, Essays and Speeches by Audre Lorde*, Crossing Press Feminist Series.

Maguire, P. (1987) *Doing Participatory Research: A Feminist Approach*, Center for International Education, University of Massachusetts, Amherst, Massachusetts.

Martin, M. (1994) 'Developing a feminist participatory research framework: evaluating the process', in Humphries, B. & Truman, C. (eds) (1994).

Mezirow, J. (1995) 'Adult education and empowerment for individual and community development', paper presented at the Conference on Adult Education and Local Development: Global Lessons, Saint Patrick's College, Maynooth, 24 May.

Mies, M. & Shiva, V. (1993) *Ecofeminism*, Zed Books.

Mohanty, C.T. et al. (eds) (1991) *Third World Women and the Politics of Feminism*, Indiana University Press.

Moser, C. (1993) *Gender Planning and Development*, Routledge.

Mulenga, D. (1993) 'Participatory research in Africa: a critical appraisal', in de Koning, K. (ed.) (1994), pp.33-37.

Parker, I. & Shotter, J. (eds) (1991) *Deconstructing Social Psychology*, Routledge, London.

Reinharz, S. (ed.) (1992) *Feminist Methods in Social Research*, OUP.

Reinharz, S. (1983) 'Experiential analysis: a contribution to feminist research', in Bowles, G. & Klein, R. (eds) (1983).

Sawicki, J. (1991) *Disciplining Foucault*, Routledge.

Weiler, K. (1991) 'Freire and a feminist pedagogy of difference', *Harvard Educational Review*, Vol.61(4), November, pp.449-74.

Welbourn, A. (1992) 'Rapid rural appraisal, gender and health – alternative ways of listening to needs', *Institute of Development Studies Bulletin*, Vol.23(1), January, pp.8-18.

PART IV PARTICIPATORY RESEARCH METHODS: FIRST STEPS IN A PARTICIPATORY PROCESS

9 Towards participatory practice: participatory rural appraisal (PRA) and the participatory process[1]

Andrea Cornwall

Almost all health research involves participation. Yet research is all too often done on participants, rather than with or by them. Conventional modes of research, from participant observation to epidemiological surveys, place the researcher in a pivotal role. Learning tends to be a one-way process, with the researcher gathering disparate items of information to be processed elsewhere. Research is often separated from action, carried out by specialists who make recommendations to be put into plans to be implemented by others. Participatory research methods offer opportunities to bring research and action, researcher and participant, together in a quite different way.

Drawing on the work of adult educationalist Paulo Freire (1972), participatory approaches emphasize the processes rather than the products of research. PR aims to substitute a cyclical, ongoing process of research, reflection and action for the conventional linear model of research, recommendation, implementation and evaluation. Research becomes one mode of a continuing process of learning. Doing is reflected upon, raising more questions which in turn create further possibilities for action. As different actors have different perceptions both of the issues at hand and of ways they might be resolved, PR methodologies aim not only to elicit these differences but to explore their effects.

Participatory approaches involve a recognition of the ways in which dominant actors and forms of knowledge render others subordinate. Health promotion has conventionally aimed to make knowledge available to those who lack it. Indigenous knowledge, often cast as folk beliefs, is all too often disregarded and treated as an undifferentiated morass of indigenous ignorance. In many places, those who are the objects of health promotion have internalized the attitudes implicit in its conventional practice. In several African countries, my attempts to open up discussions with women on their knowledge of their bodies have been greeted at first with replies like: 'What can we tell you that you don't already know? After all, you are educated'; or 'Why ask us? We don't know anything!' The subtext of these remarks was that I would probably laugh at them, find them absurd, confirm their views of themselves as ignorant.

Participatory learning methods, such as participatory rural appraisal (PRA), offer ways to open up such discussions in a non-threatening way, by focusing on local classifications, local concepts and local explanations. In doing so, the objective is not merely to find out. By actively engaging people in a process of exploring and representing what they know, the participatory research process can validate them as knowledgeable, active subjects capable of interpreting and changing their situations themselves. As such, participatory methods can set the scene for a 'learning approach' (Korten 1980) in which the conventional separation between researcher and participant is broken down. In PR, knowledge is seen not as a timeless, static entity that can be possessed, transferred or lost. Knowing is regarded, rather, as a dynamic process that takes place through action and interaction. In principle, participatory research approaches aim to create new forms of knowledge through a creative synthesis of the different knowledges and experiences of those taking part. In its more radical forms, its practitioners develop a process in which the initiators 'become redundant ... that is, the transformation process continues without [them]' (Fals-Borda & Rahman 1991). Such a process calls for changes in the roles, attitudes and behaviour of researchers, who become catalysts, facilitators and learners (Chambers 1992). Through a process of mutual learning, people are equipped with the skills to do their own research and enact their own solutions. Participatory research is, then, a personal and political process aimed explicitly at transforming current inequalities.

Participatory research methods may provide the first steps in this process. They do not always in themselves constitute it, however. Participatory methods may be used in a wide range of contexts according to quite divergent agendas (see Figure 9.1). Examples exist where research has been rooted in local knowledge and concerns and the process has been oriented at empowering local people to enact their own solutions (see, for example, Khanna 1992). But much of what currently passes as 'participatory' involves local people taking part in other people's projects, according to agendas set by external interests. And elsewhere, emancipatory principles stand in stark contrast to forms of practice that may be better regarded as collusive with or even contributory to established relations of inequality.

PRA methods can be used as tools in any of the modes of participation outlined in Figure 9.1, depending on the ends users intend to pursue. In the following sections, I focus on PRA in terms of the potential it offers

Figure 9.1: Participatory methods: means to what ends?

Mode of participation	Involvement of local people	Relationship of research and action to local people
Cooption	token; representatives are chosen, but no real input or power	on
Compliance	tasks are assigned, with incentives; outsiders decide agenda and direct the process	for
Consultation	local opinions asked, outsiders analyse and decide on a course of action	for/with
Cooperation	local people work together with outsiders to determine priorities, responsibility remains with outsiders for directing the process	with
Co-learning	local people and outsiders share their knowledge, to create new understanding, and work together to form action plans, with outsider facilitation	with/by
Collective action	local people set their own agenda and mobilize to carry it out, in the absence of outside initiators and facilitators	by

[Adapted from: Biggs 1989; Hart 1992; Pretty 1995]

for co-learning within a process oriented toward a goal of collective action. I draw on personal reflections on experiences of applications that were shared with the teams of people I worked with in different settings to explore ways in which these methods can be used to initiate a participatory process. I conclude by considering the implications of participatory research for interactions between health professionals and the communities with whom they work.

Participatory methods: tools for learning

A vast amount has been written on the participatory research methods used in PRA (see, for example: Chambers 1992; IIED 1988–present). What concerns me here is not the how-to-do-its, but the possibilities these methods offer for opening up dialogue and for facilitating co-learning. I would like to focus my discussion on techniques involving visualization, from drawings, maps and charts, to drama and other performances. I suggest, following Chambers (1992), that visualization offers a powerful strategy for working with those whose voices are rarely heard, as well as for bringing about critical awareness and self-confidence among participants in the process.

In both qualitative and quantitative research, interviewing is a central research strategy. Questions, drawn from a questionnaire or posed as part of an open-ended discussion, set a frame of reference for answers. This frame may be quite specific to a particular issue. In this way, connections respondents may make with other aspects may be left undiscussed. Interviews elicit certain kinds of verbal commentaries. There are many things, however, that cannot be shared verbally. These may concern the ways in which things are done, in practice, or may refer to things people take for granted. Sensitive or emotional issues may be difficult to discuss. Styles of interaction, from strategies of domination or resistance to the complex processes of persuasion and power in decision-making, cannot easily be described. For those working through translators, linguistic issues can muddy interpretation. Terms may be assumed to have a shared referent when people mean quite different things. Metaphors may be interpreted literally and what people say may seem incoherent or incomprehensible.

In interviews, whether with groups or individuals, information flow is usually one-way: towards the researcher, who records responses and takes them away to analyse elsewhere. The ephemeral nature of the spoken word limits the potential for analysis in these settings. The principle of visualization is to offer a means by which information is not only collectively produced but represented in a form that remains open to collective reference, both for cross-checking and analysis. While the presence of the researcher continues to influence the production of these representations, the focus of activity shifts from the researcher to the representation.

The process of constructing a visual representation is in itself an analytic act. Reflecting on what was included and why, as well as on the interactions between various aspects, invites further analysis. The visualized product acts as a focus and anchor for discussions. Further questions arise as part of this process of interviewing the diagram that provide a starting-point for further exploration, either through discussions or in other visualized forms. In this way, mapping can lead to a ranking or the construction of a seasonal calendar, with cross-reference to and further elaboration of the map. The use of visuals enables issues that have arisen to be captured and then cross-referenced and compared, as part of the process of analysis. Through this analytic process, participants as well as facilitators make new connections and learn together. The following example, from Ethiopia, illustrates this process.[2]

> Three facilitators worked together with a group of men to construct a seasonal calendar. Using symbols chosen by the participants, an elaborate calendar was produced that showed changes over the year, including disease prevalence, market prices, food availability and labour. One of the participants, a young man, chose to represent malaria with a picture of a mosquito, which became progressively larger when incidence of malaria was high. This provoked a discussion on the causes of malaria among the group. From this, the team was able to move on to discuss other illnesses. Going back to complete the calendar, the facilitators went on to ask questions about connections between various aspects. At first, participants did not see any connection. With some probing, connections were made. Participants said, with amazement, that they had seen for the first time that some of their problems were linked to others and went on to explore ways in which they could address them.

A common assumption is that people who cannot read or write will not be able to draw, let alone conceptualize issues visually. This has been challenged by experiences of participatory diagramming in a huge range of settings (Chambers 1992). As, however, attitudes like these about illiteracy are all too often internalized, skilled facilitation may be needed to encourage people to make visual images. With gentle cajoling people can and will take up a pen or a stick and offer their representations. This is a process, however, that can depend on establishing rapport with people and, of course, depends equally on what they are being asked to represent.

Visualizations offer ways to break the ice in initial contacts with people whose previous experiences of outsider professionals may have been far from the kind of mutual learning PR aims to encourage. By providing an alternative medium for communication, visualizations can involve participants in a research process driven by their own concerns and interests, in their own ways, using their own categories and criteria. Issues that are of local importance can be given a prominence they may lack in verbal discussion. Visualizations provide a shared reference point for discussions that take place during both their production and the analysis of the images produced. They also offer ways to explore the knowledge, ideas and perspectives of different actors within the community who, in verbal settings, may remain entirely silent.

Visual representations are never merely factual accounts of how things are in the community. All representations are social acts; they speak for, as well as about the perceptions of the particular actors who produce them. This process is never neutral. The presumed agendas of those who facilitate the exercise, as well as the agendas of those who take part in it, influence the representations that are produced. Contrasting images, and different concerns emerging within them, provide opportunities for discussion and reflection on the wider issues that emerge in contexts that might otherwise be approached merely as a site for the collection of information. I would like to draw on an example to illustrate this, also from Ethiopia:[3]

> Four team members and I arrived in the village for the first time and began to gather people for a participatory mapping exercise. After the purpose of our visit and the exercise had been explained, a small group of men began to create a map, starting with the demarcation of a boundary. Within minutes, more men came to join them and a cluster of people had formed. The facilitators became the observers of an animated process. As the men marked out the terrain using sticks on the ground, a debate began on the features they wanted to include. The facilitators noted points to raise in later discussions and occasionally intervened to probe further. Soon there was a crowd of people. Women stood at the margins, arms folded and silent. Children tried to join in and were shooed away. Only men were involved in making the map. I suggested that women and children could be asked to make their own maps. Two facilitators broke away from the men's discussions to do this. The women gathered twigs and grass and started to outline the rivers and streams in the area, moving on to represent the village. As they did so, they talked of the problems they faced. The children, directed by a boy of about 14, rushed around in excitement gathering stones, leaves and twigs. They began to create a very detailed map. When the maps were finished, each of the groups in turn was asked to explain their maps to us and others present. The men went first. A woman then came forward to explain their map, while the men listened in silence. Lastly, the children presented their map. All had quite distinct and different concerns. To our interest, the children represented on their map some of the very resources men had excluded from theirs and had been complaining about, revealing the agendas of those taking part.

The facilitators were amazed that people knew about their environment in such a detailed way and at the level of detail the children had represented in their map. The map-makers were proud of their product, which had absorbed their interest for several hours. And contact was made with the participants, through the discussions arising from the map, that were continued in different activities over the next few days. The facilitators came away stunned by how much they had learned in such a short time and how quickly a rapport had been established with people. Important lessons about difference, and about the politics of the encounter with the community, had been learned.

Through facilitation, issues of difference emerge that might otherwise have been overlooked. This demonstrates the importance of exploring the perceptions of different kinds of people (see Welbourn 1991). Welbourn notes from her work in Sierra Leone how the different perceptions revealed in ranking exercises 'clearly illustrated how talking to the better-off men alone, the normal practice of most development staff, was *an entirely inadequate way* of gauging the complexity of a community's needs' (1992:89). Through an apparently neutral process of replicating applications with different groups, issues of difference can be discovered by teams of practitioners who, as part of the process, are encouraged to examine their biases.

Research strategies such as focus group discussions enable the exploration of difference in ways complementary to the use of visualization with different groups. It would be erroneous, however, to assume that because people have some externally identified commonality, such as age or gender, they constitute a defined interest group. Often the differences within notionally homogeneous groups are masked by the emphasis on differences between these and other groups (Moore 1993). Without a more subtle approach to difference and to the dynamics of interaction within communities, there is a danger that the differences that make a difference locally can be overlooked. This is a particular concern with gender difference, where Western notions of gender are often unproblematically imposed on other cultures.

Where visualization can complement and extend focus group work on issues of difference is in the use of the representations of particular groups as a means of discussing different concerns in a wider forum. As images are the product of a group process, ownership lies outside identifiable individuals. Attention is focused away from the particular individuals taking part on to an externalized object which acts as a vehicle for their views and perceptions. Discussion refers to that object, rather than to the statements of individuals, and focuses on the themes that are brought into view. The outcome of visualizations can be shown to and discussed with other interest groups, stimulating both awareness and analysis of the constraints particular groups may face. Concerns voiced through visualized media and concretized in collective visual representations offer ways to facilitate debates among those with conflicting perspectives and interests that would be hard to facilitate through discussion alone.

To draw on another example from my experience, workshops were held with women in Zimbabwe to explore their reproductive knowledge and assess the gaps in providing appropriate, culturally located health promotion on contraception (Cornwall 1990). In one of these work-shops, representations of the body, which were created by groups of women formed around age differences, were contrasted and discussed:

I asked the groups of women to draw maps of their reproductive systems together and to show on them how the contraceptive pill worked. As I had done this individually with all the women present over the course of the research, I was interested in what would emerge from the groups. Relations of respect and of kinship, as well as the different perceptions of appropriate behaviour of women of different generations, limited what could be said by individuals in the group as a whole. In self-selected age groups, women were able to express their views more freely. One of these groups, of younger women, began with a heated discussion about the problems of avoiding pregnancy and the demands of their husbands. This continued as they drew their body maps. One of the women was handed the pen as she was deemed more educated. As she drew, all of the others called out what they thought should be included. Some of the suggestions were countered by others, others elicited nodding heads and were included. When it came to presenting their map to the assembled larger group, the spokeswoman spoke confidently and explained their map. As it had become part of the group process, rather than a product of her own ideas and experiences, she seemed much more able to talk about it in such a setting. Some of the points she raised might have been difficult to speak about otherwise. And when the group of older women cried out in disapproval as a younger woman spoke about sex, she gestured at the diagram, smiled and sat down with her group.

Insights into perceptions of difference and their effects can also be gained by asking particular interest groups to create visualized images as if from the perspective of others, or around the concerns of others, and then soliciting commentaries from those who are represented in these images. Bilgi (forthcoming) worked with men on daily activity schedules of women's labour in India. Through her skilled interventions, men came to realize that not only did women work long hours, but the work they initially dismissed as easy was both arduous and sometimes dangerous. As Bilgi's discussion shows, the awareness this process facilitates can be both humbling and revealing to those who take part.

Diagrams can offer ways to raise and explore issues that go beyond the original theme of enquiry to touch on other aspects of people's lives. They serve as points of reference for discussions of views, attitudes and opinions as well as for observations about the processes that impinge on people's material well-being. Welbourn (personal communication) notes, however, from her experience in Sierra Leone that the women she worked with expressed problems that simply could not be drawn. These women drew attention to interpersonal problems, such as domestic violence and rivalry between women. And while diagrams can serve as a point of entry from which to initiate discussions on these topics, concerns about raising, sharing and analysing sensitive subjects in a wider forum resurface.

The static visual representations that can be created through PRA methods can be usefully complemented with the use of more dynamic visual forms, such as drama. Theatre has long been used in health promotion, but as a didactic tool rather than as a creative way of exploring the alternatives and possibilities articulated by local people in their own words. The use of participatory theatre methods, as a complement to the visualization techniques of PRA, offers a powerful means through which to explore issues of sensitivity, conflict and emotion (see Mavro 1991). Drama offers a space in which people may be able to say or do things that they would not normally be able to say or do and in which dramatized solutions can become 'rehearsals for action' (Boal 1995). From individual brief portrayals of what life is like as a particular person in that locale, through to dramatized scenarios in which the audience are offered opportunities to intervene and alter outcomes as 'spect-actors' (Boal 1995), theatre can offer a way of taking further the personal and political issues involved in participation. As with other visual methods, theatre can enable people to express and explore issues of difference and set in motion a process of analysis and questioning.

Visualizations, then, can be used to challenge taken-for-granted ideas and explore local perceptions of a wide range of issues that form the context for people's struggles for well-being. They offer media for learning, awareness and communication. In the context of health promotion, the insights that can be gained from the use of this approach are important. Participatory visualization methods can provide a basis from which to build appropriate interventions and construct promotion materials that make sense in local terms together with the people at whom interventions may be directed.

There are many instances in which visualization methods have revealed issues that might have been obscured if only conventional research methods had been used, with implications for health promotion. In India, a PRA team used a causal diagram to explore the factors involved in making people vulnerable to disease (Kumar 1992). People identified a wide range of causal factors that health workers, with their limited view of health, might have otherwise passed over. In Ethiopia, a PRA team used a flow diagram centred on the household to explore people's perceptions of the causes and routes of transmission of certain diseases (ACTIONAID/IIED 1992). Analysing this diagram, participants offered their own solutions for prevention of some of these diseases and the team was able to identify areas where further discussion would be best focused, to develop strategies to introduce alternative causal sequences to make potential interventions make sense locally. In Zimbabwe, body mapping helped to explain women's use of and reactions to different forms of contraception and offered potential areas where explanations rooted in women's representations of their bodies could be developed and promoted (Cornwall 1992). Matrix ranking has been used in many settings to investigate the uptake of Western medical services, preferences in treatment options for different conditions and the perceptions of different groups of the severity of particular diseases (see, for example, Welbourn 1992).

Participatory research methods can, in many contexts, be used as a complement to techniques such as participant observation or be incorporated into survey research. As such, they can enrich the understanding of the researcher as well as provide opportunities for involving people in research projects that may have less participatory components. For example, in an epidemiological survey on hypertension in Nigeria, difficulties in assessing the socio-economic status of one sample group were overcome by the use of wealth ranking (Jay Kaufmann, personal communication). This yielded not only local criteria for assessing wealth, but also located wealth in relation to perceptions of the well-being and prestige of the individuals involved in the survey. In addition, discussions generated useful insights into people's interpretations of the causes of hypertension. Conversely, there may be moments in a participatory research project where, as part of the process, surveys using standard extractive techniques may be called for.

Participatory methods and the participatory process

Participatory research methods can be used, if users are committed to exploring the solutions people suggest and if institutions are flexible enough to permit this, to set in motion a participatory process in health promotion. There has been concern about raising expectations in communities; expectations that initiators are in no position to fulfil. The complex issues involved in this revolve around not only responsibility but also response-ability, that is, the ability to respond and to change.[4] It is with the development of this ability to respond, with restoring agency to people to analyse and act, that the principles of participatory research are most concerned. And part of this may be a process of raising expectations of what could be possible. Taking responsibility for raising expectations, and awareness, is clearly important; but taking responsibility for providing what people want is another issue altogether. It is, perhaps, precisely the concern that is expressed about expectations that serves as a powerful indication of the limitations in seeing the use of participatory methods as in itself constituting a participatory process. In many of the settings in which these methods are used, the root problem is not health, defined in a narrow way, but inequality, poverty and powerlessness. Without a commitment to empowerment and to seeing the process of change as a wider project, participation soon becomes a rather empty shell. And for pragmatic as much as political reasons, without carrying the learning process into institutions and decision-making structures, participatory methods can prove to be a first step that falters and goes no further.

Putting participatory ideals into practice brings about a number of practical, political and professional dilemmas. Conventional structures may be entirely inadequate to cope with the implications of participatory practice. Far-reaching institutional changes are needed if these processes are to be supported (Pretty & Chambers 1993). Wading into communities with ideas about empowerment and representation for those who are marginalized and powerless can create all kinds of problems. These may be practical, restricting participation among those upon whom domestic duties and reproductive burdens fall. They may arise from a conflict of interests provoked by the demands of a democratic agenda, for example, the issues arising from involving women as equals in strongly patriarchal settings. Not only can this kind of research threaten established interests both within communities and within the institutions that adopt it, it can also unleash a backlash that further disempowers those taking part.

While a tension clearly exists between the demands of principle and expediency, it is important not to lose sight of the potential impact of participatory methods on practice. Their use demands a style of interaction and a change in approach that in itself opens up transformational possibilities. By bringing health professionals into communities, to learn from rather than to teach people, participatory methods open up spaces for dialogue. This experience can be humbling for health workers. Realizing that people are not only knowledgeable but also capable of generating their own solutions has, for many, been a revelation. Working together with local people, as counterparts, challenges deeply held prejudices about the poor.

Using these methods, facilitators come to see that the poor, so often lumped together as ignorant and needy, are not a homogeneous mass but individuals whose knowledges, experiences and opinions are distinct, informed and different. Even if the participatory process goes no further than this, important lessons can be learnt. These can continue to have ramifications in the planning of interventions and in the design of research projects. Participatory visualization methods offer ways in which the material and explanations used by health promotion workers can be made more sensitive to local perceptions.

In practice, many health workers draw on local idiom to make medical messages make sense to patients (Kleinman 1978). Where there is a considerable divergence between local knowledge and Western medical explanations, health workers need to find a way of managing this interface and draw on their own knowledge of their communities to do so. A process that explores indigenous knowledge in order to make messages more appropriate can also provide a starting point for exploring the dilemmas health workers may face in practice. Acknowledging these dilemmas by recognizing the many different ways in which we learn about and know our bodies (Young 1981) and bringing these considerations into the training process would be a huge step forward.

Participatory methods offer ways of sharing ideas and constructing new forms of knowledge that can bridge the gap between medical messages and local knowledge. Extending this to focus on the concerns of different people within communities, by identifying issues for further study together with local people, takes this a step further. In the context of a larger project of social transformation, these steps bring health professionals closer to understanding and appreciating some of the most important personal and political aspects of participatory research.

Being involved not as objects but as active participants in dialogues and mutual learning with health professionals can form part of a process of building confidence and self-esteem in local people. The women who told me that they were 'ignorant' quickly realized, as we started to share ideas, that they were not; the very fact that their ideas were listened to and engaged with, with interest, confirmed this. Building self-confidence among those who are all too often ignored or lectured to is a vital part of the participatory process. Participatory research methods address this aim explicitly, providing a context for the recognition of people's knowledge and abilities. By working from and with that knowledge, basing it on people's lived experiences, health promotion can be not only more appropriate but also more productive of enhanced self-awareness and self-confidence. This has important implications for health service delivery. Enabling people to express their perceptions and concerns forms the basis for a more active engagement in which they are no longer cast as silent, passive recipients.

Notes

1. This chapter draws on experiences and discussions in many settings and it would be difficult to thank all of those who have been part of my own learning process. I would, however, especially like to thank Simbisai Makumbirofa,

with whom I worked in Zimbabwe. Some parts of the chapter draw on ideas developed in collaboration with Irene Guijt, Rachel Jewkes and Alice Welbourn. Responsibility for what appears here is, however, mine alone.
2. The experience, as well as the results, of this PRA training-of-trainers course in Dalocha, Ethiopia, for ACTIONAID Ethiopia, can be found in *Look Who's Talking* (ACTIONAID/IIED 1992).
3. This work was carried out as a training exercise within FARM-Africa's Farmer Participatory Research project, for staff from FARM-Africa and other local NGOs (FARM-Africa/IIED, 1991). A discussion of the results of this mapping exercise can be found in RRA Notes 14 (Jonfa et al. 1991).
4. I am grateful to Irene Guijt for introducing me to this idea.

References

ACTIONAID/IIED (1992) *Look Who's Talking: Training of Trainers in Dalocha, Ethiopia*, International Institute for Environment and Development (IIED), London.

Biggs, S. (1989) 'Resource-poor farmer participation in research: a synthesis of experiences from nine national agricultural research assistants', *Ofcor Comparative Study Paper,* No.3, International Service for National Agricultural Research, The Hague.

Bilgi, M. (forthcoming) 'Entering women's worlds through male eyes', in Guijt, I. & Shah, M.

Boal, A. (1995) *The Rainbow of Desire* (trans. A. Jackson), Routledge, London.

Chambers, R. (1992) 'Rural appraisal: rapid, relaxed and participatory', *IDS Discussion Paper*, No.227, Institute of Development Studies, Brighton.

Cornwall, A. (1990) *Indigenous Models of Reproduction: Implications for Family-planning Education*, unpublished report.

Cornwall, A. (1992) 'Body mapping in health RRA/PRA', *Rapid Rural Appraisal Notes*, No.16, pp.69-76, IIED, London.

del Valle, T. (ed.) (1993) *Gendered Anthropology*, Routledge, London.

Fals-Borda, O. & Rahman, A. (eds) (1991) *Action and Knowledge: Breaking the Monopoly with Participatory Action Research*, Apex, New York.

FARM-Africa/IIED (1991) *Farmer Participatory Research in North Omo: Report of a Training Course in RRA*, IIED, London.

Freire, P. (1972) *Pedagogy of the Oppressed*, Penguin, Harmondsworth.

Guijt, I. & Shah, M. (forthcoming) *The Myth of Community: Gender Issues in Participatory Development*.

Hart, R. (1992) 'Children's participation: from tokenism to citizenship', *Innocenti Essay*, No.4, UNICEF.

International Institute for Environment and Development (IIED) (1988–present) *Rapid Rural Appraisal Notes*, Sustainable Agriculture Programme, IIED, London.

Jonfa, E. et al. (1991) 'Participatory modelling in North Omo, Ethiopia: investigating the perceptions of different groups through models', *Rapid Rural Appraisal Notes*, No.14, pp.24-26, IIED, London.

Khanna, R. (1992) *Taking Charge: Women's Health as Empowerment. The SARTHI*

Experience, SAHAJ/SARTHI, Baroda, India.

Kleinman, A. (1978) 'Concepts of a model for the comparison of medical systems as cultural systems', *Social Science and Medicine*, No.12, pp.85-96.

Korten, D. (1980) 'Community organization and rural development – a learning process approach', *Public Administration Review*, Vol.40(5), pp.480-511.

Kumar, A. (1992) 'Trends in health care', *Rapid Rural Appraisal Notes*, No.16, pp.48-52, IIED, London.

Mavro, A. (1991) *Development Theatre: A Way to Listen*, SOS-Sahel, London.

Moore, H. (1993) 'The differences within and the differences between', in del Valle, T. (ed.), pp.193-204.

Pretty, J. (1995) 'Participatory learning for sustainable agriculture', *World Development*, Vol.23(8).

Pretty, J. & Chambers, R. (1993) 'Towards a learning paradigm: new professionalism and institutions for agriculture', *IDS Discussion Paper*, No.335, Institute of Development Studies, Brighton.

Welbourn, A. (1991) 'RRA and the analysis of difference', *Rapid Rural Appraisal Notes*, No.14, pp.14-23, IIED, London.

Welbourn, A. (1992) 'A note on the use of disease problem-ranking with relation to socio-economic well-being: an example from Sierra Leone', *Rapid Rural Appraisal Notes*, No.16, IIED, London.

Young, A. (1981) 'The creation of medical knowledge: some problems in interpretation', *Social Science and Medicine*, No.15(3b), pp.379-86.

10 Participation and action: reflections on community-based AIDS intervention in South Africa

Eleanor Preston-Whyte and Lynn Dalrymple

These days it is platitudinous to remark that research not only takes many forms, but it is undertaken with a multitude of aims not least of which is to effect change or social transformation. When the word 'research' is prefaced by adjectives like 'participatory'[1] and 'action', we know that we are in the arena of guided change aimed at interactive transformation and, often, structural renegotiation. In South Africa, intervention models using participatory research (PR) appear to have much to offer. While enthusiastically embracing the ideology of PR, however, local researchers have not been consciously analytical about their aims or the process of their intervention. With one notable exception (Mathews et al. 1993) few South African studies have reported their failures as well as their successes and insufficient attention has been given to monitoring and reporting their sustainability. In this connection, we accept that success should be measured not so much in terms of achieving community participation in itself as of PR acting successfully as a catalyst for ongoing creative and internal change. Some, and probably much of this change may well not have been envisaged by the original research intention, but in it lies the effectiveness and sustainability of the intervention, and the justification of the methodology.

This chapter represents a reflexive and critical evaluation of a drama-based AIDS education programme which is currently being run in black secondary schools in KwaZulu. In this case, the notion of 'participatory' research does not stretch, at least in the first instance, to the whole community. It is school-teachers and pupils for whom the experience is participatory. The method adopted is for teams made up of trained drama facilitators and community nurses seconded to the project to visit the secondary schools and present AIDS information in the form of a play which they themselves have devised to suit local conditions. Thereafter they work with the young people and teachers in the classroom and help them to compose their own dramatic presentations of the AIDS message. It is these phases which represent the participatory and action component of the project. The results include not only student plays but poems, dances, mimes and, to the researchers, initially startling role reversals. The performances are presented at an open day which has taken on the character of a community celebration. It is in the latter that we see the seeds of sustainability and the justification of the claim that the drama project is participatory. It must, however, be acknowledged that neither the schools nor the wider community were consulted about the advisability either of introducing an AIDS education programme or of the manner in which this was done. This is an initiative of the KwaZulu Departments of Health and Education and is funded by them.

Theoretical underpinning: theatre, drama and behavioural theory

The concept of learning through drama, often referred to as drama-in-education (DIE) was pioneered by British drama practitioners such as Peter Slade, Brian Way, Dorothy Heathcote and Gavin Bolton. Essentially participatory in orientation, DIE asserts that learning is rooted in personal experience which is extended to assimilate and analyse new information. Important for an intervention project such as DramAide is the acceptance that active learning involves a negotiation of meaning between the participants, that is between those who initially fill the roles of instructors and the learners (in this case the scholars and teachers). The latter will eventually take over the project, both running and reinterpreting its message in locally appropriate terms. This demands the achievement of a high degree of self-confidence on their part and it is here that drama theory converges with much of the recent work done in the field of behavioural intervention. In the latter, it is argued specifically that feelings of competency and self-worth provide the necessary confidence for experimentation and for an openness to change both in attitude and behaviour.

Bandura (1982) is well-known for his emphasis on the importance of what is termed self-efficacy in allowing for and facilitating personal change. Dovetailing neatly with this are various techniques of educational drama which aim at working specifically on building self-confidence and, through engaging participants in problem-solving, seek to develop feelings of competence and control. Constituting another possible piece of the jigsaw of intervention and change are other behavioural theories such as that of Fishbein and Azjen (1975) who postulated that behaviour is based on 'reasoned action' which is, in turn, rooted in beliefs and attitudes. Together, these constitute the substratum for action and behavioural change which must be based on a real change in attitudes and the rational assessment by the individual of her or his overall social position. In terms of drama theory, engaging in role play provides opportunities for rehearsing alternative courses of action and exploring their possible consequences. These notions of the possibility of understanding and changing conditioned ways of understanding the self in relation to society are supported by the work of Paulo Freire in the *Pedagogy of the Oppressed* (1972); Augusto Boal, *Theatre of the Oppressed* (1985) and Ross Kidd's work in popular theatre for development (Kidd

& Colletta 1981; Kidd 1982). We argue, from the experience of the DramAide Programme, that the active involvement in role play may open up 'new worlds' of possible action specifically in the realms of gender interaction and sexuality (Preston-Whyte 1993a; Dalrymple & Preston-Whyte 1992). The process may, furthermore, facilitate the rethinking of previously unchallenged cultural assumptions about sexual behaviour and gender interaction. This might lead to changed attitudes and, following this, open space for behavioural change, or at least serious consideration of it and possibly experimentation.

The wary anthropologist often challenges the notion that attitudes *do* invariably control behaviour in any simple and unidirectional manner, and, more important, warns that many people cannot act in accordance with their attitudes and beliefs. Adopting safe sex may be impeded by factors at both the macro level, such as poverty, and for women, in particular, at the micro level, by domestic and gender issues. In the last resort the attitudes and beliefs of other people with power over the individual often call the tune. We have then to accept that introducing behavioural change is not as simple as some of the behavioural theories sketched above might suggest. This does not mean we believe that nothing can be done. We have looked to, and adapted, the techniques of participatory research into the fertile soil provided by the concepts of learning activated in DIE and TIE (theatre-in-education) which are, in themselves, based on very similar premises to participatory research.

We argue that what is important about the techniques of educational drama is that participation is the key concept in all its different modes. The first step is to explore the young people's basic ideas about sex and HIV/AIDS, and thereafter to challenge the factual inaccuracies, hoping to change beliefs. To explore young people's basic ideas about AIDS a play was devised on the basis of the findings of the initial research phase. The use of drama makes it possible to challenge factual inaccuracies in a much more arresting manner than the usual talk-and-chalk instruction characteristic of existing school education in KwaZulu. Second, and far more critical, is the real participatory phase of the project when young people develop in workshops their own plays, songs and poems. The young people are encouraged as participants in the project to think actively about their own sexuality and the alternative avenues of action which might be possible for them. The workshops and the plays are designed to be, in a sense, rehearsals for life. They culminate in an open day to which parents and the whole local community are invited.

Here, the term 'participatory' refers not primarily to research or community involvement as such, but to the effects which participatory drama techniques may have in putting across basic information about HIV and about how to avoid infection. The objective is to initiate behaviour change on the part of individuals and, specifically, high-school children. The link between knowledge and action is accepted to be problematic, but the contention is that the very act of acting-out, in both the sense of intellectual, emotional and physical action as well as in the Western sense of a play or performance, rather than the passive reception of information, has a substantial chance of success.

In summary, the methodology of the project is in the first instance exploratory in that it bases the intervention on conventional social research. It is, secondly, interventionist. The DramAide teams have their own agenda, awakening AIDS awareness, which they pursue through the use of drama-in-action. Third, the active participation of the children themselves and of their teachers is encouraged through involvement in developing the performances. In terms of the latter we argue that it is essentially participatory and action-oriented.

The DramAide schools project

The schools drama project (DramAide Schools Project) outlined above has to date been introduced into over 400 high schools in KwaZulu in South Africa. This region is at the forefront of the HIV/AIDS epidemic in South Africa. Research indicates that in 1993 at least 1 in 20 mothers were already infected and the rate was doubling each year. Young women and men are particularly at risk.

The aim of DramAide is to activate 770 schools over a period of three years. The basic design for this ambitious scheme is the establishment of ten regional teams made up of two drama facilitators and two local nurses who begin by contacting a designated number of schools to introduce the project. On gaining admission to a school, the first step (referred to as Phase Nought) is a teachers' workshop on AIDS and the presentation of the project in the school. Second, the drama teams present an AIDS play which they have designed to suit local conditions. This is referred to as Phase One and is followed by an intensive question-and-answer session in which pupils are encouraged to voice their reactions, to open up and to seek clarity on the issues raised in the play. Because two of the team are nurses most of the essentially medical questions are dealt with adequately.

Phase Two involves drama sessions conducted in each class in the school. Role play is intrinsic to this phase and is intended to facilitate attitude change and also to lead to the devising by each class of plays, songs, dances, poems and posters. The workshop design uses active-learning methods, including role plays, to demonstrate to participants their own ability to reduce their risk of HIV/AIDS infection. The DramAide teams promote the search for solutions appropriate to the participants' lifestyles. Because the exercises crystallize real-life experiences, cognitive learning is stimulated by the emotional impact of the situation. The teams assist young people to develop a critical conscious-ness leading to cooperative social action and self-reliance. This concept is grounded in the idea of conscientization articulated by Paulo Freire as the process in which people achieve a deepening awareness both of the socio-historical reality that shapes their lives and of their capacity to transform the reality not as recipients but as knowing subjects (Freire 1972).

Another key feature of drama workshops is to teach skills, specifically communication skills which empower young people to negotiate appro-priate sexual behaviour. The drama workshops initiate the creative work that will take the AIDS message to the community in the third phase of the intervention. This is an open day on HIV/AIDS awareness held by the school for parents and the local community. The school presents a programme of speeches by local dignitaries interspersed with the items prepared by the young people. At this point in the programme the drama team must act as a catalyst group and hand over to the school to achieve the open day. What is offered is information that must be correctly passed on in a way that is accessible to the local community and catches their attention.

Some problems

It has been difficult for the DramAide teams to gain sufficient time in some schools adequately to facilitate workshops using role play and to stimulate performances for the open day. This is because there are schools that are reluctant to give up time for activities that do not appear on the syllabus. The facilitator's role, which is designed to elicit participation on the part of the school-children, is possibly the most critical part of the programme in terms of the theory which underpins it, and it has come to fall largely on the shoulders of the teachers. In fact, very often the DramAide teams have acted as a spearhead and catalyst rather than as workshop facilitators for this phase of the programme. In terms of participatory theory, this should be a positive feature; it works, however, only if a good foundation is laid.

The drama teams have also reported that the success of the open days is directly related to the participation of teachers and the attitude of the school principal. The team must hand the project over to the school. It is quite impossible for a small group of outsiders to organize and control schools of up to 1,500 pupils. Teacher workshops are, therefore, impor-tant for the success of the project.

First attempts at these workshops followed the style of a formal talk and it was found that this did not usually elicit much response and so the concept of an active drama workshop for teachers was developed. This includes simple games and ways of genuinely working from the teacher's knowledge towards an acceptance of the team's medical information. Teachers are then encouraged to use this participatory approach with their classes, and in many cases there is great enthusiasm for simple and yet innovative alternatives to chalk-and-talk teaching methods. However, in some schools there are teachers who are not able or willing to motivate the children sufficiently to produce a successful open day. In a few cases, therefore, both phases two and three have left much to be desired, both in terms of the basic understanding of HIV/AIDS achieved, and in the vital participatory aspects of the programme.

Successes: what do the open days tell us?

Many open days have been, however, an outstanding success in drawing in participation from the local community and in heightening AIDS awareness. An open day held at a school outside Matubatuba in northern Zululand began at 7.30 with a procession that started outside a village market about 2km from the school. A brass band from the South African Army 616 Battalion was asked to lead the procession. Given the ongoing political struggle and the deep suspicion of the armed forces, this choice might have seemed surprising; however, the occasion was one calling for ceremony and performance, and what more noisy and public than a brass band? Half the school gathered on the roadside and marched behind the band to meet up with the other half which was led by drum majorettes. At the point of meeting the crowd began toyi-toying. Toyi-toyi is a political dance associated with the ongoing struggle for freedom and particularly with the role of youth in this movement. But the usual political slogans were transformed into AIDS slogans. An AIDS slogan 'After Intercourse Death Starts' had been coined as a counter to the well-known 'American Idea to Discourage Sex' and a group of children carried a huge banner with this message emblazoned on it. Other banners warned of the dangers of HIV/AIDS. There was a great air of excitement, with people coming out of their houses as they heard the noise and some joining the procession to the school hall. The programme of plays, dances, songs and speeches continued all day and was well supported by parents.

It is in the demonstration of skills and in the enjoyment of these performances that we would argue, the potential lies for having an impact on the attitudes of the school-children, and getting the AIDS message across. Self-efficacy and personal fulfilment are important parts of the confidence to initiate change or, in the specific case of young women, to resist pressures to unsafe sex and the acceptance of gender domination. For men, also, successful personal involvement in what is an important ceremonial event provides evidence of personal competence. Such feelings enhance self-efficacy, especially when this is mixed with the assurance that a credible alternative exists to the commonly accepted ideas of 'lover boy', a character in most plays who succumbs to AIDS, and dies. It is the reality of infection and death as well as the possibility of either chastity or condoms and safe sex that is being mooted as both girls and boys act out the sexual options open to them in a world with AIDS.

Within this broad canvas what are the themes which the children pursue in their plays and what does the way they choose to get their message across to their audience tell us about the likelihood of some behaviour change?

Education for Life?

There is a preoccupation in the plays with the fact that there is no cure for AIDS. In one innovative instance an HIV-positive young man seeks a cure first from Western doctors, then from traditional healers. Finally he seeks solace with a group of Christians and ends up calling loudly on God for help. The voice of God responds from amid the audience: 'I don't have a cure, you should have used ways of preventing the disease.' The message is expressed in a manner which touches the experience of many Christians, and even of those who are not regular church attenders. Most plays describe the social circumstances of the lives of the performers. Parents are depicted as being away from home, and when they are present many are authoritarian and often drunk. The threat of unemployment looms over families and the need to make money often leads girls into sex. It is true that many of these young women are portrayed as motivated by personal needs, such as clothing and a good time, but the point is made that girls are available for sex if the price is right. Older men seek sex with very young girls and especially schoolgirls. Not all plays are, however, purely negative. Some show the family uniting eventually in the face of having an AIDS sufferer in the family. Indeed, the whole progress of the disease may be shown leading to this paradoxically happy ending.

In contrast to this theme are plays which emphasize another kind of positive message. In one the narrator says: 'Even if you have AIDS, you have a bright future ahead. You don't have to cry over spilt milk since you won't be able to gather or collect it. But look ahead, there is a lot waiting for you.' This theme was introduced by the DramAide team to counter-act the negative stereotypes which they found the pupils (and some teachers) were displaying to people with AIDS.

In most of the plays the pupils present what, to the outsider, seems a simplified and unreal picture of the practical difficulties of coping with the possibility of infection. While they graphically portray the scene in bars and the way in which older men persuade young girls to have sex with them, when it comes to changing behaviour, the partners of women are eventually shown as willing to use condoms or abstain from full intercourse. Certainly, from the somewhat idealistic views presented in the plays produced so far, the pupils seem to believe that it *is* possible to change their behaviour. However, they are not yet bringing to bear on the issue any experience of the constraints of, in particular, the gendered social structure in which they live. In addition, the whole emphasis in all other teaching is on the reception of information rather than the negotiation of learning, and this may militate at present against the fulfilment of the promise of participatory techniques in the learning sphere.

This may seem to be a major criticism of the programme and it is one which is taken seriously by the DramAide team, which sees two possible ways of addressing the problem. The first appears to lie in developing the workshop phase of the participatory process: the teachers need to be motivated to raise the problems which are likely to face the pupils in practice, and to seek with them ways in which these can be dealt with. The programme has adapted the techniques developed by August Boal and Paulo Freire of using plays to trigger discussion and to pose problems. These have been introduced successfully. These techniques require expert facilitation, however, and in order to sustain its work DramAide is shifting its emphasis towards in-depth teacher training.

A second avenue which is being explored is to develop a longer-term programme which will serve to reinforce the AIDS message. At present, once the open day is over and the DramAide team moves on to the next school, there is little to suggest that the AIDS message will be kept alive. It is true that teachers have reported that pupils continue to sing the AIDS songs, and, in one instance, an observer was intrigued to see a group of girls in a school playground react to the presence of boys and their sexual innuendoes by singing 'their' AIDS song! But this is hardly institutionalized behaviour. Some formal way must be found to reinforce the message and incorporate it into the routine teaching at schools. This will mean a syllabus change and perhaps the incorporation of not only AIDS information but drama techniques of putting it across, in all standards, as a regular part of the ongoing educational process.

Community responses to the DramAide project

However, it is in the response by local community representatives that the real impact of the project may be best judged. At the open days, community leaders comment consistently on the talent for performance which is displayed and many plead that further opportunities be opened up for these talents to be used in the service of education in general and AIDS education in particular. As a result, funds are being sought in order to add another phase to the project in which work generated in the schools will be presented at other schools and to grassroots organizations. The DramAide teams are networking actively with local women's clubs, farmers' cooperatives and other locally based AIDS action groups.

Gender and performance: is something happening?

On a number of occasions, women and girls wear men's clothes and dance men's dances at open days. A group of girls may perform the usually male gumboot dance and at one urban open day a troupe of girls wore men's suits and presented a variation of tap dancing, claiming in the song that 'we are in charge of our own bodies'. This gender reversal could mean that gender lines are becoming blurred as women seek emancipation from the strictures of a patriarchal society. On the other hand, it could be a more subtle variation on the theme of 'rituals of rebellion' (Gluckman 1954) which express dissonance in the social system, but serve to contain it. Women wearing men's clothes occurs in traditional Zulu ceremonials and, as in other cultures, the burlesquing of dominant groups could be part of a carnivalesque pattern where subordinate groups are allowed to blow off steam under controlled conditions. We would hope that these occasions are more than this and may approximate to a statement of women's emancipation, or a desire for it.

DramAide and the oral tradition

One of the striking features of the ongoing project described here has been the demonstration of the power of the oral medium in rural situations in KwaZulu. Although the children are at school, much of the community is often poorly educated and many people have never attended school. Talking and acting out ideas, as well as participatory singing and dancing, are excellent ways in which to gain attention. There is a sense of gratification in participating in a cultural day which pervades both rural and urban situations and combines with a sense of pride in the past to act as a possible counter to the apathy which pervades so much of life lived by the poor and oppressed in South Africa. This in itself is a spur to action and change. Implicit in our argument is the importance of participation as the key which unlocks the awareness of the possibility of making this momentous transition. The notion that cultural forms are used as a resource both to make sense of the world and also to plan action is admirably illustrated in the way in which the participants in the open days choose to perform and stage their event. The rich variety and eclecticism of contemporary South African culture is reflected in the wide range of dances, songs and presentations, all on the theme of AIDS. Songs and dance forms include modern rap, traditional wedding songs, gospel music and toyi-toyi (political dance). These are converted into AIDS songs with remarkable ease by young people, especially those who are still in touch with their oral heritage.

Conclusions: participation or participatory?

As the DramAide teams work with young people and their teachers they move from being outsiders to being insiders. More important, through the preparation for the open day, the children and some of their teachers become the moving force in the project. Where the project is successful, the pupils and teachers take it over from the team and make it their own. Importantly, they not only stage the open day, but in the drama workshops pupils are encouraged to voice and concretize their existing opinions not only of AIDS but of sexual interaction in general. They are provided with the opportunity openly to discuss sex and sexual practice. In this sense the project aims to act as a catalyst for change. The project leaders are fairly prescriptive, stressing either condom use or abstinence and chastity till marriage. It is in how this message is conveyed on the open day that the scholars and teachers enter into participatory interactions with the team. Ideally, workshopping deals with problems over negotiating safe sex and young people are told where to obtain condoms. Participation has meant a form of interactive learning and possible experimentation with new ways of looking at the world and sexuality. In the plays and in their accompanying songs and dance routines participants show their competence to stage an open day and in so doing, it is hoped, begin to internalize the message they are offering their audience. No real community involvement is, however, achieved beyond the pleasurable participation in the AIDS-awareness open day. However, the suggestion that health festivals might be organized around the issues of AIDS and sexuality and that these could be broadened to encompass other emotive issues is being explored. Eight health festivals were, indeed, held during 1994, in regions where the programme was completed. The festivals were organized by nurses from local hospitals and included the most interesting items seen on open days. These AIDS-awareness festivals are indicators of the programme having taken root and stimulated a response from local communities.

The impact of the DramAide project on behaviour change is being evaluated using a number of indicators but in the final analysis it will be difficult to isolate the impact of a particular approach in the fight against HIV/AIDS. What is being offered through the drama approach, at one level, is tangible enjoyment and participation in a whole range of new learning situations, but at another, even less concrete level there is the possibility that these experiences might initiate real behavioural change. Perhaps this is too negative a note to end upon. The essence of both participatory and community-based research is to stimulate change as does a catalyst, not an oppressor.[2]

Notes

1. The term 'participatory' when applied to research should be distinguished clearly from participant observation, which is one of the major research techniques used by many anthropologists and increasingly by sociologists to collect qualitative data in the field. The two may, however, be linked, and I have argued elsewhere that participant observation provides an ideal basis for participatory action research in the AIDS intervention field (Preston-Whyte 1993b).
2. In 1995 the DramAide programme entered its fourth year. To date, 600 secondary schools have been activated, demonstrating the feasibility of the

intervention. The cost per scholar for this programme is estimated at less than £2. Over a million people have been contacted directly through the programme and it is believed that it has made a major impact on AIDS awareness in the region. A multi-pronged approach to evaluation has been adopted, and findings will be published in 1996.

References

Bandura, A. (1982) 'Self-efficacy mechanisms in human agency', *American Psychology*, Vol.37, pp.122-47.

Boal, Augusto (1985) *Theatre of the Oppressed*, Theatre Communications Group, New York.

Dalrymple, L. & Preston-Whyte, E.M. (1992) 'A drama approach to AIDS education: an experiment in "action" research', *AIDS Bulletin*, Vol.1(1), pp.9-11.

Fishbein, M. & Azjen, I. (1975) *Beliefs, Attitudes, Intentions and Behaviour*, Addison-Wesley, Boston.

Freire, Paulo (1972) *Pedagogy of the Oppressed*, Penguin, London.

Gluckman, M. (1954) *Rituals of Rebellion in South-East Africa*, Manchester University Press, Manchester.

Kidd, Ross (1982) *Popular Performance, Non-formal Education and Social Change in the Third World: A Bibliography and Review Essay*, Centre for the Study of Education in Developing Countries, The Hague.

Kidd, R. & Colletta, N. (eds) (1981) 'Tradition for development: indigenous structures and folk media in non-formal education', German Foundation for International Development, and International Council for Adult Education, Bonn.

Mathews, C., Everett, K., Binedell, J., & Steinberg, M. (1993) 'Learning to listen: formative research in the development of AIDS education for secondary school pupils', unpublished paper for the National AIDS Research Programme, Medical Research Programme, Medical Research Council, Cape Town (revised document accepted for publication in *Social Science and Medicine*).

Preston-Whyte, E.M. (1993a) 'Half-way there: perspectives on the use of qualitative research methods in intervention oriented AIDS research in South Africa', in ten Brummelhuls, H. & Herdt, G. (eds) *Anthropological Perspectives on AIDS*, Het Spinhuls, Amsterdam.

Preston-Whyte, E.M. (1993b) 'Women who are not married: fertility, "illegitimacy", and the nature of households and domestic groups among single African women in Durban', *South African Journal of Sociology*, Vol.24(3), pp.63-71.

11 Methodological issues in the ethnographic study of sexuality: experiences from Bombay[1]

Annie George

It is widely recognized that for women to gain control over their lives, their participation is a prerequisite in the planning and implementation of programmes which will affect them directly. It is increasingly recognized that women's participation in the research process, which usually is the precursor to any programme planning and implementation, is an integral step in the control they seek over their lives. People, particularly poor women and men, gain control over their lives through the redistribution of power and resources including the resources of information and knowledge creation. Participatory research (PR), by its methods and underlying principles, is a process through which collective analysis and ownership of information is obtained. Feminist PR usually involves women in examining issues and creating knowledge and information which enables them to have greater control over their lives.

Participatory research has been defined as a method of social investigation in which oppressed and ordinary people name and analyse collectively the structural causes of their problems, and through which they join together to take collective short- and long-term action for social change (Maguire 1987). Maguire identifies the objective of participatory research as that of transforming power structures and relationships and empowering oppressed people to develop a critical understanding of the forces of their oppression. The three main components of participatory research are reflection, action and further reflection. This process mirrors the conscientization process originated by Paulo Freire. The strongest critique of participatory research is that it had been gender-blind until the early 1990s and, by and large, women have not been involved in the creation and use of knowledge which can transform their lives.

Although there is no consensus on the definition of feminist research, research which has the specific goal of empowering women tends to have some of the following characteristics: reflexivity; an action orientation; attention to the affective components of research; use of the situation-at-hand (Fonow & Cook 1991); avoidance of the objectivity–subjectivity divide; increase of closeness to the subjects; and decrease in the researcher's control over the research.

Maguire (1987) suggested a framework for *feminist* PR, the salient features of which include placing gender at the centre of the research agenda, giving feminism a central place in the theoretical debates on participatory research and giving explicit attention to gender issues in all phases of the PR project. A feminist participatory framework would create measures to ensure that women and men benefit from the process and the product of research. (The product would include actions which result from the research.)

This chapter discusses some methodological issues which arose in the process of fieldwork for a study which used focus group discussions and in-depth interviews to understand the meaning of sexuality for the poor women of Bombay. The study was not initiated as feminist participatory research, yet we had to include several elements of the feminist participatory model to make the study responsive to ethical and power issues, and acceptable to the women participants. First, we describe briefly the methods used and then discuss in greater detail the issues and concerns we faced in the process of using a feminist methodology. We end the chapter with some thoughts and issues of the realities of practising feminist participatory research.

Brief description of the study

The aim of our study was to understand the meaning of sexuality for poor women in Bombay through the use of group discussions which focused on the reproductive and social milestones of their lives. In all, we conducted group discussions with six groups of women. Each group, which consisted of six women, was of a different religious/linguistic background. Despite a rigorous schedule of the repeated use of focus group sessions, totalling twenty to twenty-four hours of audiotape material with each of the six groups, we had a very high participation rate. It appeared that the intensive sharing of life experiences in small groups which met frequently created a strong group bond and seemed to fulfil some unmet need of the women.

We requested community-based non-governmental organizations (NGOs) to introduce us to the women they served. This group of women cannot be considered statistically representative in any sense of 'poor women of Bombay'. Yet, the common themes they discussed seem to be representative of rather pervasive facts of life experienced by a wide range of women in Bombay's lower socio-economic strata (George & Jaswal 1994).

Methodological processes: creating an environment of trust

Involving non-governmental organizations in the study

A group environment which engendered a feeling of intimacy and acceptance was essential for women to discuss sensitive and personal matters within a group. We tried to do this through the involvement of select NGOs, and through our own relationships with the women. Since we, as university-based researchers, did not have an ongoing relationship with any community of women who could participate in the study, we had to seek the help of NGOs which worked closely with women in Bombay's slums to give us access to women.

To include the different influences NGOs might have on women, we selected a range of NGOs which provided them a variety of services like community-based health services, housing rights for slum dwellers, vocational training, legal rights for women, and adult literacy. As women's views of life could be influenced by the type of NGO with which they were in contact and the duration of their contact with the NGO, we selected women from NGOs with differing ideological orientations and work strategies. For instance, some NGOs which helped us recruit women were directed towards providing services and helping women adapt themselves to their life situations. Other NGOs had an activist orientation and considered their role to be that of organizing women and enabling them, through education and conscientization, to transform their life situations.

We selected NGOs which were familiar with the university where we worked, so that the NGO staff themselves knew the organization we represented and would thus introduce us very positively to the women. We had to work hard to convince NGO staff of the relevance of the research project to them and to the larger academic and social welfare community. Researchers in Bombay often seek the help of NGOs to carry out survey research. The NGOs, seeing no useful outcome, are usually cautious about lending support to such work. We had to advocate our study and tell them that non-invasive, repetitive focus group discussions with a small group of women who were their clients would be of use to them. It would strengthen the group identity of the women, thus facilitating the formation of a group (and groups are the basic unit of work for most NGOs).

More importantly, the group's involvement in this study could lead to further work by them in the area of women's health. We promised our own expertise and resources to help the NGO conduct programmes on women's health, even after the study was over. Thus, in order to have access to the women, we had to first convince the NGO, which acted as a gatekeeper. We tried to build the confidence of the NGO in this research and to link it to their future work with women by having one of the NGO staff members participate in all the focus group discussion meetings. The responsibility for forming the group, maintaining the participants' interest in the research study and disseminating findings to the women was shared by the researchers and NGO staff.

Involving women in the study: informed participation

Once the NGO agreed to introduce us to the women, we went to slum communities and invited women to a meeting where we explained the purpose of our research study. Typically we informed women that there were very few studies done on women's health and sexuality which asked women their experiences and perspectives. We stated that we were not sure whether their participation and sharing of information would bring any tangible improvement in their own health situation or in their utilization of health services. We emphasized, however, that the information they shared would be written up and disseminated widely to other NGOs which served women like them with the goal of enabling other groups of women to analyse their life situation and to take collective action to change it.

Women were informed right from the outset that we would discuss topics which were not usually discussed formally by women, such as sexual relations, pregnancy and childbirth, and that these discussions would be taped. Women were told that if they were uncomfortable about any aspect of the process, for instance the tape recording, the taking of notes or the presence of unmarried researchers, they could inform us and we would change the situation. While we emphasized that there was no compulsion to participate and that they could leave the study at any time, we also said that the group discussions were work jointly undertaken by us which needed their regular participation and commitment. We realize that this was not a truly participatory stance, and we do not know how to resolve it. Usually the initial invitation to participate, which was made in a meeting in the community where the women lived, resulted in long and intense discussions where we were questioned about ourselves, the research process and the benefits of the research to them. We always had a time lag between this meeting and the time when the women indicated their interest in joining the study. Typically only a third or fewer of the women who attended the invitation meeting joined the study.

Structuring the data gathering: increased involvement of women
Trust was built by the repeated nature of the groups' discussion process which ensured that over a period of time, through repeated interactions, the women would get to know us better.

We introduced several changes in the data collection methods, so as to establish an environment of mutual trust and confidence. As women's regular participation in a series of twelve to fifteen focus group meetings spread over a period of six to eight weeks could not be guaranteed, we introduced the collection of data in larger and less frequent blocks of time. For instance, with three groups of women we gathered the data through the use of focus group discussions which lasted six to eight hours. We covered a series of topics in one day. From the research management point of view, too, gathering of data in less frequent, larger time blocks was more efficient.

Another difficulty we faced in fieldwork was that as the group discussions were held in the community, in a woman's home or in a room in the local child-care centre, the women could not concentrate on the discussions because they would be called by their families for short periods of time to attend to some domestic matter, or they would leave early to complete some household responsibility. This affected the concentration of the group and of the individual woman, which disturbed the group process. We decided, therefore, to invite the women to our workplace, where we had a comfortable room and adequate privacy, to share a meal with us and to spend several afternoons discussing the topics of the study. This allowed for more uninterrupted time with the women, greater concentration and involvement with the discussion, and the opportunity for us to know each other better. It created for the women a space and a time for themselves which was appreciated greatly by them.

Initially, we conducted a series of discussions which focused on a specific topic like pregnancy, childbirth, marriage and so on. There was considerable overlap between the topics; during the discussion on childbirth the women also talked about pregnancy. We felt, on reflection, that, while this approach was convenient for gathering information in topic-wise blocks, we were fragmenting the lives of women, lives which they considered more fluid and flowing in nature. We decided, therefore, to start our series of discussions with the next group of women by using the narrative, life-story approach. We requested each woman to narrate the moments of joy and sorrow in her life. In these free-flowing, unstructured narratives, each woman spoke at varying length about events in her life. Women discussed their childhood struggles to be sent to school; their experience of being one of several daughters; their coming-of-age; marriage and migration to the city, and so on. Through these narratives women revealed some painful experiences, like the extra-marital relationships of their spouses; the social trauma of being infertile; domestic violence; and the experience of seeking treatment for sexually transmitted disease.

These changes in the data collection process enabled us to see each woman's life as a complete whole; it also expanded the canvas of discussion. Following the narratives, which took several hours, we focused our group discussions on topics which were mentioned in the narratives, but which were not discussed in depth. Topics which we were hesitant to raise in the focus groups, like extra-marital relations, were discussed more easily once they had already been mentioned by a woman in her narrative. The process of coming together as a group to share intimate aspects of their lives strengthened the group identity of the women. It created the space to examine the structures in our lives which kept us in a dependent position and it gave us the opportunity to discuss the collective actions we could take to change the situation.

The use of in-depth interviews with selected women from each group was another innovation which was necessitated when we realized that depth of information was not being generated in the focus group discussions. For instance, women were reluctant to discuss certain very personal aspects of their sexual lives in focus groups.

Flexibility in the size and composition of the group and in the time spent with each group was another innovation. Certain groups of women who had long, flexible hours of work, like the rag-pickers, would not be able to attend all the focus group discussions. We learned that the life experiences of this group of women had many elements in common, though, obviously, there were individual differences. We felt, however, that the similarities in the lives of this group were strong enough for us to be flexible and have six to eight women from this group attend each session, even if it was not the same women for each session. A core group of four women attended all the group discussion sessions and another two to four women would be present for each session.

Self-disclosure of researchers: minimizing the distance

Although we were always willing to share our lives with the women, we told the first group some 'safe' information about ourselves, such as where we work and our family composition. We shared very little on topics which we wanted and expected women to share with us, topics like our experiences of menstruation, childbirth and marriage. On reflection, we recognized that the lack of sharing was a form of unequal power relations between us and the women. In our work with subsequent groups, we shared with women our experiences of childhood and schooling, work, marriage, being parents, and some of the difficulties we faced in our sexual and reproductive lives, like infertility, sexual molestation and rape. We did not share all this information with every group. The extent and nature of the information shared depended on the extent of the group's interest in us. In some groups, the fact of sharing our life stories was enough for the women to start sharing their life histories with us. They were not as interested in our stories as in the fact that we were willing to share. In other groups, particularly the activist-oriented groups, the women were interested in our stories and in how we had handled the various difficult situation in our lives. Though there is much discussion and debate on the issue of whether researchers should share of themselves with the subjects of research, we felt that this process increased the relationship of trust with the group, which was critical in obtaining the quality and depth of data we gathered.

Methodological issues in feminist participatory research

Our experience indicated that when researchers made the effort to build a relationship of trust with the subjects of the research, when the purpose of the research was repeatedly explained to the women, and when the process of data gathering was sensitive to the specific life context of the women, then the regular participation and continual interest of the women in the research study was ensured. However, the research process created some ethical dilemmas and concerns, which we discuss next.

The purpose of sharing

The nature of feminist participatory research is characterized by empathy for the participants, reciprocity of feeling and the establishment of rapport, understanding, concern and authenticity. These qualities influence the extent and depth of the material shared by the participants. Herein lies the conflict for the researcher. While, on the one hand, we wanted to reduce the distance between the women and ourselves, we were, on the other hand, guided always by concerns of research and data collection. As Stacey (1988) has observed, we faced a conflict of interest between ourselves as researchers and as participants. For instance, as mentioned earlier we shared our own life experiences with the women. The more detailed and open our sharing, especially of difficult, traumatic experiences, the more the women too shared similar traumatic experiences, which became 'data' for us. It became difficult to define neatly the purpose of sharing: should we share in order to elicit richer, detailed data; or should we share in order to be empowered by the experience of collective support and analysis of our situation. Should we not share because we know that women will respond in kind, and we feel it is a betrayal of their trust when we use their life events primarily as data? These questions remain unanswered.

Unequal power relationships in the research process

Although the process of our research project appeared to embrace egalitarian values, the power balance between the women and us was tilted in our favour at every stage of the research. The way the research was structured, with the call for proposals, and with the time frame involved, it was not practical for us to involve the NGOs and the women in problem formulation and the design of the research study. The greatest level of NGO and women's participation in our study was at the data-gathering stage. At this stage, the women's influence over the research process was seen through the various changes we made in the data-gathering process. Women had control over the process by determining the nature of the group interaction and the way the research questions were treated (the extent to which the process was discussed; what was said and what was left out; what was discussed more; and what was discussed less).

Even the NGO participation was restricted primarily to activities related to the formation of groups of women, data gathering and the dissemination of the findings of the study to the women after the research was completed. To a large extent, the restriction of the participation was due to our desire for control over the research. We feared that increased participation from the NGOs could disrupt our research agenda, methods of data collection and time frame. In reality, participation means increasing the power base of the various actors. This is a messy process which may require a lot more time than may be available to share information and resources and to arrive at a consensus on the structure of the research project, the research questions, the process of research and its outcomes. It requires university-based researchers to be more sensitive to the concerns of NGOs, and for NGOs to appreciate the requirements of research.

The question we faced is: how can research which emanates from an academic institution be more participatory? How can research be more directly useful to transform the unequal power relations in people's lives? Mies (1983) suggests that the researcher's active involvement in the struggle for women's liberation will engender the selection of research topics and methods which reduce the distance between the researcher and the researched and which serve the purpose of enabling women to increase control over their lives.

Unequal power relationships in the research product

We shared Stacey's (1988) concern with feminist research that the process and product of research was in the control of the researchers. For instance, we used ourselves and our experiences to uncover the experiences of the participants. Yet, in the final document, we did not include our voices directly. We could have presented our part of the shared dialogue in the final report but our question was: do we need to present the researcher's narrative in a report, the focus of which is the participant's experience. And, how do we responsibly report this process, this shared dialogue, such that the interactive, collaborative nature of the dialogue is represented?

The dissemination of the research product was not in the control of the participants, nor entirely in our control. Women had participated with the understanding that the final product would be used with other women's groups. However, how can we control who will use the final products? For example, we made a video film of one group's discussions after obtaining the women's consent. They expressed concerns about who would see the video. They did not want their menfolk – fathers, husbands, brothers – to see them express frank views. Neither the women nor the researchers can have complete control over this process. We wondered about the extent to which the women could apprehend that once the research products were placed in the public domain, there was not much control we could exert in terms of restricting access to the research products. We were concerned that if women did not understand the notion of public access to materials, it was a betrayal of their trust.

More equitable participation in and control over the research process and products will not occur as long as all participants in the research endeavour are not better informed about the politics of research, namely, the potential of research to be structured, designed and used to serve the interest of particular constituencies. Participatory research does not begin at the problem formulation stage of a particular research project. Researchers have to be continually committed to the process of educating their participant communities about the powers and the responsibilities of research and information creation. As Mies (1983) suggested, this is best achieved if the researcher herself is rooted in the struggles of the community.

The authoritative voice

The researcher's representation of the women to the world is yet another source of her power. Although the women were the experts, the informed insiders of their culture, they did not have the authoritative voice which we had by virtue of our academic and institutional affiliations. We were the authority both in the format of the final text and in the selection of the content. We employed some measures to involve the women in the analysis and presentation of data by, for instance: providing the women with our analysis of discussions and seeking their comments; seeking clarifications on language and meanings, and structuring the format of the research report such that the women's voices were quoted. Yet, in the final research product, the researcher is seen as the authoritative voice, the interpreter of the women to the world. The problems and responsibility of interpretation are not reduced when participants and researchers share the same gender. If researchers and participants did not share cultural norms by virtue of caste and class, and if a researcher was not sensitive to these issues, problems of interpretation and representation could arise.

Invasiveness of the research process

The research study we reported invaded the lives of the women despite our efforts. Through our transitory presence in the women's lives, we changed the network of relationships they had established, even if only for a short while. While we could remove ourselves from their lives once the research process was over, the women had to continue with the situation which the research had created. For example, the research opened up old emotional wounds which the women had spent much time healing. We do not know how the women handled the emotional work of dealing with the reopened wounds once we moved off the scene. In some cases, the research process reinforced a woman's lack of choices to make immediate changes in her life situation. The research agenda did not include ways of dealing with the changes in relationships which occurred as a result of the research process. The situation remained stressful if the NGO also did not initiate any process to help the women.

The issue that arises from the situation just described is the responsibility of the researchers to anticipate the outcomes of the research process, like the reopening of painful memories, and to provide for their resolution. One solution is to define the entire activity as part of the research project. This wide definition is extremely difficult to sell to funders and to implement as university-based researchers. Another option is to involve NGOs in carrying on the action which follows from the reflection stage, namely the data gathering, including the process of emotional support. This option involves greater power-sharing between the researchers and the NGOs.

How participatory was the research process?

University-based research activity is usually determined by a research agenda dictated from above. We may seek to incorporate elements of participation in the process, but to what extent can university-controlled research be participatory in the sense discussed by Maguire (1987) and Chambers (1992)? Participatory research has been defined as a method of social investigation in which oppressed and ordinary people collectively name and analyse the structural causes of their problems, and through which they join together to take collective short- and long-term action for social change. What role did our research study play in this cyclical process? And what was the role of the NGO? What are the necessary conditions for the successful partnership between the researchers, the NGO and the women?

Though the research agenda was primarily ours and not that of the NGOs or the women, there was enough room for collective investigation. The group nature of the focus group discussions allowed the women collectively to analyse the structural causes of their problems. Researchers are interested primarily in the analysis of the cause. Action is left to other agents. This was where collaboration with the NGO became essential. As mentioned earlier, we were given access to the women by a number of NGOs. We found that those NGOs who had an action orientation, as opposed to a service provision orientation, were more interested in the participatory action which could result from the research process.

One NGO illustrates this position. It had formed a group for women who were separated or deserted, to help them regularize their legal status. The women were facing a structural rupture point in their lives. They had analysed together the structural causes of their marital problems. For this group of women, the focus group meetings were a means in their process of analysing the various forces which were bottlenecks in their search for greater autonomy. Thus, the research process was seen by the NGO and the women as a material support to continue the process of reflection and action which they had already initiated. This group of women went on to work collectively to seek a legal solution to their problems.

The ideological orientation of the NGO, its preparedness to take on the responsibility of engendering action and the availability of human and other resources for action are all key elements in determining whether action follows from the reflection. However, researchers too have a responsibility to create the conditions where such action can take place. Researchers should define the participatory research process broadly to include the infrastructural support for action. To what extent this is possible in university-initiated research if the university does not have strong links with and commitment to the community is uncertain. We realize that we did not involve the NGOs enough in reflection, nor did we have enough dialogue with them about the potential for action. Participatory research is about 'handing over the stick' (Chambers 1992). In this case we should have handed it over to the NGOs, so that the research study could have become the first step in a participatory process.

Note

1. The data for this chapter are based on a research project which was part of the Women and AIDS programme conducted by the International Center for Research on Women, Washington DC, and funded by the Office of Health of the US Agency for International Development.

References

Bowles, Gloria & Klein Renate (eds) (1983) *Theories of Women's Studies*, Routledge & Kegan Paul, Boston.

Chambers, Robert (1992) *Rural Appraisal: Rapid, Relaxed and Participatory*, Discussion Paper 311, Institute of Development Studies, Brighton.

Fonow, Mary Margaret & Cook, Judith A. (1991) 'A look at the second wave of feminist epistemology and methodology', in Fonow, Mary Margaret & Cook, Judith A. (eds.), *Feminist Scholarship as Lived Research*, Indiana University Press, Bloomingdale.

George, Annie & Surinder, Jaswal (1994) *Understanding Sexuality: Ethnographic Study of Poor Women in Bombay*, International Center for Research on Women, Washington DC.

Maguire, Patricia (1987) *Doing Participatory Research: A Feminist Approach*, Center for International Education, Amherst.

Mies, Maria (1983) 'Towards a methodology for feminist research', in Bowles, Gloria & Klein, Renate (eds) (1983).

Stacey, Judith (1988) 'Can there be a feminist ethnography?', *Women's Studies International Forum*, Vol.11, pp.21-27.

12 An experience in the use of the PRA/RRA approach for health needs assessment in a rural community of northern Gujarat, India[1]

SEWA-Rural Team

SEWA-Rural (Society for Education, Welfare and Action-Rural) is a voluntary service organization working for overall development in a predominantly tribal population in Gujarat, a state in western India. The organization has been working for the last thirteen years running various programmes in areas such as health, income generation and education. The project area of the comprehensive health care programme of SEWA-Rural comprises around 38,000 people in 30 villages spread around Jhagadia, the base village. These services replace government services, including a primary health centre. A 75-bed base hospital in Jhagadia village provides referral curative care. Over the years, there have been substantial increments in the utilization of health services by the people of the area, and several indicators of the health of the population have shown significant improvement (Khanna et al. 1991). A weak link for a long time has been the relatively small involvement of the community in its activities. Several initiatives in different fields of development have been reported in recent years, where innovative activists have systematically elicited people's involvement in a variety of areas (Chambers 1992; Shah 1991; MYRADA 1990). The recent introduction of PRA methods in its research programme has provided SEWA-Rural with an opportunity systematically to explore the possibilities of involving people in health programmes.

In 1992 *Mahila Samakhya*, a government-sponsored organization for women's awareness and empowerment (Government of India 1991), approached SEWA-Rural for help in introducing a health component into its existent activities. The work required an understanding of both health problems and solutions, and the pattern of working of the *Mahila Samakhya* programme. This programme is based on a cadre of village-level workers, who are called *sakhis*, supported by a cadre of *sahayoginis*, one for every 10 *sakhis*. Although it has been conceived as a national-level programme, there is much decentralization of decision-making and most of the administration and planning takes place at the state and district levels. The main thrust is to organize women and encourage them to demand their due from the society in general and from different government-sponsored services in particular, and at the same time become self-reliant and contribute significantly to a fair and peaceful rural environment. The approach is to create awareness among rural women about various issues that they face in daily life and organize them into groups called *sanghas* around these issues. Broad areas of work are predetermined, for instance, economy, literacy, the law. But the contents, priorities and pace of work are determined by the *sanghas* under the leadership of the *sakhis*, who are also women from the same village. The *sahayogini* acts to ensure that the process remains participatory.

Given this background, it seemed best not to introduce a top-heavy health programme but instead to involve women at the grassroots in the planning of the health activities. Hence, it was decided to conduct a rapid, cost-effective assessment of the health needs of the communities with which *Mahila Samakhya* works using appropriate techniques, and in the process initiate a dialogue with the community about its health problems and needs. The idea was to learn from the people, to begin with what they know and believe and to help them build upon this base. This chapter describes our experiences in starting such a process in a village in Gujarat.

Choice of area and methods

The *Mahila Samakhya* programme functions in three districts in Gujarat state: Rajkot, Baroda and Sabarkantha. In mid-1992, in a major review of its activities, the programme organizers decided to restructure the work under five main headings: literacy, economic issues, the law and women, child care and health. It was around this time that SEWA-Rural got involved in the programme. The state-level functionaries apparently felt that with its extensive experience in community health, SEWA-Rural could play a useful role in the evolution of the health component of *Mahila Samakhya*, which was being introduced for the first time. Following a series of meetings, a broad understanding was reached, whereby SEWA-Rural would have the main responsibility for designing a health intervention for the project area, and would be involved in training *dais* (traditional birth attendants, or TBAs) of concerned villages. After consultations among functionaries of districts, it was decided to start the health activity in Sabarkantha district. The main criterion for this choice was the felt need for such work in the *sanghas* at the village level in this district, and a readiness of the functionaries to take up this work. A poor government health network in the area was another good reason.

The scene thus shifted to Sabarkantha. This is a district in north Gujarat, known to be a relatively dry region, leading in some places to an extreme scarcity of water. In these areas the otherwise fertile soil has become virtually barren and is barely able to support cattle-rearing, one of the main occupations of the people here. Compared to the industrialized regions of the state this place is rather underdeveloped. About 105 villages of the district have a presence of the *Mahila Samakhya* programme. Almost half of them are situated in Khedbrahma Taluka (subdistrict). Selection criteria of a work area for the programme include, among other things, aspects related to underdevelopment. This area is no exception as it has low female literacy and is poorly developed economically. Since there was little first-hand information of the kinds of health problems in the region, it seemed a good idea to begin with a health needs assessment. Obvious sources of information were the village and higher-level *Mahila Samakhya* functionaries of the district, and extensive discussions were held with them regarding this matter. It seemed clear to all present that a realistic picture of health problems would best be obtained by actually going to a sample of villages, talking to people there and seeing for ourselves. At the same time, being conscious that the basic approach of *Mahila Samakhya* was participatory, we decided to retain this character and try to involve people in the health component right from the outset. It thus seemed a sensible idea to use methods of assessing health needs that were naturally participatory. Our relative familiarity with qualitative research methods, including PRA, influenced the choice of methods we used.

The major constraint was the large distance of the chosen area from our own work area. It was quite obvious from the outset that our methods would have to be efficient, and depend on data from only a small sample of villages that we could possibly visit. It was decided to begin with a couple of villages and add more later as the need arose. On the basis of their knowledge of the spread of the population, the *Mahila Samakhya* functionaries indicated that there were two kinds of villages: those on the roadside and those in the interior. We decided to approach one of each kind. Mavatpura was selected in the interior and Mithiwedi on the roadside. It was decided to visit Mavatpura first. In addition to the visits, groups of local *dais* functionaries of *Mahila Samakhya* working in these villages were interviewed separately when they visited Jhagadia for training. The other village could not be visited. This chapter deals with experiences in Mavatpura and with information gathered at different times from different levels of functionaries of the programme.

The primary objective was health needs assessment; it was also an opportunity to try out PRA/RRA techniques in a situation apparently tailor-made for their use. A combination of various techniques was employed to discuss different issues with the people.

The experience at Mavatpura

It was decided that a team of facilitators, including functionaries from the *Mahila Samakhya* and from SEWA-Rural, would visit Mavatpura together. The villagers were informed about the visit in advance by the functionaries of *Mahila Samakhya*. The village is about 40km from Khedbrahma, the *taluka* headquarters, which in turn is 140km from Ahmedabad, the largest city in Gujarat. The approach is by road. The farthest it is possible to travel by bus from Khedbrahma is a town called Lemadia from where, if one can afford it, a jeep takes one to a point about 3km off the main road. From here, it is a brisk hour's walk over an undulating, lonely landscape to Mavatpura. For the people of Mavatpura, Lemadia is the gateway to the outer world.

Two members of our research team were involved in this exercise, a social worker and a senior field supervisor, both having considerable field experience. The first visit was the shorter one. We arrived at the village by mid-day, and remained there for about five hours. The second was an overnight visit with interactions occurring late at night and early next morning. *Mahila Samakhya* functionaries did not accompany us on the second visit. A summary of the methods used and the broad areas covered by each method is presented in Table 12.1. The information collected during the course of these visits is summarized in Table 12.2. A brief description of the process follows.

The first visit At Mavatpura, after some preliminaries, we requested women to gather at a convenient place where we could talk. A couple of women of the village (*sakhis*) who had attended the previous meetings were aware that we wanted to discuss the health problems of the women and that we might conduct some diagramming exercises. A large house was chosen and the women came in over the next hour, in ones and twos. As the crowd grew its composition changed, adolescents gradually making way for older women. In the meanwhile, after some small talk, the topic of discussion veered around to women's health problems and a short list of women's illnesses was made. Some discussion about healthcare-seeking practices also took place. We then requested the women to make us a map of the village so we could understand better the lie of the land. They began tentatively, but soon picked up momentum and, in about two hours, a fairly large, detailed map was ready. The map was drawn on the floor with chalk, exclusively by the women. Around 25 women were present during this exercise.

Several health-related questions were then asked of the women. They used the map effectively to answer these questions. They marked out the previous year's childbirths and deaths (including causes of death); women who had experienced difficult labours (including descriptions of causes of difficulty); cases of blindness or poor vision (including night blindness); adolescents or 'girls ready for marriage'. They refused to mark out cases of diarrhoea, leucorrhoea, and scabies, saying there was no point since virtually every house had a case. The visit ended abruptly, because we were anxious to get home before dark. A number of other areas we had intended to explore had, therefore, to be postponed to the next visit.

After the first visit, we took stock, reviewed the data collected and the process we had initiated, and decided that we needed to go back and continue the dialogue. Several areas were identified that needed further exploration. For this we made a tentative list of methods that could be useful. We also attempted to identify mistakes we had made and to take corrective steps. Several reasons forced a postponement of the second visit a number of times before it materialized about four months after the first visit.

The second visit Learning the first lesson from the previous experience we decided to spend a night at the village the second time. On this visit we were more relaxed and had plenty of informal interactions with the people. The data gathering was a much more spontaneous process, with some of the interactions being totally unplanned.

The first night we had informal discussions with many women and men about their day-to-day life: how they manage their funds, their caste system, the power supply to the village, and we heard some interesting fables. A group of three men began a long conversation with us about caste. They then got interested in the map made by the women during the first visit (we showed them a copy). One of them began identifying houses on the map which led to questions about numbers and, soon, we were into an hour-long exercise of an armchair census of the village, which included a household-wide listing of all adults and children, females and males. We had been intrigued by a repeated mention of polygamy which, they explained, was due to sterility. They also discussed issues of alcoholism, and the smoking habit. The lack of a regular school in the village was mentioned. Some of the deaths listed during the previous visit were reviewed.

The next morning, a key informant accompanied us in a walk through the village that helped confirm the accuracy of the map and their census, and we came to know some of the features of the village we had earlier missed. For instance, the only well they had drawn on the map was apparently representative of not less than 20 wells in the village! In the previous visit, we had not noticed that the village had a supply of electricity and we had assumed it did not. In this visit we noticed a huge electricity pole just outside the house where we had spent four hours during the drawing of the map, and that there was a regular supply to the same house! Later, with a small group of women, we explored the issue of extra- and premarital sexuality. The women readily discussed this and revealed that this was not uncommon; the larger group during mapping had staunchly denied the existence of such 'immoral' practices.

One of this group, a *dai*, described at length many of the practices they followed in conducting deliveries, and commonly perceived perinatal problems and common menstrual practices. All the deaths that had been listed in the previous visit were reconfirmed, deaths occurring in the intervening four months were added and causes of death noted. The talk shifted to the prospects for the crop that year and from there to general patterns of farming. Sensing the opportunity, we initiated a seasonality exercise in which a few men joined. The group described, among other things, the variation of incidence, and severity of different illnesses from month to month, with some understanding of the reasons for this variation. Some of the terms the women had used in the previous visit were unknown to us and clarifications and explanations were obtained during the second visit. The group also talked of the range of health services available at Lemadia.

Some weeks later, we talked to a group of around twenty *dais* from the same area of Sabarkantha who had come to Jhagadia for training, including one from Mavatpura. They talked about the caste structure and hierarchy in the villages, the consumption of alcohol by women on festive occasions and types of *dokras* (local traditional healers). We then had them give us lists of illnesses in the area. Later we asked them to rank them by severity of illness. All this added to the information gathered during village visits.

Thus, the process of interaction was completed over two visits and some informal interactions, in around 12 working hours (24 person-hours). For the facilitators, this was the first independent use of PRA methods for such a purpose. As Table 12.2 shows, a large amount of information could be collected by a few persons in this short time. More importantly, a basis had been secured on which a dialogue could continue for building in a relevant and acceptable health care programme.

Discussion

After achieving amazing success in the field of agriculture and natural-resource management (Chambers 1992; KRIBHCO 1992a&b; Scrimshaw & Gleason 1992; Welbourn 1991), PRA methods are now invading the field of health. A number of experiences have been described in the last few years (Scrimshaw & Gleason 1992; *RRA Notes* 1992; SPEECH 1991). This chapter adds to this growing field. In a situation where much of the organized health care is highly medicalized, and consequently full of concepts quite alien to rural people, and where high-tech curative care is far more lucrative for health care providers than preventive or positive health (Antia 1990), it is asking for too much to expect people to participate enthusiastically in a health programme. How, then, can people be persuaded to take greater control of their own health and health programmes? PRA methods and attitudes could be an important mode of breaking away from the top-down thinking that characterizes health care planning today. It also could be a good medium for interlinking various fields of development at the grassroots levels.

Before we accept the usefulness of PRA methods, however, we need to be convinced about certain crucial issues: is data collected with the help of PRA methods valid? What are the specific advantages of these methods in action programmes, particularly in the health field? Several recent articles attempt to answer these questions (Chambers 1992; *RRA Notes* 1992). We can only add to these on the basis of our limited experience.

The question of validity has been raised repeatedly by users of these methods (Chambers 1992). Judging by their experiences and ours, perhaps the strongest arguments in favour of validity could be listed as follows:

- The strength of the data arises from the extensive use of triangulation, a multipronged approach to obtain and cross-check a piece of information. Given the way the data are collected, the source of data is seldom a single individual or community. Each piece of data passes, as it were, through several filters – the many participants, the onlookers, the critics and the sceptics, each of whom is at equal liberty to intervene in the proceedings and opine. This open process is not automatic, of course. The facilitators have to ensure that such an atmosphere is created and maintained. One also has to look at the data and its sources critically, and deliberately employ different ways of checking the information. The strength of these methods lies in recognizing the value of triangulation, and providing psychological space and methodological freedom for such processes.

- Through the intense interaction of researchers with the people and the different methods used, the researchers are confident about what they have seen and felt. The data are not so much a set of figures, as a live memory of people's concerns, expectations, opinions and feelings in relation to the subject under exploration. The information is qualified by a precise understanding of the circumstances in which it was collected. This is backed up by the possibility, often, of being able to return and check out any doubts.

- The people in the community perceive the information as true, their own, not alien. Neither the methods used nor the way the information is recorded or interpreted is usually beyond their understanding. Most communities find data collected by closed methods like surveys suspect; they are not sure, not having been witnesses, who has said what and why. PRA/RRA methods leave little scope for such suspicion or doubt; all questions can come to the fore, get talked about and, usually, resolved to a fair degree of general satisfaction. There are generally effective ways to tackle domination by some individuals and the reticence of others. Hardly anyone feels left out.

- Besides answering questions about what and how much, a wealth of understanding of how and why also emerges. These latter aspects often help detect potential errors in the hard data by revealing logical inconsistencies and improbabilities.

Far from being mere research tools, PRA methods are concerned with eliciting and sustaining people's active involvement, participation in and sense of ownership of activities that directly concern them and their lives. In our experience at Mavatpura, for instance, at every step during mapping, diagramming, transects (systematic walks observing diverse conditions on route) (Chambers 1991) or interviews, the people's involvement was active and enthusiastic. Most of the women found 2–3 hours to stay on during the mapping exercise, and some of those who had to leave to attend other work hurried back at the earliest possible opportunity. One old woman, too tired to sit, lay down on the floor beside the map rather than go home. All this was done on their own accord without prodding or requesting by the facilitators. The facilitators often found themselves forgotten by the women working on the map. Such involvement also makes the work lively and enjoyable for the facilitators. The women readily described and discussed the various aspects of their lives that we touched. The dialogue was conducted at a healthy mature level, devoid of bickering and personal or political animosities. The women's involvement in the process was complete. It is possible to imagine that, were the process to be carried to its logical conclusion of planning people-centred programmes, the same level of involvement would continue. That would be a true indicator of the utility of this approach.

How crucial are specific techniques like mapping and diagramming to such processes? Would it make a difference if the processes were conducted without the aid of such tangible exercises? Common sense and our limited experience tell us that such concrete exercises are useful in enhancing people's involvement. For instance, it is a common experience that, in general, villagers tend to get distracted and bored with conversation lasting more than half an hour, while such exercises as mapping are able to sustain people's interest for hours together. In any case, it seems likely that the use of these techniques purely for research, without giving the people anything in return, could prove more frustrating for them than the use of standard survey tools, since such participatory exercises raise collective expectations much more than do survey methods. It is possible to envisage a situation where, being emboldened by the awareness that such exercises undoubtedly create, a local initiative may take root and grow into a people's movement. [2]

Table 12.1: Methods used for exploration of health needs of the community

Technique	Participating group	Areas covered
Community mapping	Representative group of women from different parts of the village	Total houses. Births in a year. Deaths with causes. Difficult deliveries. Locations of cases of diarrhoea, leucorrhoea, night blindness, cataract, etc. Number and location of adolescent girls, dais.
Seasonality diagramming	4 women, 3 men, a few children	Local vocabulary for months, seasons. Seasonality of cropping patterns. Sources of their income. Seasonal illnesses.
Transects	Village people.	Census cross-check. Resources. Observation of village life.
Focus group discussion	Adolescent girls and women of Mavatpura, 5 dais + 2 sahayoginis of Sabarkantha district. 3 men, 3 women Trainee dais of Sabarkantha district.	Free listing of illnesses. Their understanding of each illness. Health-seeking behaviour and available health services Sexual behaviour. Pregnancy and delivery-related illnesses. Beliefs regarding diet. Participatory census. Cross-check of village map. Sterility and polygamy. Tuberculosis. Extramarital and premarital sexuality, illegal abortions.
In-depth interviews	Two dais of Mavatpura village. Key informant (woman) Key informant (woman). Trainee dais of Sabarkantha district.	Perceptions and practices related to menstruation, sexuality, unwed pregnancies, illegal abortions, etc. Confirmation and expansion of death-related information. Clarifications of confusing local terms. Alcohol and tobacco consumption. Map cross-check. Mode of savings and health security. Village structures, including caste system. Free list of illnesses in local terms. Ranking of illnesses. Pregnancy-related illnesses. Traditional healers. Family planning. Alcohol.

Table 12.2: Summary of health information of the area

Demographic and general aspects	Mavatpura has 88 huts (from map), housing 98 families (households; from participatory census). Total population 598, enumerated by household, sex, marital status, ethnicity. A house-to-house check of roughly 10% of households matched exactly with data from participatory census. No major discrepancy found during cross-check of previously drawn map by different group of villagers 4 months later. Highest-educated woman is a girl currently in 8th year of school; 2 men have finished school - both employed in far-away cities; most of rest involved in farming. Virtually every family owns at least a small piece of land.
Available health facilities and treatment preference	In Mavatpura: Anganwadi-worker (AWW) (Anganwadis are village pre-schools having health care responsibilities) supposed to stock and dispense medicines for common ailments. But AWW very irregular; no one from village mentioned her as an option for health care. Sarpanch (executive head of local government) offers branding for limited ailments. No traditional healer lives in the village. Near village: Traditional healers (dokras) of seven kinds practise in nearby villages, categorized according to specific ailment that each handles (including one for maternal health). Primary health centre at Lemadia, a 10km walk away, with one allopathic doctor. Nearest private doctors at Lemadia - 4 doctors: 2 non-allopath, 1 quack running a sterility and VD clinic, 1 allopath (the PHC doctor, who also runs a private practice). Nearest hospital at Khedbrahma, 40km away. Information regarding preferred treatment for around 20 common illnesses.
Morbidity	Over 75 conditions of ill-health listed in local terms and common illnesses ranked according to relative dangerousness. This includes 15 illnesses related to menstruation, pregnancy and fertility, besides other reproductive tract illnesses. Detailed description of around 40 of the conditions in local terms, including beliefs about causation. Specific treatment preference/sequence for 13 of the illnesses. Seasonality of some common illnesses. Detailed information about childbirth difficulties. Goitre commonly noticed by us, but women apparently unaware of it. Women were totally unaware of oral rehydration therapy (ORT) in the treatment of diarrhoea, although they considered diarrhoea dangerous.
Births, Deaths	Exact number with names and households, for all births and deaths which occurred over last 12 months, according to whether the mother belongs to village. Age at death, causes of death in local terms. All confirmed with same women at second visit 4 months later.
Promiscuity and illegal abortions	Prevalence and attitudes to extramarital, premarital sexuality; commonly used methods to induce abortion; costs of illegal abortion.

Notes

1. The team is grateful to the women and other people of Mavatpura village on whose lives this chapter is based, and who contributed so much to the team's understanding of participatory research.
2. There is a rapidly growing body of literature on this topic, much of it yet outside the commonly read journals. The most comprehensive compilations of recent articles on the topic of the application of PRA/RRA methods to health can be found in two recent publications (Scrimshaw & Gleason 1992; *RRA Notes* 1992).

References

Antia, N. H. (1990) 'Medical education: in need of a cure', *Economic and Political Weekly*, 21 July, Bombay.

Cernea, M. (ed.) (1991) *Putting People First*, Oxford University Press, USA.

Chambers, R. (1991) 'Shortcut and participatory methods for gaining social information for projects' in Cernea, M. (ed.) (1991).

Chambers, R. (1992) 'Rural appraisal: rapid, relaxed and participatory', *Discussion Paper* No.311, Institute of Development Studies, Sussex.

Government of India (1991) *Mahila Samakhya. Education for Women's Equality*. Department of Education, Ministry of Human Resource Development, Government of India, New Delhi.

Khanna, R., Mehta, N. R. & Bhatt, Anil (1991) *Voluntary Effort in Community Health. Review of the Community Health Project of SEWA-Rural*, SEWA-Rural, Jhagadia 393 110, Gujarat, India.

KRIBHCO (Krishak Bharati Cooperative Limited) (1992a) *Report on Participatory Rural Appraisal at Jaliyapada Village*, KRIBHCO Indo-British rainfall farming project annual review mission, Dahod 389 151, Gujarat, India.

KRIBHCO (Krishak Bharati Cooperative Limited) (1992b) *Report on Participatory Rural Appraisal at Nagalwat Choti Village*, KRIBHCO Indo-British Rainfed Farming Project Annual Review Mission, Dahod 389 151, Gujarat, India.

MYRADA (1990) *PRA-PALM Series*, No.3, MYRADA, 2 Service Road, Domlur Layout, Bangalore-560071, India.

RRA Notes (1992) 'Special issue on applications for health', IIED, No.16, July.

Scrimshaw, N. S. & Gleason, G. R. (eds) (1992) *Rapid Assessment Procedures: Qualitative Methodologies for Planning and Evaluation of Health Related Programmes*, International Nutrition Foundation for Developing Countries (INFDC), Boston, MA.

Shah, A. C. (1991) 'Shoulder-tapping: a technique of training in participatory rural appraisal', *Forests, Tree and People Newsletter* No.14, Aga Khan Rural Support Programme (AKRSP), India.

SPEECH (1991) *Report of a Workshop on Participatory Rural Appraisal for Planning Health Projects, October 2–5, 1991*, Society for Peoples' Education and Economic Change, 2/96-A, North Car Street, Tiruchuli 626 129, Kamarajan District, Tamil Nadu, India.

Welbourn, A. (1991) *The Social and Economic Dimensions of Poverty and Ill-health*. Department of International Community Health, Liverpool School of Tropical Medicine, UK.

PART V DIFFERENT METHODS OF PLANNING AND EVALUATING PR

13 Towards a sustainable and participatory rural development: recent experiences of an NGO in Bangladesh[1]

Maurice Bloem, Dulal Biswas & Susanta Adhikari

The Christian Commission for Development in Bangladesh (CCDB),[2] a non-governmental organization (NGO), has been involved in development since 1973. Initially it was engaged primarily in welfare and charity work, addressing relief and rehabilitation needs in response to the devastation and destruction caused by the liberation war. Since then its role has expanded, and today it has seven major programmes. Research findings, studies and critical observations revealed the shortcomings and pitfalls of development programmes of the dominant paradigm. A growing need for just and sustainable progress led to a quest for an alternative approach.

According to the CCDB, sustainable and participatory rural development is a continuous process carried out and controlled by rural people at their own expense in terms of resources, knowledge, understanding, skills, wisdom, labour, cultural ethos and experience. This development process may be helped with inputs in terms of money, training, information, infrastructural and other supports by governmental or non-governmental agencies. The People's Participatory Planning (PPP) process began in October 1990. The thematic design of PPP encompasses 'Recollecting the past, analysing the present and visualizing the future'. The PPP process is part of the comprehensive method called participatory action research (PAR).

The basic ideology of PAR is that critically aware people, those who are poor and oppressed, will progressively transform their environment by their own praxis. In this process others may play a catalytic and supportive role but will not dominate (Rahman 1991).

Sustainable development

Sustainable development is an often-discussed topic nowadays and much has been written about it. The same can be said about definitions of sustainable development. Many of them have been vague, inadequately capturing the environmental imperative to cease exhausting natural resources. Labonté, in one of the most interesting essays of the past few years on this subject, uses the term 'econology', a neologism that combines economy and ecology. Econology is the science, or rules, of managing the planet, and the human social systems that depend on the planet's resources. In other words, the principles of sustainable development. Using this term, Labonté tries to explain that ecology and economy cannot be seen as separate systems. Sustainable development is still a matter of balancing environmental protection with sustainable economic growth:

> The notion that sustainable development is having our cake (a healthy, resource replenished planet) while eating it, too (economic growth, increased purchasing parity, no decline in consumer goods or choices), is pervasive. (Labonté 1991:47)

The problem the world is facing at the moment is the belief that a 'green' (as stated by Labonté) economy can be achieved with little effort and without a changing of attitudes. Within the CCDB, it is believed that an isolated or fragmented focus on tecological and environmental sustainability alone is inadequate, as has been the case with the present, dominant economistic paradigm of development:

> Sustainable development is seen as a process of holistic transformation of the society for self-reliance and the well-being of all. This holistic transformation can take place by minimizing the gap between the existing level of knowledge and knowledge needed for appropriate sustainable society. The knowledge gap can be decreased by importing appropriate training facilities at all levels. The process is essentially related to all spheres of human existence. As such the process of transformation will have to ensure social, cultural, economic and political sustainability together with ecological and environmental sustainability. This is expected ultimately to lead to a holistic development of society. (CCDB 1991:8)

To be a genuine alternative, this development has to be a process planned not by experts but by the people themselves. They have to assess their own local environment and its possibilities. People-based development means that not only the questions but also the answers must come from the people. These answers should come from within their own space and time, from their own cultural, social, economic and political reality. This is the essence of the PPP process. To be sustainable, PPP will have to recreate the systems of life and existence of the oppressed and marginalized peoples, particularly of the landless, tribal peoples and women in Bangladesh (CCDB 1991).

Besides working for the sustainability of the society, we will also give some examples of how the CCDB tries to keep the process itself sustainable or continuous. The monitoring of this process is especially important. Since October 1990, the CCDB has faced a lot of difficulties, but has also had good results. Here we give an idea of the experiences of all people involved in this ongoing process.

The people's participatory planning (PPP) process

A working definition on which the PPP process is based emerged from a CCDB workshop:

> People's Participatory Planning (PPP) is a just and empowering social process in which the poor and marginalized are democratically involved in collective action, strive to articulate and design the vision, goal, objectives, path, direction, content, magnitude and process of a holistic social transformation in their favor, recollecting and analysing the past experiences, focusing on the present situation and projecting the future. This process is based on their own value-orientation, knowledge, critical awareness and skills, through rediscovery, regeneration and generation, elaboration, evaluation, consolidation and sharing of people's own knowledge as well as other relevant knowledge. (CCDB 1990)

An important characteristic of PPP is that it is not value-free. It takes a position in favour of the poor and marginalized.

The twelve modules of the PPP process

The PPP process consists of twelve modules or stages that will lead ultimately to a people's plan of action. This plan is designed to identify future programme and activity needs by and for the people themselves. In summary, the modules contain the following topics:

Module 1:   Informing the people about PPP. (What is PPP? Why? Do people agree? Why does the CCDB turn to this practice? Selection of Convenor, Animator and Recorder [CAR] team).

Module 2:   Inauguration of PPP. (Great festival organized by the somity[3] members to discuss the new concept.)

Module 3:   Recollecting the past and our journey towards development. (To recollect and identify past events and adjoining areas with a view to learn lessons. To identify the trends to extrapolate into the future. To rediscover indigenous knowledge, skills and ability etc.)

Module 4:   Our village today. (To map the various physical resources in a village and locate the financial and social resources and other institutions. To identify the present social, political and economic resources and other institutions.)

Module 5:   Analysis of the societal structure of the village. (Analysis of the social and class structure of the village. Identification of inequality.)

Module 6: Analysis of the micro–macro relationship. (Examine the relationships, problems etc. between villages, unions, districts, Bangladesh and other countries. Is there an impact of outside problems on the existing problems of one's village?)

Module 7: Analysis of the causes of the problems. (What are the root causes of the structural problems? Why is this a factor?)

Module 8: Responding or addressing the problems. (Responses of the villagers, CCDB and government should be marked separately and the similarities be compared with what comes from the critical analysis.)

Module 9: To determine physical and financial resources. (Determine physical and financial resources and how much people can utilize for their development. Make people aware of their own resources. To learn what kind of assistance would be made available from the government and other organizations.)

Module 10: Our aspired society. (Visualize the societal state. To know our need and expectation for our future. Utilize people's knowledge and skills.)

Module 11: People's participatory plan. (Identify programmes and activities. After preparation of plan, conduct feasibility and viability studies of each activity as part of PAR and, finally, verify whether the activity is congruent with people's needs, aspirations and perspectives towards their development.)

Module 12: Monitoring and evaluation. (Continuous action, reflection and action. The activity component should be completed in a planned manner within scheduled time. Feedback from the field.)

In all the modules, the findings can be described in pictures, songs, poems or drawings. These modules are the tools to produce and to make new and rediscovered knowledge where the people themselves are the main actors.

The modules in action

To give some idea about how the twelve modules are exercised in practice, we will give a few examples of the outcome of the modules that the CCDB plans were based on up to 1995:

Recollecting the past and our journey towards development

Module 3: Participants reviewed the events of the past 20 years dividing the span of time into several junctures. All the major political and social events with the focus on the economic system and the natural disasters of the period were discussed. The people divided the last t20 years into five junctures: the liberation war of 1971, the famine (1974–79), drought (1979–84), food (1987–89) and political change and the cyclone (1989–91).

The analysis of the five periods revealed that the existing system is causing an increase in poverty and engulfing more and more people into the vicious circle of poverty as the rich become richer. As a result, the sufferings of the poor from hunger, malnutrition and ill-health are becoming acute. (CCDB 1993)

Our village today

Module 4: The village situation was depicted through graphs and pictures elaborating the living pattern of the people. Graphs showed a very disappointing situation in the village. Torn-out houses, ill-health, damaged roads, polluted water, population pressure, a decrease in livestock, birds and animals were found as the salient features of the village. It was found that about 70 percent of the villagers are landless. The traditional village culture is disappearing. In most villages there is communal harmony though sometimes it is disturbed by the religious leaders and the rich. Traditional values are being changed and many of the age-long village rituals have disappeared. Statistics on numbers of people, schools, sanitary latrines, amounts of land, sharecroppers etc. were provided. With the extension of habitation due to population increase, cutting of wood for fuel has caused reduction of rural vegetation, according to the participants. Also they described how the soil is dying due to overuse of chemical fertilizers. Also the fish population has reduced in the villages. (CCDB 1993)

Analysis of the causes of problems

Module 7: In exercising this module people found out the various levels of causes of problems including the main or root causes. We will only summarize the causes of malnutrition and ill-health. Malnutrition is in the first instance caused by lack of knowledge and awareness, lack of adequate food, overpopulation, idleness, illiteracy and superstition. These factors are closely related to poverty and exploitation, but the root cause of malnutrition was seen to be society itself and the unequal distribution of production. The causes of ill-health were considered almost the same as malnutrition, except that initial causes were slightly different. Participants mentioned lack of consciousness, lack of knowledge and illiteracy as the causes in the first phase.

Responding to and addressing the problems

Module 8: During module 8, the people analysed the responses of the government, CCDB and themselves and assessed the justification of these responses. Many problems were discussed; again we discussed only the problem of malnutrition and ill-health. The people said that they had tried to create some awareness of the problems of malnutrition and ill-health. The government is implementing some programmes and the CCDB is providing training on nutrition and distribution of vegetable seeds. Still, the justification of these responses is considered minimal.

PPP and the CCDB staff

The inception of the PPP started a process of transition in the CCDB itself. A series of training courses, workshops and seminars was arranged in order to orient the staff to PPP, its conceptual framework, modules and methods of facilitation. The basic intention was to develop a set of trainers responsible for introducing village-level PPP exercises. These trainers would be equivalent to the 'cadres' of Fals-Borda (1991b). CCDB's Human and Organizational Potential Enhancement (HOPE) programme is important in the development of the trainers and in helping people move along with the process so that they become familiar with the necessary know-how to rebuild their lives and futures. At this stage, organizational strengths and weaknesses were reviewed, and a process of reflection and action was also entered upon. The outcome was an holistic consensus that helped establish a new vision of people as the key factors and supreme authority in planning and implementing their own development. 'Participation' became the basic value premise. Consequently target-oriented practices were replaced by process-based efforts that generated the urgency to change the traditional roles of the staff members. They had to become the facilitators of the participatory process which required attitudinal change.

Initially there had been a sense of apprehension among staff members. A misconception of the process had led many staff to believe that they would lose their jobs. A lack of trust in people's power and ability was felt by many staff. Many, even in the decision-making body and donor community, were suspicious about the practical effectiveness and future of the process. With the deepening of understanding, people's commitment towards the process became more visible. The nature of training, i.e. creative sharing, 'people's questions being answered by people', opportunities for self-disclosure and, finally, the total participation i.e. openness and shared decision-making, helped to reduce staff anxieties and uncertainties.

Somity level

To facilitate the PPP process at somity level 216 convenors, recorders and animators (CAR team) were trained from 72 different societies. While the

PPP process was in progress, the tornado, cyclone and flood of 1991 occurred. A total of seven project areas were severely affected. Despite these constraints, participants tried to carry out PPP in 5 percent sample somities.

Especially at the beginning of the exercises, the people had rather mixed feelings and reactions to the PPP ideology. After primary orientation, a large segment of the selected somity was enthusiastic; a considerable number were, however, critical. The latter feared that CCDB would narrow the scope of material assistance.

Although the purpose of the modules is actively to involve the people, people showed passivity. Thus the process was slowed down, but the continuity of the exercises led to a gradual improvement in the situation. During the exercises, many participants became emotional when telling the stories of their lives, stories about suffering and social pressure from influential people in the village. It became clear that people can both analyse their own situation and themselves make plans.

Organization and management
The nature and practices of PPP required a new management and organizational style within the CCDB itself. During the various workshops and training sessions, several of the organization's management strengths and weaknesses were identified. The question arose: what kind of management style and structure should the CCDB practise within the organization consistent with PPP at the grassroots? The organizational set-up and staff roles were redefined to ensure the proper implementation of the PPP process. A management committee was formed at central and project levels to look after the emerging management concerns created by issues like staff domination of the people, the ignoring of participatory values and the displaying of a controlling mentality. The openness of the CCDB after accepting PPP provided the moral ground on which to oppose these bad practices and take collective decisions to overcome them through organizational measures. For psychological and behavioural adjustments, the CCDB organized PPP reorientation courses.

Monitoring and evaluation
There was a need to educate the PPP facilitators about the process of monitoring and evaluation. To meet these requirements, a trainers' training on monitoring and evaluation was held. In general, the participants discussed four groups of problems, issues and concerns: understanding and internalization of PPP; implementation of PPP in CCDB; PPP and CCDB as an organization, and PPP training. The outcome of the discussions and analysis of group number one specified at somity level: lack of time for informing people about PPP, lack of continuous adequate attendance in the exercises, CAR team did not carry out their

responsibilities, many facts remained unexpressed during module 5 (the structural analysis) for political reasons. The involvement in the lengthy process of the exercise created economic hardship for many of the participants which reduced the attendance correspondingly; the plan was not accurate for the whole village and the lack of skills and experience of the CAR team hampered the process. They discussed the problems of these four areas and participants tried to identify solutions.

Despite the fact that the CCDB has a strong belief in the process, the organization acknowledged that it is necessary to follow the whole process critically. During the development of the monitoring framework the following questions seemed important:

• is the CCDB really only facilitating the process?
• what changes have occurred in people's lives due to PPP?

The monitoring activities of the CCDB were not as expected at the initial stages of the PPP. Through regular project reports and case studies, attempts were made to try to follow the process. Recent analysis of both these past reports and the PPP exercise reports show a positive picture of the events at that time. The CCDB has to acknowledge that these past reports gave a too-positive view of that situation, although a lot of very promising events and changes did occur during this time. A functional analysis team, comprising two members, was appointed in each project. These teams were supposed to collect information, classify, compile and analyse data and prepare reports on the status of PPP within the respective projects, but they did not function as expected, due to a lack of clarity about job responsibilities. People's monitoring and evaluation of their plans and actions took place both at somity and forum[4] levels by involving themselves, from the beginning. The main problem was record-keeping.

The PPP is supposed to create an environment that will improve the wellbeing of people. To monitor the changes due to this process, five research areas are identified: agricultural growth; non-farming activities; labour and employment; women and gender issues; nutrition. Asaduzzaman and Westergaard (1993) used these areas in a review of growth and development in rural Bangladesh. They state that agricultural growth, non-farming activities, and labour and employment are mainly economic activities. The People's Economic Activities Study (PEAS) tries to track down the changes within the economic activities of the people. The Women and Gender Issues Study (WAGIS) is supposed to describe the overall economic, social and cultural contexts in which half the people live (and die). According to Asaduzzaman and Westergaard (1993), economic, social, cultural and gender factors play a role in determining nutritional status. Health and nutrition are key subjects within the People's Health and Nutritional Assessment (PHNA) where both quantitative and qualitative methods are being used. The People's Participation Study (PPS) is trying to give answers to 'facilitation–participation' problems. A special task group of the CCDB developed guidelines based on the model of Rifkin et al. (1988) and the rapid assessment procedures (RAP) handbook by Scrimshaw and Hurtado (1987) to measure the level of participation. Indicators were identified to find out if the people's plans of action are really an outcome of a participatory process or still based on the dominance and the presence of the CCDB. The somities are in most cases still not able to keep records. Forum workers are paid by the people to write the minutes and records. Some somities are not completely satisfied with this solution, because in the past the CCDB paid these workers. Nevertheless, it seems satisfactory for the time being.

The studies of the identified areas give a good idea of the present status of the process. The tools used within the monitoring studies are often participatory and the results reflect the opinions and practices of both the people and the CCDB. This does not imply that participation is total and perfect. The reports and the experiences of the monitoring studies have shown that it is worthwhile for all concerned. That is why the CCDB will proceed with these studies in the future in an effort to follow the process closely.

The CCDB acknowledges that many changes are necessary to improve the PPP process. For example, to monitor their own actions and plans, the reference people are using reflection-action, but the CCDB's role as a facilitator is in demand. The CCDB should help the reference people in making records, so that they become less dependent on people with writing skills. Some of the methods used in the monitoring studies would be proper for the somity members themselves, or maybe somity members can develop new monitoring tools by themselves with the help of the CCDB trainers? Providing somity members with a pictorial monitoring book could be a point of discussion. With the help of the monitoring studies, this problem could be solved in the next phase of the CCDB's journey towards a participatory and sustainable development.

The functional information analysis teams will be made functional again in order to strengthen the CCDB's monitoring capacities. This will allow the individual projects to make the monitoring studies even more relevant to their own specific situation (CCDB 1994). The CCDB will also try to improve vertical and horizontal communication within the organization to strengthen its participatory management efforts and its monitoring framework. More attention will be paid to following the suggestions of the several sections, projects, forums or somities (CCDB 1994).

The majority of methods used are based on PRA (participatory rural appraisal) techniques which are designed to combat bias, stimulate openness and provoke analysis of the programme's problems. Besides these techniques, formal and informal interviews are also used. The interviews, discussions and PRA exercises are done by the Mobile Action Research Team (MART). The adoption of participatory methods is a way of making the evaluation process more open, diminishing remarkably the degree of formality by using the analytical capabilities of the people concerned and establishing a new quality of relationship between the the CCDB and the reference people. Keeping the main focus on participatory techniques does not exclude the use of other practices. For example, CCDB joined the Nutritional Surveillance Project initiated by Helen Keller International in collaboration with a number of other non-government organizations, the Institute of Public Health and Nutrition (IPHN) and UNICEF. Anthropometric, socio-economic and health data are collected with more conventional data collection techniques. The information is used within CCDB's PHNA. (For more insight into these monitoring studies we refer to PPS, PHNA, PEAS and WAGIS reports and a more elaborate paper by Bloem, Korim and Quader (1994).)

Discussion and conclusions

PPP derives its philosophy from the belief that human beings have the strength and potential to learn from their own fundamental beliefs, value systems and attitudes, in order to differentiate facts from myths. The continuous process of reflection and action can enable people to change and transform from one level of functioning to another. The process assumes that people have the potential for transformation and that they should direct their own change at a speed that is desirable for the individual at a given period of time in life. The process of transformation is not only for individuals, but also for organizations. Through cooperation they can both transform the community and society. PPP has a value premise and ideological base that must lead to a social transformation process.

After the analysis of the PPP ideology, a few constraints or pitfalls may be identified. One may question if it is possible for the people to analyse the macro situation. Although the influence of the media is expanding enormously, the input of external information, due, for example, to illiteracy, seems insufficient to this end. Analysis of the meso level seems the maximum that can be achieved. There is also the enormous burden on the facilitators, the 'agents of change', because they can only facilitate, but may not impose their own views on the people. Proper communication is a prerequisite in enhancing this kind of development process.

Another constraint concerns the macro-economic situation of Bangladesh. The country often faces crisis situations and, because of that it is almost continuously fighting a struggle for survival. For example, every year there is a seasonal food scarcity, and research shows that during those periods even the children of the landowners suffer from malnutrition (HKI 1993). Nevertheless, PPP may be very important during the other periods of the year.

Abacassis (1990) has doubts about participatory approaches as an alternative for Bangladesh, because of the enormous hierarchy and 'faction'-thinking still heavily present within the country. It would be helpful to further research these religious–cultural constraints.

The CCDB is giving a lot of emphasis to people's-institution(PI)-building as an important element of participatory and sustainable development. Selected somity members have formed Somity Representative Forums (SRF) which are maintaining links with the CCDB. These forums are still not functioning properly. A concern is what will happen with the somity and forum if the CCDB terminates its savings and credit facilities. Money seems to be an important factor in keeping the groups together.

One can agree with Rahman (1991) who claims that participatory research at this stage may be viewed more as a cultural movement, independent of political movements for people's liberation, rather than as a political alternative in itself. As mentioned at the beginning of this chapter, out of the culture of participatory research ideologies such as PPP, elements emerge that help benefit the initiatives of the people.

Despite these constraints, it seems that the CCDB has shown that it may be worthwhile to proceed with PPP. The ideology has the potential to succeed, but it must be constantly criticized by in- and outsiders. There is always the need for careful vigilance and (self)-criticism. As soon as this approach conjures up slogans like 'PPP is the solution for all your problems', it makes the same mistake as all the other paradigms. PPP has potential for Bangladesh, but it has still a long way to go.

Notes

1. We gratefully acknowledge all CCDB staff, sharing agencies and reference people. Many thanks to the Education Resource Group of the Liverpool School of Tropical Medicine for their great editorial help. This chapter would not have been written without the generous financial assistance provided by the British Council Dhaka, British Council London, and Dutch Interchurch Aid.

2. Although it is a Christian organization, the religious diversity and ethnic distribution within CCDB is equal to the overall picture of Bangladesh. Thus, the majority of the staff are Muslim.

3. The term somity refers to the formal institution of CCDB reference people. In general, somity consists of five groups having at least five members each.

Each somity has its chairman and secretary, selected for a given period of time by the somity members themselves.

4. A forum, or Somity Representative Forum, may be formed from twenty-four representatives from six somities under a field office.

References

Abacassis, D. (1990) *Islam and Human Development in Rural Bangladesh*, UPL, Dhaka.

Asaduzzaman, M. & Westergaard, K. (eds) (1993) *Growth and Development in Rural Bangladesh*, UPL, Dhaka.

Bloem, M., Korim, D. & Quader, M. (1994) *Monitoring and Evaluation in CCDB*. Paper presented during Round Table Meeting 1994, Dhaka.

CCDB (Christian Commission for Development in Bangladesh) (1990) *Proceedings of the Workshop on Participatory Planning Process of the Christian Commission for Development in Bangladesh*, Dhaka, 15-20 October.

CCDB (Christian Commission for Development in Bangladesh) (1991) *Towards a Decade's Perspective for Sustainable and Participatory Rural Development. An Indicative Program Proposal for July 1992 - June 1995*, Dhaka.

CCDB (Christian Commission for Development in Bangladesh) (1993) *People's Participatory Process in CCDB, A Spade Work*, CCDB, Dhaka.

CCDB (Christian Commission for Development in Bangladesh) (1994) *Towards a Decade's Perspective for Sustainable and Participatory Rural Development. An Indicative Program Proposal for July 1995 –June 1998*, Dhaka.

Fals-Borda, O. (1991b) 'Some basic ingredients', in Fals-Borda, O. & Rahman, Md. A. (eds) (1991)

Fals-Borda, O. & Rahman, Md. A. (eds) (1991) *Action and Knowledge. Breaking the Monopoly with Participatory Action Research*, Apex Press, New York.

HKI (Helen Keller International) (1993) *Seasonality of Nutritional Status in Bangladesh*, Nutritional Surveillance Project (NSP) data.

Labonté, R. (1991) 'Econology: integrating health and sustainable development. Part one: theory and background', *Health Promotion International*, Vol.6(1), pp.46-65.

Rahman, Md. A. (1991) 'The theoretical standpoint of PAR', in Fals-Borda, O. & Rahman, Md. A. (eds) (1991).

Rifkin, S.B., Muller, F. & Bichmann, W. (1988) 'Primary health care: on measuring participation', *Social Science & Medicine*, Vol.26(9).

Scrimshaw, S.C.M. & Hurtado, E. (1987) *Rapid Assessment Procedures for Nutrition and Primary Health Care: Anthropological Approaches to Improving Programme Effectiveness*, UCLA Latin America Center, Los Angeles.

14 'Planning together': developing community plans to address priority maternal and neonatal health problems in rural Bolivia[1]

Lisa Howard-Grabman

This chapter is based on a three-year demonstration project in maternal and neonatal health in the rural province of Inquisivi, Bolivia. The project was implemented by Save the Children Federation/USA Bolivia field office (SC/B) under a subcontract to John Snow, Inc. and was funded by the United States Agency for International Development (USAID) MotherCare Project. The Warmi Project (*warmi* means woman in Aymara, the local language) was initiated to determine how a community-based approach could be used to improve maternal and neonatal health in a very remote setting, in which there is little access to adequate formal health services.

Results of the project to date include a significant decrease in perinatal and neonatal mortality from 75 deaths out of 639 total births at the beginning of the project (1988–90) to 31 deaths out of 708 total births (1991–93). Families demonstrated positive changes in health practices, such as increased immediate breast-feeding, tetanus toxoid vaccination, hygienic birth, immediate care of the newborn, and increased use of contraceptive methods.

This chapter focuses on SC/B experiences in participatory planning, a process that we call Planning Together. Since every setting has its own particular characteristics and resources, replicating the process presented in this chapter will require some adaptation.

Background

SC/B began MotherCare Project activities in 50 communities in Inquisivi Province of the La Paz department in July 1990. The goal of the three-year project was to reduce maternal and neonatal mortality and morbidity through affecting the range of behaviours that influence the outcomes of pregnancy, delivery and the neonatal period. A major strategy used to achieve these objectives was the organization of women's groups to increase women's knowledge and awareness of specific maternal and neonatal health problems and of the locally available resources that could be used to address these problems.

General characteristics of women in Inquisivi, Licoma and Circuata communities

The Warmi Project worked in three geographic zones of Inquisivi Province (Inquisivi, Licoma and Circuata) that vary widely in their socio-cultural characteristics. The families in the Inquisivi zone tend to be more well-established, more traditional and more resistant to change than those of the Licoma and Circuata zones. In contrast, the communities in Licoma and Circuata zones are newer, or, if old, have a number of recently immigrated families. Though these new families are also descendants of highland people, the fact that they are a self-selected group of immigrants who initiated change implies that they are more interested in, and accepting of, change in their lifestyle.

Men and women in Inquisivi Province are bound by a tight family structure and rigid sexual roles. Traditionally, women have not participated in the community decision-making process; it is usually the husband who has a voice and vote in the monthly community meetings and, if women attend, they are never heard. The village authorities are elected or serve in turn; the only time a woman is found in this position is if she is a widow of a former member and if she owns land.

Not only are the communities led exclusively by men but, in the family, it is the man who most often makes financial decisions. Not infrequently, husbands decide that it would cost too much to send a woman with complications during her labour or pregnancy to the hospital (3–7 hours by road, not including the time spent trying to gain access to transport). The cost of a Caesarian, for example, may represent six or more months of cash income. This not uncommon scenario contributed to the high maternal and perinatal mortality rates in the province.

Organizing women's groups

The isolation of women in such dispersed communities leaves many feeling powerless and alone. One of the first activities of the Warmi Project was to identify existing women's groups and to strengthen those that were interested in continuing to work together. New groups were also organized. The purpose of this strategy was to raise women's awareness that their individual problems are often common to others and that together they are more likely to find solutions.

The women's groups consist of approximately 10–30 members each and meet at least once a month. Many groups meet weekly. The groups function as a forum for learning, decision-making, social contact with others and as a diversion from the hard life shared by all the members.

The role of project staff

Philosophy

In keeping with SC/B's participatory approach to its work, the role of project staff is seen as a facilitatory rather than an educational one. Staff are viewed as project 'beneficiaries', along with project participants, in the full belief that one of the project goals is self-development for all those involved. Taking the approach that the only lasting form of development is one where the participants take control of their situation and make collective decisions on improving it, project staff then assume the role of assistants in this process, facilitating and aiding the participants in making their decisions and in converting them into actions.

The underlying philosophy relating to staff is the central importance of respect for the project participants and of belief in the latter's ability to identify and find solutions to their own problems.

SC/B continuously assesses the learning taking place in the areas of knowledge, attitudes and practices, both of project participants and of its staff. Constant self-evaluation and openness to learning have led to better acceptance and integration of staff within the women's groups and the community, and, ultimately, to more self-development within the groups. They have also resulted in greater understanding on the part of SC/B of the reality of the women's situation and of the essential need for appropriate local solutions to their problems.

Training

In the initial stages of the project, much work needed to be done to enable staff to understand the difference between 'educating' and 'facilitating'. Some staff members found it quite difficult to make the transition from taking a directive role to adopting the stance of listener and facilitator. With continual practice and training, however, their approach changed considerably, and they learned how to facilitate the problem identification and planning processes rather than direct them. Staff also received training in technical issues, including pregnancy, birth, post-partum care, care of the newborn and family planning.

The approach taken with project staff has been one of learning through actually doing. Initially, many staff members were inhibited in their work, believing that they should have answers for every question (which, of course, they hadn't). The project has fostered the idea that there is no one correct answer to any question nor any one solution to a given problem. It is only through a process of collective decision-making and action that an issue affecting a community can be resolved.

In the course of the project, staff became more confident in their roles as people who are there to help the group open up and to realize that the group can influence what happens in members' lives. In the process, the staff also realized that they did not have the answers to the group's problems. This realization proved to be particularly important in preventing staff from making promises that SC/B could not fulfil and, thereby, falsely raising the group's expectations. In addition, staff developed the ability to try different approaches with the groups and to accept that they, too, can make mistakes and should not be afraid to do so. Considerable staff development and learning took place through their contact and work with the groups.

Programme strategy

SC/B developed and implemented this project in the context of the agency's established methodology of Community-based Integrated Rural Development (C-BIRD). This methodology is based on the premise that long-term, sustainable development depends on the capacity of community groups to determine local priorities, plan projects, acquire necessary resources and assume responsibility for the administration and coordination of development activities.

Community-level problem solving

The SC/B Warmi Project developed a simple model for community-level problem solving. A diagram of the model, the Community Action Cycle, is presented in Figure 14.1. This cycle was the basis for all programme intervention. This chapter focuses on the Planning Together phase, presenting each step of the process as SC/B carried it out, together with a short summary of the results.

Figure 14.1: A Community Action Cycle

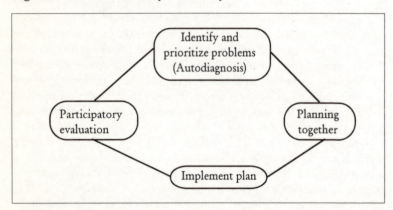

The cycle might be considered obvious by some readers. However, SC/B found that stating the steps explicitly and drawing the diagram, as in Figure 14.1, was a breakthrough in understanding the process, both by staff and community members.

The steps of this cycle were implemented as follows:
1. *Identification and prioritization of problems* An exercise called the autodiagnosis was developed for use with women's groups in identifying and prioritizing their maternal and neonatal health problems.
2. *Planning together* The women's group carries out a planning meeting together with other members of the community and local authorities to develop strategies and actions to solve their problems.

3. *Implementation* The communities implement their plans based upon their agreements from the 'planning together' exercise.
4. *Evaluation* The community evaluates the results of its actions taken during the implementation phase. Based on the evaluation, problems should again be identified and prioritized, as the cycle begins anew.

It is important to note that, in the area of maternal and neonatal health, many interventions to prevent mortality rely on secondary- and tertiary-level medical care which is often not readily available to impoverished rural communities. The autodiagnosis motivates women to look for solutions *within their community context,* trying to make the most of their local resources. In the case of Inquisivi, the effective referral hospital is 4–6 hours away, in La Paz. This implies that different strategies are needed to confront the problems in these remote communities than in communities that have fairly easy access to services.

Autodiagnosis: a basis for planning together

Autodiagnosis is a participatory, qualitative research process in which women's groups identify their maternal and neonatal health problems. As such, it allows both the community and the field staff to learn about how women perceive these problems and how they respond to them. Whereas in other, more quantitative study methods the interviewers seek specific, quantifiable data, in the autodiagnosis method there are no right answers, only what the women themselves believe, understand and do. In addition to raising women's awareness of specific maternal and neonatal health problems, a major goal is to foster the women's confidence in their ability to gather information from their neighbours about topics that concern the community and to learn to prioritize the problems that are identified.

Autodiagnosis consists of four sessions of three to four hours each, not including external interviews with other women in the community. The four sessions are divided into nine steps. The process may vary, as a result of individual group differences and circumstances. The priority problems that women's groups most frequently identified in Inquisivi included too many children, haemorrhage, retained placenta and malpresentation.

The autodiagnosis process was not developed solely for the purpose of identifying maternal and neonatal health problems. It serves, more importantly even, as a means to empower women through self-reflection, through greater communication, and through learning to make decisions as a group. It is also an essential first step in identifying and prioritizing problems prior to solving them.[2]

Planning together: the process

Planning Together is the second step of the Community Action Cycle that is designed to result in community-based action to resolve identified problems.

The Planning Together methodology was developed through a series of field trials and adjustments until staff and communities were satisfied with the results. Several exercises included originally in the sessions had to be discarded because they confused the community members or because they distracted the group away from the session's objectives. One interesting example was an exercise that was designed to help the group look for root causes of problems that contributed to maternal and neonatal mortality. This exercise was not going well and staff realized eventually that it was because in Aymaran culture there was no concept of 'cause' as Western culture understands it. In fact, nobody could translate the word 'cause' into Aymara! The exercise was removed from the session and more emphasis was placed directly on how problems occur in daily life. This helped the process enormously.

The objective of Planning Together is to define strategies and actions to resolve the problems identified by the women's groups through a process of planning together with the group, with local authorities and with other community members.

The Planning Together process requires a meeting of at least 3–4 hours' duration; more time may be needed. It is important that people with some understanding of maternal and neonatal health problems and/ or political influence attend the meeting as they can help to look for realistic solutions and formulate action plans that can be implemented.

Preliminary phase

The group needs to prepare prior to the planning meeting. The group members who participated in the autodiagnosis should review the results and decide how they are going to present them to other community members during the planning meeting. They should consider the following questions: what priority problems did they choose? why did they choose them? who can best explain the process to the group? would it be better for several people to make the presentation? who will do what?

One way of sharing and identifying barriers to problem solving is the use of a socio-drama. The women's group should choose some of their members to prepare a skit, taking as the main theme the problems identified in the autodiagnosis. It is important when preparing the socio-drama to consider that the scenario presented to illustrate the problems must be a real one. The skit should also present difficulties or barriers to solving the problem so that the audience can identify them. The group must take into account that they will need to stop the skit for a few moments whenever the participants identify a barrier. The actresses will need to rehearse in preparation for the meeting; the rehearsal will also enable them to feel more secure and confident in their roles.

We found it helpful to consider the following questions in advance: how will the women present the autodiagnosis, its results and the skit? who should attend the planning meeting? when will they meet? Availability of the people attending the meeting must be considered. Who will invite the participants? How will they be invited? What materials will they need to conduct the meeting? Who will be responsible for preparing the materials? The women need to organize all of these details.

The step-by-step process

The process is flexible and should be changed if the group has a special need. The facilitator must rely on her or his creativity to discover techniques and methods which suit the group.

Step 1: Problem presentation by the women

Aim: The group will learn about the problems identified by the women and will know why they are priority problems.

Activities:

1. The facilitator introduces the women to the audience, explaining that they have carried out good work in investigating and identifying problems with maternal and child health during the first month of a baby's life.
2. The women present their autodiagnosis experience according to their plan.
3. The facilitator asks the audience for comments or questions on the presentation. S/he congratulates the women on their presentation.

Step 2: Identifying barriers to solving the problems

Aim: The community participants will understand what a barrier is and will identify barriers to solving the problems portrayed by the women.

Activities:

1. The facilitator demonstrates what a barrier is, using real-life experiences of those present. (10 minutes)

   Possible questions:
   - What is a barrier?
   - Can you give an example of a barrier that you have in your life?
   - What are the barriers to solving our problems with maternal and newborn health?
   - Why do these barriers exist?

   (Examples of some barriers: people do not recognize that there is a problem; people do not think that the problem is important; there is no transport available; there is not enough money or people do not want to spend it on medical services; maltreatment by health personnel.)

2. Presentation of the skit.

A red card is handed out to each participant. Once everyone has a card, an explanation is given:

- 'The women will now present a skit showing what can happen in reality when the problems we have identified occur in the family. Every time you (the audience) notice a barrier to solving the problem, you should hold up your red card. The skit will stop while we write down the barrier on the sheet of paper. The skit will then continue.'

- The group that prepared the skit begins their presentation. When the audience identifies a barrier, the actors 'freeze'. The facilitator notes the problem that has been identified on a piece of flip-chart paper. The skit continues until it is finished, with the facilitator making a list of all the barriers identified by the audience.

Step 3: Identifying strategies and realistic, concrete actions

Aim: The community will identify strategies and concrete, realistic actions which will help to lessen or overcome the barriers identified.

Activities:

1. All community participants (including the women's group members) divide into two groups, one group of women and the other of men so that the women will be more likely to participate actively because men will not dominate their discussion. Both groups work with the list of identified barriers, taking each one in turn and discussing how the community can deal with them. At this stage the facilitator should stress that the plans they come up with must be very practical and realistic. The participants themselves will be putting the plans into practice and must therefore develop strategies and decide on actions to which they will be able to commit themselves.

Facilitation questions:

- What resources does the community have to deal with this problem?
  material resources
  people
  other (eg. time)

- What else do we need in order to confront the problem?

- Is it possible to get what we need? How? Who can help us? When? (specific dates, times if meetings are to be held, who will be responsible)

- What results do we expect to achieve through this strategy? (measurable objectives)

- When they have finished, the two groups present their strategies to the whole group.

- The facilitator asks if everyone agrees with the recommendations.

The participants discuss whether the recommendations are realistic or not and whether they will solve the problem.

- The group reaches consensus on the strategies and actions to be put into practice.

Step 4: Formalizing the agreements in a written document

Aim: The group will draw up a written document of the agreements they have reached in order to put into practice the strategies and actions for dealing with the barriers to problem solving that they have identified.

Activities:

1. Using the strategies prepared in the previous step, the group writes up a final document of all the agreements. The document must contain at least the following:
   - Specific identified strategies with concrete, detailed objectives and actions.
   - Dates (and hours, if applicable) of every action (including the date of the evaluation meeting to assess progress towards achieving their goal).
   - Person(s) responsible for each action.
   - Names of all the participants.
   (It is suggested that the participants organize themselves into working groups or 'committees', with one person responsible for each group. These working groups may be written into the document as a formal mechanism for carrying out the work plan.)

Step 5: Closure of the Planning Together meeting

Aim: The participants formalize the agreements among themselves.

Activities:

1. The facilitator congratulates the group for its good work and reminds the participants that these are real agreements. If they want to solve the problems that they have identified, they must fulfil the promises upon which they have agreed.
2. Everyone signs the document. If participants are pledging the participation of an institution, they can include their official seal as well. The document should be made as formal as possible (with signatures, seals, stamps) to project the seriousness of the participants' commitments.
3. The facilitator states that the group will meet on the date set to evaluate the results of the actions they have taken. It is always advisable to set the date for the next meeting during the planning session.

Actions taken by communities in response to identified problems

The next step in the Community Action Cycle is to implement the strategies developed in the Planning Together sessions. Several examples of actions taken by various communities to improve maternal and neonatal health are listed below:

- Developed a midwives' manual and four booklets for women on reproductive health (pregnancy, labour/delivery, post-partum care and care of the newborn) with technical assistance from SC/B and Centro Interdisciplinario de Educación Comunitaria (CIEC), a local NGO.
- Produced safe-birth kits and sold them to pregnant women in the community.
- Held training/education sessions on topics such as family planning, haemorrhage, retained placenta.
- Solicited and succeeded in initiating family planning services in Inquisivi province through an agreement between SC/B and a local service provider.
- Established emergency funds through women's group income-generating projects such as: communal gardens, sewing mosquito nets, and running general stores.
- Solicited and are now implementing a credit programme for women.
- Solicited and are now implementing a literacy training programme with women's group representatives serving as the literacy trainers.
- Local authorities invited women to participate in general community meetings to which they were never welcomed before.
- Wrote to the Ministry of Health to request improved health services and offering a community counterpart contribution.
- Selected community midwives (not traditional in Inquisivi) who were trained in safe birth practices at the referral hospital in La Paz and in ongoing classes in Inquisivi. (One zone's authorities decided to establish a price scale for the midwives' services, thereby legitimizing their presence and their services.)

Many of the communities participating in the Warmi Project were involved in the Planning Together phase at the time that this chapter was written. SC/B is field-testing a facilitation guide for the next phase, participatory evaluation.

Conclusions

At the time of writing, over twenty communities have participated in the Planning Together phase of the Community Action Cycle and have developed their own plans and strategies to confront maternal and neonatal health problems at the community level. This process was new to many of the women who participated in it, and through it they have learned that they have a voice and can set the community agenda. Many men learned that women can be important community resources and they have seen the value in women's organizations to help promote community development. In a Warmi Project evaluation in May 1993, community authorities were asked to prioritize the project's interventions according to what they believed to be the most important for improving women's lives and health. With few exceptions, the leaders chose 'organization and strengthening of women's groups' as their first priority.

Group planning was a foreign concept to many of the women who took part in Planning Together. Although planning is often done at the individual and family levels in such context as planting and harvesting, most women found the process a new, sometimes intimidating and sometimes liberating experience. It was often necessary to use small groups, dividing women and men, to enable the women to participate fully in strategy development. When the large community group served as the decision-making mechanism for strategy formulation without prior input from smaller, same-sex groups, the women's participation diminished noticeably.

Though it seems obvious, the Planning Together experience in Inquisivi demonstrated the importance of developing methodologies within a cultural and gender context, taking into account basic concepts of causality, planning and the role of fate in other areas of community life.

The qualitative goal of women's empowerment was a guiding force in the development of the Warmi Project methodology. When certain methods were judged possibly to result in a lowering of women's self-esteem, they were discarded, and other methods sought. The willingness of SC/B field staff and community members to admit that methods were not suitable, and to suggest new ones, helped to improve the entire process and contributed to staff and community members' personal growth.

In conclusion, the Warmi Project shows very positive trends. Communities have begun to take action and families have chosen to substitute some of their more harmful reproductive health practices for new, improved ones that they have determined to be both realistic and acceptable. As a result of this, maternal, perinatal and neonatal mortality are on the decline in these communities.

Notes

1. The work upon which this chapter was based was funded by the US Agency for International Development under a subcontract from John Snow, Inc. to Save the Children Fund/Bolivia under the MotherCare Project, Contract No.DPE-5966-Z-00-8083-00, Project No.936-5966.

2. Details on the autodiagnosis methodology are in a working paper, *The 'Autodiagnosis': A Methodology to Facilitate Maternal and Neonatal Health-Problem Identification and Prioritization in Women's Groups in Rural Bolivia*, (Howard-Grabman, L., John Snow, Inc./MotherCare Project, March 1993).

15 Rhetoric or reality? Participatory research in the National Health Service, UK

Grindl Dockery

It is questionable as to how far the concept and practice of community participation is a realistic or achievable option in public-sector organizations such as the United Kingdom (UK) National Health Service (NHS). The term 'public participation' is often used in the rhetoric of such public authorities, but how this term is defined and put into practice varies widely. The following discussion draws upon my involvement with the NHS in the UK and, more specifically, on several training and community-based research projects in which I have been involved. I will use them to highlight problems and possibilities in advocating the adoption of participatory research approaches within what are essentially non-participatory organizations.

Changes and the NHS

The NHS in the UK is a public service, funded through taxes and national insurance (NI) contributions, which has provided a free health service at point of use to members of the British public. The last few years have seen major structural changes within the NHS that have formalized the separation between those who make decisions on what health services communities need, now known as *purchasers*, and those who are providing the services or care in the community, known as the *providers*. Although there has also been an emphasis on increased choice and autonomy for patients, Shackley and Ryan argue that 'it is the purchaser–provider split and the pursuit of efficiency in the newly-created health care market that have tended to dominate the discussion and debate in the new NHS' (1994:520). In line with the market-led approach to health care, patients and service users have come to be viewed as 'consumers' whose needs are addressed through initiatives such as the Patients' Charter which guarantees new 'rights' in relation to issues such as hospital waiting-times and waiting-lists (Liverpool Health Authority 1992). The focus is on improving the efficiency with which services are provided. In light of the political emphasis on efficiency, it would seem that it is crucial for purchasers and providers to have a greater understanding of how and why patients, or 'consumers', make choices and decisions about their health.

However, to think of health service users as consumers suggests that health care is a commodity, that the use of health services is determined by factors such as cost, benefit, effectiveness and efficiency, and that the role of communities within the NHS is only to make choices about consumption, in the same way as people consume fridges and washing machines and videos. In this context, it is perceived that people's views on health care can be identified through market-research techniques – the choices of what type of service people prefer, whom do they want to be cared for, what do they regard as being their priority problems – thus treating the health services in a similar way to people's choice of toothpaste flavours. Hence there is an increased interest in focus group discussions, initially a tool of market research, by purchasers and providers. Shackley and Ryan argue such techniques have their limitations: 'at best they produce an ordinal ranking of interventions which reflect the direction of people's preferences. They do not provide information on intensity of preference' (1994:521). More importantly, they treat people as passive receivers of health services, and whilst such research may serve as a methodology for transmitting the views of local people to health care planners, it does not address how these people might be involved or participate in the planning and shaping of the health services.

Before changes in the NHS, local people's views were represented to the health authorities by Community Health Councils (CHC), which had a statutory role as the voice of the user. This role has been reduced dramatically with the NHS reorganization. Members of my local CHC feel that they now have less say in decision-making and the planning of health services, and in the implementation of health strategies in response to community need. Whilst the powers of CHCs have been reduced, the government has issued a series of documents which offer political directives to health purchasers and providers to consult communities. In the *Health of the Nation* (Secretary of State 1991), it is suggested that achievement of the key objectives identified in the document necessitates: 'involving people more ... at both strategic and operational levels in discussion and decisions about options and priorities, and through that involvement generating a shared commitment' (p. viii). The NHS Management Executive, in its document *Local Voices* (NHS Management Executive 1991), also encouraged purchasers to take more note of the preferences of local communities when identifying health care priorities and this has been taken up by many health authorities. For example, Salford Health Authority says:

> Any real assessment of health needs must take account of the views of Salford people themselves. The purchasing Health Authorities will need to find new ways of talking to local people about health needs. If they achieve nothing else, the proposed service contracts ought to make the dialogues between the Authorities and the people of Salford, whom they serve, much more explicit than has hitherto been the case. (1990:91)

What is unclear is what is meant by the term 'involving people more', how much involvement are we talking about, and what is the difference between involvement and participation? Is involvement, as I suspect, less radical?

Participation and research in planning services

Some health authorities, in their role as purchasers of care, are trying to find ways of consulting communities in identifying their needs and preferences, for example when there are proposed changes in provision of care or when funds are being allocated to a particular part of the health service. This raises issues about: how are 'consumers' or local communities consulted? how can communities participate or be involved in research and who decides what is to be researched? who has the needs and who decides there are needs?

The danger for the term 'participation', now quoted widely in the rhetoric of various health agencies or individuals, is that it comes to be seen as simply another popular concept. Thus, it may be adapted and adopted within the current system of delivering and planning services, rather than being used as an approach to joining and sharing power with oppressed groups, to reflect and create knowledge and take collective action. A participatory approach would demand a fundamental change in the way health authorities conduct health service research. Despite the written commitment to participation, health authorities generally adopt conventional non-participatory approaches to research when, for example, assessing community needs or identifying people's preferences in the planning and provision of health care.

Whether research is participatory or conventional will be reflected in how the research population is identified and what methodology is used to conduct the research. In conventional research, local people and communities answer research questions and it is the researchers, the professionals, who design and implement the research process. Structured instruments, such as questionnaires, where respondents have no control over the questions being asked or the answers they give are frequently used. (These are pre-determined by the researcher.) Potential respondents are identified either by sampling techniques or, in qualitative approaches, purposely chosen because they have characteristics relevant to the topic being investigated. As Hilary Graham says, 'respondents would be approached without their knowing who else was also being invited to take part' (Graham & Jones 1992:239). This isolationist approach acts against collective reflection, analysis and action.

There is an emphasis in conventional research on statistical validity and the avoidance of bias, with the ensuing analysis being conducted in isolation from community respondents. This emphasis on validity can expose the division between community and professional realities; for example, a hospital consultant questioned the finding in a survey which demonstrated that unemployed people, when compared with employed people, were more likely to use public transport rather than private cars when travelling to Accident & Emergency services!

Conventional methods involve the production of a research report outlining findings based on the researcher's analysis. These are not usually disseminated back into the community or to those respondents who 'participated' in the study. In this context, information is taken away from the community, without it having any control over the outcome of the research or the subsequent planning decisions which may be taken by the purchasers and providers of health care. In cases where the data are deemed sensitive (for example, because they are critical of the quality of service provision), reports may be marked 'confidential'. The result is that neither community members nor other health care professionals have access to the information. In contrast, in one project in Liverpool, involving a CHC, findings were fed back to the community members who had been interviewed in the research. This enabled them to comment and make changes to the researcher's initial analysis, thus influencing the findings as presented in the final report and giving them a greater sense of ownership in the research process. However, this is not common and, even with the existence of CHC, as described previously, there is limited access for users to voice their opinions. Often CHC members are only present in planning discussions on the invitation of the local health authority concerned, rather than by right.

Participatory research (PR)

The concept of participation as defined by people such as Paulo Freire in *Pedagogy of the Oppressed* (1972) means acknowledging the political structures and practices which disempower marginalized groups in society, and finding ways in which such processes can be challenged and transformed by those groups. Participation is about facilitating processes whereby people can reflect, analyse, plan and take action. It also enables people to develop new, or build on existing skills and knowledge and increases confidence. This facilitates the process of empowerment, which leads on to potential changes at a structural as well as personal level. Participatory research attempts to redress the balance of power which traditionally exists between the researchers and the researched and to challenge in practice those processes which disempower people.

Power and institutions

PR acknowledges the processes of power which operate not only in the act of conducting research but at all levels and in all spheres of the private and public lives of communities or individuals. This usually means taking sides.

The influence and practice of institutions, legal frameworks, informal relationships and culture inform people how to behave. In other words, the ideologies active in our society influence how we behave and respond to situations, the difference being that the dominant ideologies are usually oppressive or manipulative, whereas the empowering or liberatory ideologies are marginalized and reinterpreted in line with the vested interest of those in power. (Dockery 1991:90)

This has implications when working with or in the formal sector, particularly in relation to how the concept of participation may be used for manipulative and oppressive reasons by institutions.

The NHS is one of the largest bureaucracies in Europe and, as a bureaucracy, is hierarchical by nature and in practice. This raises the question of how its practice can be changed in response to the rhetoric of public participation. The Liverpool Public Health Observatory refers to Pollit (1988):

[who] notes that the encouragement of greater consumer responsiveness in a public service cannot be simply a 'bolt-on extra' to be fixed to the most appropriate part of the organization while all else goes on as before. Sir Roy Griffiths (1988) states that it must be seen as 'part of a total management and organizational philosophy'. (Ubido & Snee 1992:2)

This still does not acknowledge the existing fundamental problems and changes that need to be addressed to prevent participation becoming simply that bolt-on extra. Frances Baum also highlights the contradictions which exist between the principles of Healthy Cities projects, which are potentially radical in the way health is defined and acted upon, and their close allegiance with bureaucracies.

Healthy Cities projects around the world appear to be using the language of radical social movements, with their emphasis on change through conflict, but operating within a bureaucratic logic that stresses consensual, incremental change. ... The danger in this approach is that the term ceases to have meaning. Concepts have meanings because we attach values to them. (Baum 1993:32)

The issue of accountability in the NHS between the medical profession and its employers was brought to the public's attention recently in a widely respected national newspaper. A well-known NHS trust chairman was quoted as saying 'that doctors' first duty is to the organization they work in, while their second is to ensure that they themselves are properly organized and trained' (Brindle 1994:2). This, of course, drew objections from various quarters including the medical profession, which responded that the patient is always their first responsibility. The problem here is that the health professionals' commitment to serve and give priority to those in their care, the patients, is frequently paternalistic, with a reluctance to share their knowledge and work *with* people rather than *for* or *on* them.

Pure PR, or what is possible?

It would appear from the discussion so far, that if we want to apply PR in its purest sense and without fundamental reforms, we face an impossible task within the NHS bureaucracy. Whilst we might aim for the ideal participatory community research project, it is important to acknowledge there are constraints on achieving the ideal in institutions like the NHS. Rather, we should be looking for opportunities, no matter how small they may seem, within the research process where participation can take place. We could liken participation to a continuum, where different entry points for participation are identified: these are not fixed, but move backwards and forwards according to the particular research situation you are involved in. What is important is that we look purposefully for entry points where participation can be facilitated and attempt to push the boundaries further along the continuum towards the ideal. As Maguire argues:

> while participatory research may be one tool with empowering, emancipatory potential, it is not the only tool ... we might absolve ourselves of some unspoken requirement that all research be 'pure' PR [and] instead we might look at ways to move deliberately along the participatory continuum. ... I am as much an advocate of participation itself, as both a means and end, whether it be more participatory education, evaluation, management or research. (Maguire 1994:7)

Needs assessment (NA)

The current vogue in the NHS to conduct needs assessments (NAs) highlights the ethics about who decides an NA is necessary, whose needs are being met and to what end?

> Producing a body of knowledge that identifies the health needs of a local population does not in itself ensure that those needs will be met. ... Social and economic barriers do not simply evaporate in the face of community needs assessment. (Wainwright 1994:29)

The commissioning process that is evolving with the current reforms in the NHS is directed to purchasing services that will improve the health of the nation. Hunter and Alderslade argue that 'there are several stages which effective commissioning should go through'. They identify the second stage as the analysis of health needs. They suggest these needs are 'complex social constructs which have to be analysed, interpreted and given meaning and priority in conversation with the population served'. They feel that the mechanisms for these conversations to take place are 'crude and poorly developed' and suggest adopting such techniques as rapid appraisal (RA) and focus group interviews (1994:22). The reality however, is that these conversations are usually a one-way process, from community members to health professionals, and there is often a belief that the information the community provides through these methods is anecdotal and unscientific.

This attitude towards qualitative-research approaches was highlighted in some of the comments made after an NA was conducted by health workers using RA methods. Concern was expressed in the final report about the validity of respondents' experience, as expressed in the interviews through anecdotal and descriptive discussions (Leach & Bradley 1993:20). It is not uncommon for professionals to have difficulty in seeing community perceptions and experience as useful and meaningful knowledge for policy formulation and planning services (Williams & Popay 1994). The majority of us are taught that quantitative methodologies are more scientific and factual, or even more truthful, which may explain why there was a desire by some to quantify what was essentially qualitative data.

In my experience, some communities are refusing to participate any further in such research as they feel they have been 'needs-assessed to death', without any tangible response in terms of resource allocation. The purpose of NA should take into account what potential resources are available in response to the needs being identified. In a participatory approach, it is the community which would participate in the research-planning process, deciding what needs to be assessed and to what end. It would be participating also in the planning and implementation of actions to take place in response to the findings. 'The research problem must be generated by people living in these communities reflecting on their own experiences. It should be a community-defined problem' (Graham & Jones 1992:236).

The two examples below reflect the different approaches taken to plan an NA. In one project, initial discussions with managers revealed the aim of involving and transferring skills on to health workers who would be conducting the NA, the hope being that they in turn would be able to involve the local community more effectively in their programmes. Despite this concern and interest, the topic or focus of the NA, mental health, was chosen by the managers. Neither the health workers who were to be trained nor the community to be involved had any say in this. The managers were under pressure to produce an annual report containing local survey data and the topic was based partly on the belief that substantial funds were to be made available on mental health issues by the government in the future.

In contrast, another NA initiated by community members evolved from their concern about the proposed closure of a health clinic in their area. Public meetings, organized by a local voluntary agency, were held in order that the community could express its opposition to this proposal, and the health authority (HA) was persuaded to make a commitment to conducting research before any final decisions were made. Through later discussions with a small group of community representatives and with suggestions from the HA representatives present, the decision was made to broaden the scope of the research to include not only the proposed clinic closure but also the provision of health services generally in the whole area. The HA responded to the community's demands and was willing to provide some funding for the research to be done, although the broader research remit decided on, finally, was what the HA wanted.

Intersectoral collaboration

Identified health needs may be seen only as those which can be addressed by the health and/or social services; others beyond the remit or resources of these services are ignored or not seen as legitimate. This raises the issue of intersectoral or interagency coordination and cooperation when identifying needs and planning allocation of resources. The Liverpool Public Health Authority states that if a commitment to community participation is made then there is also a commitment to intersectoral collaboration and to various agencies working together. This is essential because '(p)eople see their health problems not in isolation, but rather as deeply embedded within the social and economic fabric of their lives' (1992:2). This analysis is consistently endorsed in my research findings, especially concerning research in deprived communities.

Process and methods

Institutions often put much more emphasis and importance on research methods than on the actual process involved. Research techniques alone cannot guarantee or ensure ongoing participatory and empowering processes, nor does it follow that communities will own and control the information once it is collected. Local participation should extend beyond the decision about where and what to research, to include the community's ongoing role in the planning and implementation of health care. As Srinivasan says: 'it is not the technique itself but the underlying principles that matter' (1990:12).

In recent years, there has been increasing interest in the rise of alternative approaches to conducting community research, and the popularity of RA is no exception. The development of RA methods began in the agricultural sector, primarily in countries of the South, and it is only recently that the methods are becoming better known in the North. Despite the promoted merits of RA there are problems, in what appears to be a predominant emphasis on the methods as empowering to those participating in the diagrammatic exercises which are a feature of the practice. Whilst the literature demonstrates the participatory and innovative nature of these methods, there is little theoretical exploration of the whole RA process and its ongoing outcome for those community members who participated.

When considering PR it is important to address the whole process and the community's ongoing role in the planning and implementation of health care activities. As Patricia Maguire (1994:6-7) argues:

> each PR endeavour attempts, at however micro a level, to transform not only the particular problem-posing process but also decision-making and resource-allocating institutions and processes.

An approach towards fulfilling this ideal is demonstrated in a Healthy Cities project. Local people had identified various community initiatives, including a large sheltered housing scheme. Community members were involved in planning and negotiating funding for the schemes, working with different sectors under the control of local authorities; they also supervised the implementation of the schemes.

Time and money

PR addresses the issue not only of who has control over and ownership of the research process but, based on the research findings, of who will make the ongoing decisions and plans for action. It can be seen, therefore, that PR is not rapid, but a gradual process from one step to the next. People need to feel confident and skilled enough to participate, especially if they are to control and own the process. The progression from disempowerment to empowerment is usually a slow, reflective and action-oriented process which can take years.

Alongside the ideological and political constraints on PR within the NHS, there is also often a lack of time and funding to develop and facilitate such participatory processes. For example, in a training exercise where health workers were being prepared to conduct a needs assessment using RA methods, the research timetable was very limited, which restricted the possibility of any meaningful community consultation. It was clear that the 'rapid' in the rapid appraisal approach adopted was what appealed to the managers. Whilst financial considerations are important, they should not be the dominant reason in deciding whether participatory research should be undertaken.

Professionals in PR

Participation involves professionals being able to work in partnership with local communities, where they are obliged to view health problems through new eyes. It does not involve professionals either teaching community members or volunteers how to think or imposing their interpretations on the expressed experiences of local communities: *'they must also radically alter their own perspective.* The main disadvantage is that they are often constrained by the institution or statutory agency in which they work' (Wainwright 1994:29). For example, a group of health workers which was to be trained to conduct an NA was selected by the participants' respective managers rather than themselves volunteering, and as a consequence some did not have the necessary commitment to new concepts and methods which facilitate or enable participatory processes to take place. It is important that more opportunities are made available for health workers to develop new skills and learn new concepts; it is crucial, however, that they are given adequate time and relief from normal duties to participate in such ventures.

Health professionals are trained in the medical model which includes a view of research and education as being empirically based. More importantly, they receive little or no education on empowering and emancipatory approaches to health issues generally. They often face difficulties in conceptualizing different approaches which may challenge their own professionals beliefs and perceptions. The role of many health professionals is to a large extent based on giving advice, explaining medical conditions and supervising others. Robert Chambers suggests that conventional education has a major impact on the habits, ideas and values that professionals adopt (Chambers 1983). This means that the change from telling others what to do to discovering what others feel and think involves a reversal of roles. The teacher becomes the learner and the learner the teacher.

There is a real need for health managers to have a greater awareness and understanding of the various research methodologies available to them when deciding to commission community research. They could facilitate opportunities within the research process for greater participation among those communities they want to investigate, and also support creative and innovative approaches to conducting such research.

Whilst health professionals may act or behave in ways which disempower local people, they are also disempowered by the structures in which they have to work.

A training process I was involved in attempted to address both those problems, by presenting a range of different theoretical models, including a participatory research paradigm, to enable participants to develop a critique of current research practice. The models were used to look at different aspects of the research process and the type of relationship health workers have with local people. This can be a useful method raising awareness of issues of power and knowledge, and identifying ways in which health workers can facilitate greater participation by local people in research.

Planning framework

A participatory planning process was introduced into the training of health professionals who were involved in assessing mental health needs of the community. The planning process validated and enabled participants to use their knowledge and experience in the planning of the research. A planning framework adapted from work in the Cameroon served as a useful tool to initiate the participatory process (de Koning & Bichmann 1993:3).

The framework (Figure 15.1) consists of a series of columns starting with aims, then the secondary data for review, specific objectives, the key issues arising and to be addressed, informants or interviewees identified for interviews according to the research objectives, the methods to be used in collecting the information and a final column for details and notes on final arrangements to be made.

Figure 15.1 Planning framework

Aims	Secondary data	Sub-issues	Objectives	Check-list	Informants	Methods	Notes/organization

Adapted by: G. Dockery & K. de Koning.

To identify the content of the framework, brainstorming and group exercises were carried out, for each column in turn. It was sometimes necessary to review previously completed columns as new issues were raised and decisions taken on what was feasible for the research team to cope with, considering the existing time constraints and level of experience within the team. The majority of participants expressed concern about the increased workload caused by the expectation of carrying out their normal duties as well as conducting the research.

The focus of the research was used as a basis for the group exercises to develop the appropriate interviewing and listening skills and to practise other rapid-appraisal diagrammatic methods, such as ranking, seasonal calenders and community/body mapping.[1]

Through interview role plays, participants tried out the different questions they might use in the interviews in order to develop further their skills in probing for in-depth information. This experience led to an acute awareness of what it means to have to answer what are frequently very personal questions; participants often became deeply involved, forgetting that it was an exercise. It further bridged the gap between what they, the informants with mental health problems, might experience and the trainees' own perceptions or experience of mental health problems.

Applying a practical, participatory planning framework and introducing RA methods into the training context provided opportunities for people to rethink the way they do things and how they approach local communities. Although the ideal PR approach was not achieved, the training did provide an opportunity for change and reflection amongst participants. Some thought about how they might use and expand further the ideas generated in the training, and integrate these within the planning and implementation of their own programmes. Later comments elicited that fact that some workers were already applying the ideas and skills they had developed through the training in their ongoing activities, whereas other participants in the training programme found the challenge of a different approach and new concepts a problem.

Conclusion

There are no easy answers or solutions to the constraints on PR when working within a bureacratic environment. In my experience, community participation becomes a reality when there is already a long-term political commitment to change, with active participation taking place in existing programmes or projects. To promote and facilitate participatory processes within non-participatory systems, utilizing any opportunity that arises, no matter how slight, is a challenge that exists for all practitioners. Using the official rhetoric, where appropriate, is one way of encouraging managers and health professionals to make changes. Finding practical frameworks or tools which encourage reflection and active participation in research and health care planning is important if we are to put theories into practice. Keeping community groups or organizations informed of potential projects or decisions being made at policy level provides an opportunity for them to respond, and challenge those in power. Participation is about seeking to influence those processes or agencies which affect our lives.

Note

1. There are various publications regarding RA methods. See, particularly, *RRA Notes* (1992) and Welbourn (1992).

References

Baum, F.E. (1993) 'Healthy Cities and change: social movement or bureaucratic tool?', *Health Promotion International*, Vol.8(1), pp.31-40.

Brindle, D. (1994) 'Trust's first NHS chief condemned', *Guardian*, 14 November, p.2.

Chambers, R. (1983) *Rural Development: Putting the Last First*, Longman Scientific and Technical.

Dockery, G. (1991) *Power and Process in Development Theory, Decentralisation and Primary Health Care*, M.Ed Dissertation, University of Manchester.

Freire, P. (1972) *Pedagogy of the Oppressed*, Penguin Books, London.

Graham, H. & Jones, J. (1992) 'Community development and research', *Community Development Journal*, Vol.27(3), pp.235-41.

Griffiths, R. (1988) 'Does the public service serve? The consumer dimension', *Public Administration*, Vol.66, pp.195-204.

Hunter, D. & Alderslade, R. (1994) 'Outward bound', *Health Service Journal*, 27 October, pp.22-3.

de Koning, K. (ed.) (1994) *Proceedings of the International Symposium on Participatory Research in Health Promotion*, Education Resource Group, Liverpool School of Tropical Medicine, UK.

de Koning, K. & Bichmann, W. (1993) 'Listening to communities and health workers: a participatory training process to improve the skills of health workers in Cameroon', *Learning for Health*, Issue 3, pp.3-7.

Leach, J. & Bradley, S. (1993) *Mental Health in Central Manchester – Views from the Community*, Department of Public Health, Manchester.

Liverpool Health Authority and Family Health-Services Authority (1992) *The Patient's Charter.: Raising the Standard*.

Maguire, P. (1994) 'Participatory research from one feminist perspective. Moving from exposing androcentricism to embracing possible contributions of feminisms to participatory research theory and practice. Voices and Visions', in de Koning, K. (ed.) (1994), pp.5-14.

NHS Management Executive (1991) *Local Voices: The Views of Local People in Purchasing for Health*.

Pollit, C. (1988) 'Consumerism and beyond', *Public Administration*, Vol.66, pp.121-4.

RRA (Rapid Rural Appraisal) Notes (1992) Vol.16, International Institute for Environment and Development, London.

Salford Health Authority/Family Health Services Authority (1990) *Beyond the Stethoscope*.

Secretary of State for Health (1991) *The Health of the Nation*, HMSO, London.

Shackley, P. & Ryan, M. (1994) 'What is the role of the consumer in health care?', *Journal of Social Policy*, Vol.23(4), pp.517-41.

Srinivasan, L. (1990) *Tools for Community Participation*, PROWESS/UNDP, New York.

Ubido, J. & Snee, K. (1992) *Consumer Participation: Directory of Projects. Merseyside and Cheshire*, Observatory Report Series, No.12, Liverpool Public Health Observatory.

Wainwright, D. (1994) 'On the waterfront', *Health Service Journal*, 7 July, pp.28-9.

Welbourn, A. (1992) 'Rapid rural appraisal, gender and health – alternative ways of listening to needs', *IDS Bulletin*, Vol.23(1), pp.8-18.

Williams, G, & Popay, J, (1994) 'Lay knowledge and the privilege of experience', in *Challenging Medicine*, Routledge, London.

PART VI USING PARTICIPATORY METHODS TO ESTABLISH COMMUNITY-BASED INFORMATION SYSTEMS

16 A Zimbabwean case

Ravai Marindo-Ranganai[1]

The concept of participatory research gained currency in the late 1980s as a symbol of fresh perspectives towards equitable involvement of rural or indigenous populations as equal partners in research. The idea behind participatory research can be understood as an agenda of active participation, empowerment and poverty alleviation (Scoones & Thompson 1993). It is not quite clear whether participatory research is pointing to a fresh and new direction which defines social research or is simply an academic bandwagon soon to be forgotten.

This chapter discusses the use of participatory modelling in gathering demographic data on fertility, population size and mortality in a semi-nomadic community of Zimbabwe, for the purpose of creating a community-based information system. Using a case study of the Tembomvura people of Zambezi Valley, northern Zimbabwe, an attempt will be made to show how participatory modelling was used in drawing maps of the research area as well as in collecting quantitative data on children ever born and children dead. The study will highlight the gender and age differences in participation and some of the impacts these have on the research process. In addition, by discussing the practical problems experienced in the modelling process, the study will attempt to show how these problems were tackled on a practical level.

Current issues

Before discussing the modelling process, an attempt is made to highlight some of the theoretical problems that provide a background to our understanding of participation. Because participatory research is a new perspective, clarification is needed on some of the issues that might assist in understanding the dynamics of the process. For example, what defines participatory research? Is it the method, the theory or the field actions? Does the presence of one of these factors make a piece of research participatory?

With relation to the actors in the process

Who defines that a piece of research is participatory? Is it the researchers or the indigenous people that we work with? How can we be sure that our definition of participation is the same as that used by the participants? Is participation a two-way process, or is it one where we expect villagers to participate without referring at all to what is expected of the researchers? Are researchers not falling into the trap of defining what is good for the villagers?

These and other questions are raised not as an attack on the concept of participation but as an attempt to raise awareness of the need to develop theory and clarify concepts. Academic disciplines have grown through the examination, debate and critical analysis of issues pertinent to the subject matter.

The importance of indigenous knowledge

An outstanding feature of participatory research in combination with the use of participatory rural appraisal methods is an attempt to make indigenous knowledge legitimate in the research process. The idea that local people can be sources of information is not new. Anthropologists and sociologists working with illiterate indigenous communities have recorded and used indigenous knowledge, sometimes redefining it to fit their own models of what is rational and intelligent or using it to confirm their ideas on the inferiority of the native. Scoones and Thompson (1993) provide a detailed account of the way rural people's knowledge has been represented in agricultural research and extension services, and their work could fit easily as a review of literature on indigenous knowledge for many social science disciplines. What participatory rural appraisal methods offer is a chance for indigenous people to present their perception of their problems, or their world, in their own models and diagrams, and to communicate, these models. The use of drawings, models and drama and other non-formal methods of communicating provide a forum for sharing indigenous knowledge.

The need for community-based information systems in demographic studies

A challenge for most demographic and epidemiological studies carried out in Africa and other developing countries is the need for collecting relevant and reliable data. The lack of continuous vital registration data has made demographers rely on census and survey data collected by using quantitative questionnaires. Although efforts have been made and continue to be made to improve questionnaires by providing elaborate instructions and making questions as culturally sensitive as possible, most demographic data collected from most rural communities in Africa remain unsatisfactory. Van de Walle (1968), Brass (1975), United Nations

(1983) and Ramachandran (1983), among others have emphasized the poor quality of such African data. One major weakness of the quantitative and long questionnaires normally used in collecting demographic data is that research problems are defined out of context and questions are brought to the indigenous population regardless of whether they consider the research problem relevant to their situation.

In recognition of this weakness of quantitative questionnaires, suggestions have been made to use micro approaches in collecting demographic data, approaches which use anthropological, ethnographic and other qualitative methods (Caldwell et al. 1988). In spite of this suggestion, qualitative methods have not been popular in demography because of the need for large sample sizes.

Data collection could be participatory if the indigenous people take part in defining the problem, suggesting ways of collecting the data and analysing them. In that way, ownership of data is increased and data become useful to them as a tool that can change their situation and empower them. A combination of quantitative and qualitative data-gathering approaches can provide comprehensive data which can inform policy.

Methods used in the study

Figure 16.1 shows the participatory rural appraisal (PRA) methods used in the information-gathering process in setting up a continuous registration system together with the sources of these methods.

Figure 16.1 Participatory methods, sources and characteristics of the participants, Tembomvura Survey 1992

Method	Source of method	Characteristics of the participants
Participatory area modelling	Mascarenhas et al. (1990)	All individuals from the four villages of Chiramba, Chitombo, Chaguruka and Nsansa
Modelling of size of population, of concepts of healthy children, etc.	Researcher	Men and women aged 30 years and over
Setting up local community register of births and deaths by using seeds	Researcher	A sample of adult men and 10 adult women
Modelling of children ever born and children dead	Researcher, based on an original idea by Brass (1968)	Only women who had ever had a live birth

A brief background to the population studied

The Tembomvura people are a group of 780 semi-nomadic hunters and gatherers who reside in the Zambezi Valley, Zimbabwe. Their area of residence lies between two game reserves: the Dande safari area and Chewore game reserve. Figure 16.2 shows the geographical location of the Tembomvura area. Their livelihood is based on the clandestine hunting of wild animals, the gathering of wild fruits and the selling of their labour to a neighbouring agricultural community.

The Tembomvura people have been isolated from the urban centres. The 384km distance from the capital city, Harare, most of which is dust road, has made contact difficult. Malaria and tsetse flies have made the area unpopular with researchers. This study is the first attempt at gathering demographic data among the Tembomvura.

The Tembomvura have also been marginalized, socially and politically. Their hunting-based livelihood makes them different from the other ethnic groups in Zimbabwe which are cultivators. Their hunting lifestyle has also put them in direct conflict with government officials attempting sustainable utilization of wildlife resources. The Tembomvura are very poor. They have not been exposed to formal education. Government efforts to this end were seen as an effort to remove the community from its livelihood in order to protect animals.

In 1992, when the study was carried out, the community was experiencing one of the worst droughts ever in Zimbabwe, which had started in 1987 and continued until 1992. As food shortages escalated, the poverty and marginalization began to be defined in demographic terms and fears of dying-out were expressed by the elders.

From this background it became clear that methods that allowed for an expression of local knowledge in as informal and non-authoritative way as possible had to be used. The creation of a rapport which allowed for a building of confidence and respect for each other's limitations became central to the whole research process. The use of a demographic questionnaire alone was not the best approach. The International Institute for Environment and Development (IIED) provided some publications and ideas as to which PRA methods could be used during the data-gathering process. In the next sections, the practical aspects of carrying out participatory modelling are discussed in detail.

Practical application of PRA: involving the villagers in the definition of the research problem

At an initial meeting with the elders, I introduced myself and informed them of my interest in studying Tembomvura fertility. The response was unexpected:

That is not our problem, we do not care about how many children are born, what we want to know is why our men and our children are dying. We are dying out.

Figure 16.2 Tembomvura villages and some important man-made features in Chapoto ward

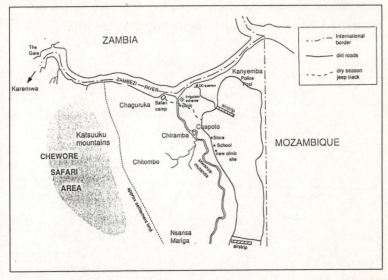

The meeting with the elders of the community indicated clearly that they had their own problems. Their fear was that they were dying out as a community because of excess mortality. A suggestion was made, therefore, to redefine the whole project and focus on mortality rather than fertility. Through a process of negotiation and explanation I managed to emphasize the idea that the death of a population does not depend only on the number of people dying but also on whether the births are replacing the dead people. The study had to examine both mortality and fertility.

Designing a map of the area
Because this was the first study in the area, there was need to draw a map showing location of settlements and footpaths, and some of the areas frequented by dangerous wild animals. When the idea of modelling the village was brought to the elders, there was initial resistance. I decided to work with the children, using leaves, stones, mud and some paints to build a model of the village on the ground. As the model-building continued, the elders watched and then began correcting and making suggestions about the children's efforts. With time, the elders became involved. The men and women argued about location of dwellings, places

of significance and even about the direction of the main distinguishing features like the Zambezi river. Without the researcher suggesting anything, the women and men split up and each sex drew its own map of the village.

Sex differences in the perceptions of the area

Figures 16.3 and 16.4 show the female and male maps respectively. The maps differ in a number of ways.

Figure 16.3 Female area map from participatory modelling

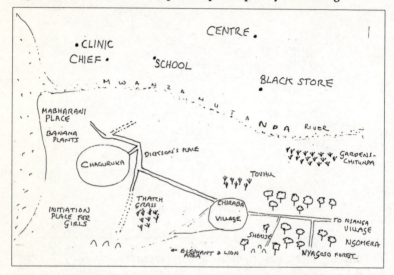

Figure 16.4 Male area map from participatory modelling

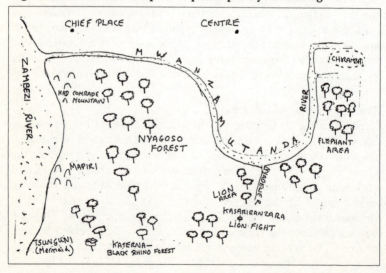

The female map is a more contemporary depiction of the Tembomvura area as it is currently and it shows other places of significance, like the school, the grinding-mill and gardens. The male map seems to be a depiction of the area as it looked in the past. The lack of detail of contemporary features as well as the presentation of large forests with wild animals both tend to suggest that men provided an historical rather than contemporary map of their own area.

Another difference was that the male map was incorrect, the direction and position of the Zambezi river being reversed. Although some hints were made by the women as to the position of the river, the men insisted that was how they saw the area and that their model was correct. When village walks were taken, however, the men had a very good sense of direction.

Differences in participation by age and sex
The area modelling was started by working with children, but as the elders got involved, they took over the children's map and excluded the children. The children were not prepared to start a new model and became destructive at some point, putting some funny locations on the women's map. After some time, the children lost interest and went back to their play. In a way, the loss of the children in the process made the models less spontaneous and slower than originally. Communication between children and adults was in one-way format, with elders commanding the children and never listening to children's ideas and the children looking frustrated that their views were not included on the map.

From this study, I realized that adults probably subscribed to the view that children should be seen but not heard. This behaviour in the community led to loss of valuable information from the children.

Gender differences
During the participatory modelling, women initially appeared uninterested. Their start was slow and they tended to be bullied into silence by the men when they worked on a combined model. However, when the women and men split up and worked on different models, the women appeared to work in unison. A difference between the old women and the young women was noticed. The old women did not have a good sense of places far from their own village. For example, they were not sure of the location of the clinic and the grinding-mill. The young women appeared more knowledgable about places in other villages and made the women's map more detailed. Older women, however, quickly admitted their lack of knowledge. Although there was respect given to the old women, for example they talked longer and their views were listened to, the younger women insisted on and supported each other about recent developments in the area. The old women would then back down, shake their heads and

mumble: 'When did they build the school? Who built it? Who needs a grinding-mill?'

The men's approach to model-building was both fascinating and frustrating. They appeared organized, sitting and planning and throwing ideas at each other, but at the end of the day little would appear on the ground. Some of the old men began by telling long stories which were unrelated to the area modelling. The men also had a tendency to laugh at the women's map, pointing at what they defined as ridiculous locations of places. There was a lot of mental activity among the men but the resulting map was disappointing. It also became clear that they did not take kindly to suggestions from women, including me. Sometimes the women retorted by pointing out that men were good at only one thing, talking all the time and not producing results.

Villagers in control and a different world view

The process of letting the villagers take control of the mapping exercise had its problems. Arguments among men and women led to the group splitting into two by sex. Other unforeseen problems, such as power struggles between individuals and age differences which affect the way old and young people work together, delayed the modelling exercise. Pressure was placed on me not to interfere and 'organize' the modelling in a more 'efficient and methodological' way.

Three critical issues came out during the mapping exercise:
1. Villagers had a different time-scale to mine, in which things were done slowly.
2. The villagers' maps were not drawn according to the cardinal points N, E, S, W but were based on their understanding of the position of rivers and mountains. These maps demanded a process of unlearning from me as I realized that the villagers had key points of relevance which depended on what they considered important in their own village.
3. Men and women had different concepts of what were important landmarks in their own area. Villagers are not necessarily homogeneous in the way they perceive things.

Was area modelling participatory or simply mechanical?

The process of area modelling took four months. Bits and pieces went on being added to the maps with time. The process was not mechanical. People shared ideas, argued about location of places and tried to put forward their images of the area as they knew it. There was a lot of talking, and I discussed not only the model but the historical development of the area, where the people came from and their culture. They, in turn, asked about the city and about places outside the country. It is impossible for this process to be mechanical because villagers meet, design a model, break this down and create a new one. In this way they construct images, and a kind of empowerment comes from the realization that they have this information within them and that it can be depicted in a form that is understood by other people outside their area.

Fertility and mortality data: the challenge of quantification
After area modelling, the second part of the study involved collection of mortality and fertility data. Calculation of mortality levels and trends requires numeric data. In developed countries the sources of data on mortality are vital registration records which are normally complete and useable. In most developing countries, vital registration data is urban-based, hence cannot be used in rural populations. It is this recognition of the deficiency in data that has led to the development of indirect methods of estimating mortality levels and trends based on data collected from retrospective surveys. Brass pioneered this approach in 1968.

The popular method uses information on children ever born by each woman, and the children dead. Although the detail required from this approach is not much, there are still practical challenges in gathering this data.

How does one collect numeric numbers of children ever born from illiterate women with no recording traditions?

Participatory modelling of demographic data on fertility and mortality
Using the seeds of two popular and abundant fruits in the area, ziziphus Mauritania and Tamarindus Indica, each woman was assisted in modelling her children ever born and children dead, by sex. Tamarindus indica (believed to be a male aphrodisiac which increases potency) was used to represent male children, while ziziphus mauritania represented female children. Dead children were represented by stones. A woman's fertility record obtained from participatory modelling could look like that in Figure 16.5.

Figure 16.5 A woman's fertility record obtained from participatory modelling

Son	Daughter	Son	Son (dead)	Daughter
TI	ZM	TI	stone	ZM

Dramatization
For some women, fertility histories were reconstructed through dramatization. Using children from neighbouring houses, a woman would be asked to arrange the children in order as if there were her own daughters and sons, leaving gaps for those who died. A demographic questionnaire was completed during the modelling and dramatization. Table 16.1

shows the data collected from all women, using a combination of modelling and dramatization, and direct questioning. The raw data were later used to calculate estimates of total fertility rate and probabilities of dying.

Table 16.1 Children ever born and children dead by age of mother, Tembomvura women 1992

Age group of women	Number of women	Total children ever born	Mean no. of children ever born	Number of children dead	Prop. of dead children out of total children ever born
10-14	62	1	0.016	0	0.000
15-19	46	19	0.413	8	0.421
20-24	33	74	2.242	23	0.311
25-29	32	147	4.594	57	0.388
30-34	33	182	5.515	52	0.286
35-39	27	202	7.481	70	0.347
40-44	24	200	8.333	73	0.365
45-49	19	149	7.842	54	0.362

Is the population growing or declining?

Adults were asked to model the changes in the size of population. Using seeds of the trees tamarindus indica and ziziphus mauritania, the elders modelled the size of the population and the changes in mortality and fertility that they experienced from their childhood compared to the their adult years.

Indications are that the adults perceived the population as experiencing higher childhood mortality, high male adult mortality and a stable female adult mortality. Suggestions are that the recent period had seen the threat to the extinction of the community through perceived excess mortality. The major cause of this accelerated death was reported as a change in lifestyle as well as the drought, poverty and marginalization. Men reported that they were dying at a faster rate than the women because men could not live without eating meat. Women, on the other hand, were believed to be surviving because they were used to a diet of leaves, and the ban on hunting did not affect their health. It is surprising that when the data on mortality were analysed, female and male mortality was found to be very similar, both sexes having experienced more severe mortality in the recent past. In addition, the data also showed that the Tembomvura population was not facing extinction, either in the current year or in the near future.

Creation of a continuous register of deaths and births

As a concluding part of the community-based information system, an attempt was made to collect data on births and deaths which occurred in the village according to seasons. Tins were painted in different designs to represent different seasons. A group of ten men and ten women was selected from the village and asked to be in charge of the tins. For each season there were two tins, and each time there was a death during a particular season, a stone was thrown into the particular tin; for a birth, seeds of the Ziziphus Mauritania tree would be thrown into the birth tin.

There are four seasons during a Tembomvura year: hot–dry, hot–wet, cold and the windy. The seasons are distinct, and even when there is a drought they are identified by other factors, such as the position of the sun as it comes out, the direction of the winds and the behaviour of wild animals. The register was very crude because the sex of the children could not be determined in this procedure, but it provided a good basis for a community-based vital registration system.

Lessons learned

On a practical level, this study found that the following considerations were important when attempting to carry out participatory work with a community:

- discussing all aspects of the study from the initial stages because indigenous people have good ideas of the relevance of some of the work that we try to carry out in their community;
- humility and a desire to consider all angles and suggestions, recognizing your own limited knowledge;
- respect for local power structures and beliefs, because the community members have to continue to survive in their own way after you have gone;
- creation of rapport is important, and sometimes working with children can help in breaking the ice and easing involvement for adults;
- an empowered group of villagers is not necessarily an easy group to work with. As rapport was created, I found the villagers' criticisms sometimes very harsh and this made the research process at times rather difficult.

How can participatory research be evaluated?

Participation is a process and a process cannot be judged by dichotomous variables. Participatory research can be understood as a process whose overriding aim is empowerment. In evaluating this process, research can be seen as less participatory or more participatory rather than not participatory. Evaluation should be based on a continuum.

Participatory rural appraisal techniques – are these mechanical tools which can be applied blindly by researchers?

At a symposium on Participatory Research in Health Promotion held in Liverpool 1993, experts in participatory research raised the fear that researchers were 'blindly' applying participatory rural appraisal methods 'mechanically', hence their studies were not participatory. This chapter challenges that view and asks instead: 'How can PRA techniques be applied mechanically in the field? Is it feasible for researchers to obtain maps and models of the way people perceive their environment or their bodies through a mechanical process?' Models and diagrams come from people, and no amount of researcher power can make people produce those diagrams or models. The weakness may be in applying PRA as an end in itself because researchers fail to make clear the link between the process of information gathering and its empowering potential. Do participation and empowerment exist simply because researchers articulate the empowerment agenda in their studies?

For people not used to writing, the ability to express their knowledge through PRA methods may be empowering. Researchers who have worked in communities with no recording traditions, and produced models and diagrams with villagers, identify with the intensity of emotions that accompany the design, articulation and final communication of a problem that happens between the researcher and participants. One woman in this study expressed the following feeling: 'And we thought we were so foolish because we could not write. Yet look, we had all this information inside us.' Having been alienated for so long by their lack of formal education, they saw the use of PRA as a positive change.

The paradox: data requirements and policy making

In theory, policies are made on the basis of local people's needs and problems. This kind of data would best be collected through participatory methods that reflect the problems as they are reported at grassroots level. On a practical level, however, policy makers demand that data be from large representative samples provided with standard errors and confidence intervals. Those kinds of data look professional and convince those who decide about resource allocation even though they might not represent the way villagers perceive their problems.

For most researchers in quantitative disciplines, participatory research is synonymous with qualitative research, characterized by small sample sizes, irreplicability and a lot of unsubstantiated rhetoric. This 'weakness' has been used as a weapon deliberately to ignore findings which represent to a large extent the reality of normally the poorest and most marginalized in the community.

Participatory research, in combination with proper use and analysis of data obtained through PRA methods, is a powerful tool that legitimates the knowledge of the illiterate and can challenge the way in which surveys can sometimes misrepresent the problems of those who cannot count or read. This kind of research deserves a more respectable position in academic disciplines than it enjoys currently.

Conclusion

This study has shown how participatory modelling was used to collect demographic data and how an attempt was made to set up a community-based vital registration system. Some data on fertility and mortality were collected and analysed and showed that people's perceptions were not necessarily supported by the quantitative data but provided the context within which results such as high mortality levels and trends in population growth could be understood and discussed. The community-based vital registration system needs further improvement but the study suggests that it could be a good starting-point for organizing a community-based information system.

Note

1. The author would like to acknowledge the useful comments of Basia Zaba and Jamie Robinson of the London School of Hygiene and Tropical Medicine, and Ian Scoones of IIED for an earlier version of this chapter. This study forms part of a major demographic survey aimed at studying the population dynamics of a semi-nomadic community in Zimbabwe. The major study was funded by UNFPA-New York and the fieldwork was funded by the Population Council, New York.

References

Brass, W. (1975) *Methods for Estimating Fertility and Mortality from Limited and Defective Data*, based on seminars held 16–24 September at Centro Latinoamericano de Demografia (CELADE), San Jose, Costa Rica.

Brass, W., Coale, A., Demeny, P. & Van de Walle, E. (eds) (1968) *The Demography of Tropical Africa*, Princeton, New Jersey, Princeton University Press.

Caldwell, J.C., Hill, A.G. & Hull, V.H. (1988) *Microapproaches to Demographic Research*, Kegan Hall International, London.

Ramachandran, K.V. (1983) 'Errors and deficiencies in basic data: overview of methods of detection, evaluation and adjustment', in RIPS: *Fertility and Mortality Estimation in Africa*, Occasional Publication of RIPS, University of Ghana, Legon.

Scoones, I. & Thompson, J. (1993) 'Beyond farmer first. Rural people's indigenous knowledge, agricultural research and extension practice: towards a theoretical framework', *IIED Research Series*, Vol.1(1).

United Nations (1983) *Indirect Techniques for Demographic Estimation*, Department of Economic and Social Affairs, Sales No.E.83.XIII.2, New York.

Van de Walle, E. (1968) 'Characteristics of African demographic data', in Brass, W. et al. (eds) (1968).

17 Participatory community-based health information systems for rural communities[1]

H. M. Oranga and E. Nordberg

Participatory methods of generating information aim at bridging the gap between those who collect information for development and those who are meant to benefit from it. This chapter describes an operational framework outlining the phases and actors in the development of a community-based health information system, involving community participation in planning, implementation, evaluation and utilization of the final system. A case study of a community-based health information system in a rural Kenyan population is discussed.

In this time of declining per-capita resource allocation to the health sector, it is unlikely that the health system will be able to expand its planning and monitoring capacity. It is therefore important that communities take a larger role in planning, implementation and monitoring of their own primary health care (PHC) services. The involvement of local communities in the generation of health information is, therefore, necessary. Participatory community-based health information systems (HIS) also help communities reduce dependency on the health system to identify their needs, set their priorities and monitor progress.

Participatory methods are associated more with community-based than with facility-based HIS. Health information is required by managers in order to make informed decisions during planning, implementation, monitoring and evaluation phases of projects and programmes. An effective PHC manager must be aware of the changing health conditions, coverage of health services, utilization of services and the amount and quality of resources (human, physical and financial) available to meet the objectives of the programme. PHC is based on a central strategy of community participation, including participation in the planning, implementation and monitoring of PHC services.

Methodology

The systems process
A health information system is a combination of people, equipment and data collection and processing methods that are coordinated to produce useful information needed for planning and management of a health-care delivery system. The participatory approach invites the involvement of the communities who are the intended users in the study design, implementation and evaluation; this increases the likelihood of acceptance and use of the study findings. Questions to be addressed therefore,

when developing community-based participatory research (PR) include: who plans the research? who is the community? what is the involvement of the poor, the less educated and the women in the participatory research? Who influences the next phases in the process?

Participatory research involving communities occurs at three levels: (i) *utilization* of the services and facilities provided by the project: (ii) *cooperation* with the initiatives planned by an outside agency: and (iii) *involvement* in planning and managing activities. While utilization is not itself considered true participation but rather a precondition, involvement is the highest form of participation and is usually what is meant by community participation. Without utilization, however, further participation is unlikely to occur. Most PR projects are of the cooperation type.

The success of community participation (CP) will depend on several attributes related to the community concerned. In past studies conducted in Latin America (PAHO 1984), the following characteristics of the community were found to influence the level and extent of its participation: geographical distribution (urban versus rural); how it was formed and developed; openness to change; a strong sense of social cohesion dictated by the degree of cultural heterogeneity; a high level of education; spatial concentration of the community; adequate communication and transportation facilities; presence of dynamic and enthusiastic leadership; community consciousness of its rights and responsibilities with regard to development; prevailing attitudes towards local community practices (e.g. traditional beliefs and practices).

The conceptual framework for PR in community participation helps structure a systematic analysis of projects in three dimensions: (1) mechanism/mode, i.e. the channels or structures through which CP occurs and how it occurs (individuals or organized groups, informal or formal, spontaneous or requested/imposed from outside); (2) breadth of CP, i.e. who participates (leaders, élites, women, minorities, youth)? how many? continuous or sporadic?; and (3) areas of CP: (a) planning, (b) implementation, (c) evaluation, including formal and informal ways of expressing community opinions regarding health activities. Studies have revealed that formally organized mechanisms appear to be more effective channels for CP than informal ones since they tend to be more lasting and conducive to group action. Further, the more closely linked to the community the mechanism is, the more likely the effectiveness in promoting participation. If a programme's aims include community involvement, responsibility and widespread behavioural change, very broad participation by a large proportion of important community groups will be necessary.

Implementation phase

Use of a community-based HIS comprises the following key activities:

- community mobilization and sensitization
- identification of community health information needs and priority setting
- appraisal and allocation of local resources to the system
- harmonization of implementation with Ministry of Health (MOH) system
- data collection
- data analysis
- management and supportive supervision of the system
- information dissemination and feedback systems
- use and storage of information generated.

Community mobilization and sensitization   Community mobilization should be conducted through public meetings, seminars and workshops facilitated by community leaders in the villages. Local administration officials (chiefs and their assistants) and councillors should also be asked to inform and mobilize the respective communities on the HIS by enlightening them as to its goals, objectives and coverage, including anticipated benefits.

Identification of community health information needs and priority setting The merits of a participatory community-based HIS rest on a number of hypotheses: people are more likely to take action on decisions which they have made; since community members have a broad image of their environment, their involvement will enhance their capability of conducting rational health care planning and management; and further, CP will improve awareness of the local health situation and the likely effects of various interventions, and improve the willingness of communities to initiate relevant health development activities.

A first step in establishing the system could be brainstorming discussion between parties involved, i.e. project implementers, extension workers and selected community leaders. This would involve sharing experiences and problems related to the aims of the HIS system. Communities are capable of assessing their own situation, evaluating options and opportunities and choosing the right course of action. However, they require the external support of professionals to facilitate the evaluation process. Participatory qualitative research techniques, such as participatory rural appraisal (PRA) and rapid rural appraisal (RRA) methodologies involving the researchers, extension workers and members of the community, should be used. The two approaches are often used to determine the needs and priorities of the community, with regard to health (Ramakrishna et al. 1993). The community at large should be consulted now and then, through key informants, focus groups and public meetings, on issues related to the system as the implementation progresses, and it should also be involved in the project work itself.

Household interview baseline surveys could, in addition, occasionally and sparingly be used for collecting the needed information. Other qualitative group methods, such as Delphi[2] panels and nominal group techniques (NGT), could also be applied.

Appraisal and allocation of local resources to the system   In order to put up a system, resources (human, financial and supplies) are necessary. A community-based HIS must be planned on the basis of locally available resources. After identifying the types and volume of information required, the question is what resources are needed and/or available locally for the implementation. The qualitative methods of PRA and RRA are again very helpful at this stage and are therefore recommended.

Nomination of the interviewers should be done by all members of the community at a public meeting while under professional guidance from HIS specialists. Interviewers should, where possible, be selected from members of the community within the village. The selection of interviewers from within the cluster has several advantages, namely it:

- promotes a sustainable and community-friendly HIS system
- ensures lower cost of implementation
- is more convenient to the work of the interviewer since he/she is at home
- improves the friendliness and working relationship between interviewers, supervisors and the community
- promotes accelerated interaction and information feedback within the cluster
- fosters interest of the key players in the HIS system
- encourages more use of the information collected
- establishes the sense of ownership of the system by the community

The selected interviewers and their supervisors must be trained before deployment to implement the system. They should be given orientation and taught how to conduct household interview surveys and how to use the information collected. In particular, the areas to be taught should include:

- how to approach a respondent
- ways of enhancing public relations and rapport with the respondents
- how to conduct a successful interview and
- techniques of minimizing non-response rates.

For every HIS instrument and techniques to be introduced, interviewers must be re-trained and exposed to a field pre-testing exercise before being left on their own. Every interviewer should conduct at least one interview during the pre-testing exercise. In order to promote smooth supervision and system efficiency, interviewers should be trained regularly, probably at intervals of two years. Some findings have shown that mere re-training of health workers like community health workers (CHWs) is all that is needed for sustainability and reduced attrition rate, rather than direct incentives like salaries and allowances.

There are some methods of data collection such as the Delphi technique, focus group and informal interviews with key informants which cannot be handled by the interviewers as these are beyond their capabilities. Their supervisors, that is, health workers at the nearest health facilities, should be trained so that they facilitate the implementation.

Harmonization of implementation with Ministry of Health system   There are two types of health information systems, namely facility- and community-based HIS. In order to understand the structure and functioning of the Ministry of Health (MOH) system, a descriptive study should be undertaken by interviewing key informants and policy makers of the ministry's health system.

Given that any community-based system is supposed to support the facility-based source, compliance with the MOH is mandatory and important for the long-term sustainability of the system. For such a system, the local health workers at the facilities should be placed such that the information generated passes through them for any referral and prompt action that may be necessary, as in the case of an epidemic outbreak. It is normal to engage the nurses and clinical officers in charge of the nearest health centres and dispensary as first-level supervisors of the community-based HIS. Eventually, all the data collected must be accessible to the same health workers in charge before onward transmission to the higher levels of authority in the government. The harmonization process is not costly.

Data collection   Techniques and instruments for data collection are among the most important components of a community-based HIS. The methods and questionnaires for data collection should be simple to understand, easy and cheap to implement and fast to analyse, comprehend and interpret. They should be capable of producing timely information without unnecessary cost, bearing in mind the meagre financial and physical resources available in developing countries. Moreover, people in these communities are semi-literate and hence should not be loaded with complex statistical survey methods and bulky questionnaires. The number of questions included should be minimal and should solicit only the information identified by the community as its priority need for local health care management and planning. Do not overload the questionnaire with questions aimed at collecting the ideal data necessary for such activities. The questions should be simple, clear, precise and unambiguous. It is only then that valid, consistent and comparable information can be collected on a long-term basis.

Operational research studies have shown that longitudinal surveys should be avoided as much as possible in community-based health information systems. They are more complicated to design, implement and analyse. They require a fair amount of experience and management capability, and also active participation of people. Longitudinal studies consume huge financial outlays of resources that are beyond the financing capacity of such communities. Moreover, the methodology is characterized by a growing amount of respondent fatigue and frustration over time. Where the information is highly desirable, as is the case when monitoring health conditions and care-seeking behaviour, longitudinal surveys should be undertaken only at the district level, every 4–5 years and with a one-month interview-recall period (Oranga & Nordberg 1992).

It is recommended that cross-sectional surveys be incorporated into the community-based HIS and be repeated every two years. The surveys should be designed to solicit information on:

- demographic characteristics;
- socio-economic conditions;
- nutrition and environmental factors;
- morbidity and mortality of chronic health conditions; and
- disability conditions.

Household interviews exploring illness episodes should ask probing questions on a small number of illness categories in order to overcome respondents' memory loss and their own inability to interpret reported symptom combinations. A list of 8–10 broad illness categories should be printed on the illness-recall questionnaire in order to facilitate classification on the basis of experiences with reported symptoms. Based on flow charts, interviewers should be trained to diagnose the conditions.

The Delphi technique described extensively by Delbecq et al. (1975) and Masser and Foley (1987) is likely to reflect more of the truth regarding mild illness episodes and conditions, which are not seen at health facilities for one reason or another and do not, therefore, appear in facility-based morbidity statistics. We see good reasons to make selective use of the Delphi method, locally adapted, and to focus more upon otherwise hidden and poorly known issues, such as chronic conditions, permanent disability, mental illness and socio-cultural factors associated with disease perception, self-care and care-seeking behaviour. The Delphi technique is cost-effective (Oranga & Nordberg 1993). Collection of data by Delphi methods should be facilitated by local health workers with support from the district-level professionals. A Delphi study should be conducted at the same frequency as the cross-sectional surveys, that is, repeated every two years.

The Delphi technique is a qualitative research methodology. If more detailed, quantitative information on the way local people perceive causes and management of different diseases is required, and if appropriate preventive and curative counter-measures are needed, then a small-scale socio-cultural study could be implemented. Even though the questionnaire and interview schedule could be fairly exhaustive, thus providing adequate information, some of the health problems, such as healthcare-seeking behaviour, need ethnographic methods of data collection, using focus group discussions, intercepts, informal interviews and participant observation. A combination of different methods would strengthen the validity of the data. As in the case of the Delphi technique, focus group discussions and informal interviews with key informants should be undertaken with the professional health workers.

Data analysis At the village level, interviewers and their supervisors should be trained in how to analyse part of the data in less detailed form, as totals, averages and associations. The information should be presented mainly in the form of graphs, charts and pictograms. Important series of information should be identified and analysed routinely. Generally, data to be analysed at the village level should include:

- demographic patterns and profiles, e.g. number of births by age and sex;
- morbidity, e.g. number of persons ill by type of illness, age and sex and types of disability;
- mortality by age and sex;
- nutrition by age and sex;
- environmental health, i.e. water and sanitation; and
- immunization.

The rest of the data emanating from the system should be analysed at divisional or higher levels.

Management and supportive supervision of the system Management of the HIS system should be under the village health committee (VHC) whose composition should be determined by village members at a public meeting and irrespective of age, gender, legal, political or socio-economic status. Since over 80 percent of the rural population consists of women and they are the people who are confronted with the myriad of health problems, women should be proportionately elected into the VHCs. Because of their gender roles, most women are either too busy to take on additional roles or are illiterate. Hence a majority of the VHCs are run by men. The VHC becomes responsible for the management of the system but with facilitation from the health personnel in the division or district. Smooth and conducive supervision of the HIS can be achieved by:

- Incorporation of village elders (ex-officio members of VHCs) and respondents into the keeping of records/diaries of the days when visited by the interviewer.

- Asking the interviewers to programme and develop long-term plans of when it would be convenient for them to visit specific households. The roster should be kept by all the parties involved in the HIS, i.e. interviewer, village elder, supervisor, respondent and the VHC chairperson.
- Frequent visits to the community by MOH officials, especially from the district level through the divisional structure.
- Follow-up of identified complicated cases of ill-health conditions needing referrals by the local health workers.

Supervisory activities should involve making field spot-checks by the immediate supervisors and members of the district-level MOH to ensure that implementation is within an agreed plan. Internal consistency and completeness of information should be controlled through rigorous editing of completed questionnaires by supervisors, both in the field and office. Interviewers should forward completed questionnaires to their supervisors for scrutiny before analysis is done.

Information dissemination and feedback Every properly designed HIS system must have well-defined and efficient channels of information dissemination and feedback. Given that consumers of the information are primarily community members, the majority of whom are semi-literate, the form and means of disseminating the information must be easy and simple to understand. More graphical and pictorial presentations are recommended for such an audience.

Throughout the implementation of the HIS, a lot of information is generated. This information is often required for other intermediate interventions to be instituted. Hence the feedback channels should be connected to all the activities going on within the system. They should be efficient and dynamic enough to monitor changes taking place at any given time and at the same time revise the database promptly for the next actions to be taken.

Dissemination of the information must be done carefully. Confidentiality of the information relating to individual households must be ensured. According to most Statistical Acts, it is an offence to disclose to the public any information relating to one or two parties without their prior written consent. This means, therefore, that only summaries or totals involving at least three respondents could be disclosed for public consumption. Interviewers should be made aware of this important legal requirement during their training.

In order for the information to reach many users, the dissemination should be carried out during public meetings; social and religious gatherings of women's groups and churches could be alternative avenues. Wherever finances allow, seminars and workshops for community leaders should be organized. In some cases, establishment of community information resource centres has been recommended. Such centres should store information relating to sectors other than health. At the centres, notice-boards should be put in place and any relevant and routine information generated by the HIS displayed for the general public. The more detailed information should be locked away.

Finally, it is important that information generated by the systems is forwarded to the district level in order to solicit support and appropriate interventions by mobilizing the resources set aside for the activities in the district. The feedback system should send back views and responses from the higher levels through the same channels. This latter flow of information is most appropriate in the government system. It stimulates and encourages greater community participation, ensuring the greater success of the project.

Use and storage of information generated One central assumption related to community-based HIS is that access to broader health information will motivate the community, improving its ability and increasing its willingness to analyse local health problems and formulate appropriate interventions. Proponents of community participation also believe strongly that dependency on community contributions will enhance local community involvement in programme development and monitoring.

Members of the VHC should be trained in the use of information generated by the system for their local health care planning and management. During the training, emphasis should be laid on the role of health information for the general management (resources and HIS system), epidemiology, short- and medium-term planning and health programming.

A case study in rural Kenya

The Integrated District Diagnosis and Health Planning Project was a three-year study carried out in Kibwezi Division, Makueni District in eastern Kenya between 1989 and 1992 (Oranga & Nordberg 1992). The purpose of the study was to test a broadened but low-cost community-oriented HIS with the overall goal of helping health care become more in tune with the needs of local communities through locally identified priorities. The project proposal was conceptualized and formulated by African Medical and Research Foundation (AMREF) after several consultations with health workers and MOH officials, together with field visits to the area. No PRA exercises were conducted to solicit information on the needs and priorities of the community, in terms of information requirements for local PHC management and planning. The drawback of not conducting the PRA was manifested clearly by the resolutions of the end-of-project seminar discussed below.

Household-health interviews were conducted in 390 households from 12 clusters (villages). Twenty-six non-medically trained persons, comprising 15 men and 11 women, were recruited as interviewers from within each cluster, with medically trained health workers from the nearby local health facilities as supervisors. The literate adults and CHWs emerged as the best personnel, in terms of dedication, trustworthiness and community acceptance. Respondents in the household interviews were the heads of household; for illness, only those affected were interviewed. For children below 15 years of age, however, mothers were interviewed as proxies.

Public meetings were held in the respective villages in order to inform community members and local leaders about the aims and objectives of the study, and about their expected roles and the possible benefits for them. It was at these public meetings that nominations for candidates to be engaged as interviewers were held, by the communities themselves in accordance with certain minimum-required qualification criteria set by the project leader. The final selection was conducted by the project leader after a written examination.

Although in this project interviewers were paid some field allowance for their efforts, other financial incentives were avoided. Some incentives should be provided by the community itself, however. At the reporting seminar organized at the end of the project, the community leaders in attendance suggested the annual provision of special gifts and privileges, through funds raised by the community. It was reckoned that such incentives were necessary for the long-term sustainability of the system.

In order further to ensure its sustainability, the community-based HIS was designed to fit into and supplement the existing MOH system. Hence there was early involvement of the local health personnel, divisional extension personnel, the district health management team (DHMT) and the local-government administration officials. Health workers in charge of the local health facilities participated as first-level supervisors in the system. These interviewers were instructed to refer any seriously ill cases to the nearest health facilities. The referral system was operationally effective.

This case study revealed that longitudinal studies are very costly and should be undertaken only rarely in community-based HIS systems (maybe at the district level at 4–5 yearly intervals). The study found that for any longitudinal study monitoring illness conditions and healthcare-seeking behaviour, an optimum recall period was between 1 and 3 months. It was found, however, that a cross-sectional survey conducted at intervals of 2 years, at the same time, supported by a Delphi panel, was feasible. A socio-cultural study was also found to be useful, particularly when supplemented by such techniques as focus group discussions and key-informant interviews.

In order to disseminate the project's findings, two reporting seminars were held at the end of the project; the first for the project field implementers (interviewers and supervisors), and the second for the community through its leaders (local administration, politicians and women's groups), including those running and managing the local health care system. The use of group-interviewing methods such as Delphi panels also contributed significantly to enlisting more participatory commitment (Oranga & Nordberg 1993). The role of the interviewers was noted as significant. The majority of the interviewers admitted that they had become accepted in the community as 'doctors', since most sick individuals were approaching them for consultations when ill. Quite often, they were asked for their opinions on health issues and epidemics in the village, as well as PHC development issues. It was evident, therefore, that for a community-based HIS interviewers should be trained in the basic principles of PHC. In this context, a literate adult in the village who is trained in PHC could prove to be a better and more reliable interviewer than a CHW recruited as an interviewer from within the cluster. This is because a CHW working in her/his own cluster would tend to fix the collected data to suit the expected situation.

At the end-of-project seminar, the community leaders identified as priority information, required for their local health care planning and management at community level, data on: demography, morbidity, immunization coverage and nutrition, a very important function which could have been achieved by conducting PRA at the beginning of the project as described above. The community representatives recognized the need to establish information resource centres in their respective villages for the dissemination of the generated information. This was a sign of the impact of their involvement and participation in the study right from the start. They had now realized and recognized that it was their responsibility to initiate such activities for their own well-being. They, however, requested some assistance in terms of professional support from the government and AMREF, to enable them to establish the HIS before being left on their own. Thus, while the 1989-92 study involved development and testing of the HIS, the next phase of the project will be concerned with the implementation of the system by the communities themselves.

Conclusion

Many project failures have been attributed to the fact that important project actors and partners were not fully involved in the project management process, including project planning. The early involvement of the community and local health workers in a participatory HIS will help develop commitment to the project and facilitate the project's implementation.

It is feasible technically and practically to establish a participatory community-based HIS in developing countries where the general population is resource-poor and less educated. The community must be involved right from the project conception stage and during the planning phase. Although the idea for a research project normally originates outside the community, it has to address the problems or needs related to the community at hand. A community-based HIS must collect only relevant information needed by the community for its own use and should avoid gathering too much unnecessary information which is not of immediate use. It is mandatory, therefore, that PRA be conducted at the initial stages of implementation in order to involve the community in identifying the information needs and priority settings as relevant and essential for local health care management and planning. The researchers should spend some time educating and sensitizing the community on the goal(s) and objectives of the project. It is also strongly recommended that group-interviewing techniques such as focus groups, Delphi panels and nominal group technique (NGT) be incorporated into the systems. At all levels of implementation, a flexible and dynamic information feedback system also should be put in place in order to enhance efficient and timely use of the generated information as well as providing back-up to the management and supportive supervision of the system.

At the community level, local administrators and politicians such as assistant chiefs, councillors and village elders are more useful during the time of awareness creation, education and sensitization of the community than are the senior administration officials and extension staff. The long-term sustainability of a participatory community-based HIS is ensured mainly by providing some incentives to the interviewers. Wherever possible, the HIS should utilize the locally available resources and avoid too much dependence on external support. The idea of a community-based HIS is feasible. The system should be designed operationally to be cheap, simple, easy to implement and replicable in other parts of the country.

Notes

1. The International Development Research Centre (IDRC) and the Swedish Agency for Research Cooperation with Developing Countries (SAREC) provided the financial support for the study. Contributions from local administration officials, health workers, other government extension staff in Kibwezi Division and all members of the project team are highly acknowledged.
2. The Delphi technique, developed as a forecasting technique at the RAND Corporation in the US around 1950, generates and combines written judgements from individuals on a particular question, with the aim of forming a consensus. First-round judgements are aggregated and then presented individually to each of the respondents who respond without face-to-face

contact with other panel members, all of whom remain unknown to each other. This process may continue through several rounds until a satisfactory degree of consensus has been reached.

References

Delbecq, A.L., van de Ven, A.H. & Gustafson, D.H. (1975) *Group Techniques for Programme Planning. A Guide to Nominal Group and Delphi Processes*, Scott, Foresman and Co., Glenview, USA.

Masser, I. & Foley, P. (1987) 'Delphi revisited: expert opinion in urban analysis', *Urban Studies*, Vol.24, pp.217-25.

Oranga, H. M. & Nordberg, E. (1992) *Integrated District Diagnosis and Health Planning (Kenya)*, Final Report, African Medical & Research Foundation (AMREF) (Mimeo).

Oranga, H. M. & Nordberg, E. (1993) 'The Delphi panel method for generating health information', *Health Policy and Planning*, Vol.8(4), pp.405-12.

PAHO (Pan American Health Organization) (1984) *Community Participation in Health and Development in the Americas. An Analysis of Selected Case Studies*, Scientific Publications No.473, Washington, DC.

Ramakrishna, J., Chung, K.R. & Bentley, M. (1993) 'A participatory approach to identifying food and nutrition security', paper presented at the International Symposium on Participatory Research in Health Promotion, Liverpool School of Tropical Medicine, 17–21 September.

PART VII PARTICIPATORY RESEARCH IN THE WORKPLACE

18 Using participatory research to enhance health in the work setting: an Australian experience

Jan E. Ritchie

Australian society is probably viewed by much of the rest of the world as egalitarian, having progressed beyond the defined class system of our British forefathers and currently offering what are seen to be unequalled opportunities to anyone living in this so-called lucky country. Behind this initial bright picture of equality, equity and mateship lies however, a more sombre portrayal of those who have and those who have not. We are doing a relatively poor job in addressing the needs of Aboriginals, of women, of lower-income workers, of the unemployed and of people from non-English–speaking backgrounds. This lack of care and resources for members of these groups is generally true for basic needs, and no less for health.

The participatory action research described in this chapter evolved in an attempt to explore more effective ways of improving the lot of one of these groups, that of lower-income workers.

Background

Epidemiological research in recent years has indicated the links between health status and socio-economic factors in the Australian scene (National Health Strategy 1992). But while the quality of the research has been high, studies demonstrating what we in Australia are doing about these problems show very few results for our efforts. While the health of all Australians continues to improve, the gap between the well-resourced and well-educated and those more disadvantaged remains (Ritchie et al. 1994).

On this basis, it seemed to make sense to attempt to explore these issues further and consider innovative approaches that the literature was suggesting needed to be researched. One of the settings that attracted my attention as a potential intervention base was the work setting. An organization employing large numbers of unskilled or semi-skilled workers might prove to be an appropriate place in which to explore these issues. People spend a third of their day at work, the social and ecological factors in their environment can be relatively easily explored, and it appeared to be an appropriate way for me to reach a disadvantaged group such as low-income workers. The work setting as such is a defined community, one where I could legitimately explore community-based strategies.

Over the past fifteen years I have undertaken many health promotion programmes in the workplace. The conventional approach in Australia has followed the US model, consisting of measuring the health risks of a group, offering education, information or counselling on what lifestyle changes should be made to reduce these risks and then re-measuring (Terborg 1988). I was disillusioned with this approach. Not only did management decisions on health promotion favour programmes for executives rather than workers, when workers were included the pro- gramme was rarely tailored to their needs. Evaluation of this type of programme has shown poor results (Ritchie et al. 1994).

The Australian work setting brings with it some traditions that assist in enhancing the health of its inhabitants, epitomized in the New South Wales (NSW) legislation which states that 'every employer must ensure the health and safety at work of his employees' (OH&S Act 1983, Section 15). In addition, the current workplace reform that is occurring in this country is based on guidelines that are consistent with health promotion principles of community participation and intersectoral collaboration. Together with the principles of promoting the health of individuals and communities as outlined in the Ottawa Charter (WHO 1986), a broad health-promoting agenda could be pursued that might be much more effective than the conventional approach I had rejected.

Along with my desire to address the needs of low-income workers, I was aware of another problem. Part of my recognition of the need for the research arose from my daily interactions with the health profession- als that I teach in the WHO Regional Training Centre for Health Development at the University of New South Wales. Our students are all health professionals of various disciplines – nurses, doctors, allied health personnel, dentists, pharmacists – and come from a great variety of cultural backgrounds, for example Asia, the Pacific nations, Australia and elsewhere. Some come to us for a short-term learning experience; more undertake higher degrees over a longer time period. All intend to use their newly gained higher qualifications to assume key positions in administra- tion, education and human resource development in the public health systems of their own countries.

As I worked with this diverse student body over a period of some years, I came to realize that what I was teaching made sense theoretically to these people trained in conventional Western medicine and health sciences, but that they were unable to see easy ways to apply this new knowledge because it did not fit with their previous experience. In most cases, their undergraduate training had focused to such an extent on their becoming experts in their field that it had succeeded in building a barrier between them and the communities they wished to serve. They were trained actively to provide care and cure, to make decisions on behalf of patients and community members, and to act with authority. They were accustomed to instructing, directing or, at the very least, guiding patients. Community participation and all it stood for did not fit into their daily view of their work. They all wholeheartedly agreed with the WHO definition of health promotion as 'a process of enabling people to increase control of and improve their health' (WHO 1986), but when we came to explore how they would undertake this process of enabling, they were unsure of how to proceed.

I needed to find out what this process consisted of in order better to teach it. Theories and conceptual frameworks abounded on all facets of community involvement. What was lacking was a systematic observation of the constituents of a supportive environment for health. Just as importantly, it seemed imperative to identify the components of this dynamic process of enabling, particularly in the cases where the enabling was done by people with very different characteristics from those whose health they wanted to help improve.

In summary, then, this study was prompted both by a desire to see more constructive approaches to promoting the health of those most in need in Australia, along with a desire to teach health professionals the principles of enabling. What eventually evolved was a study which took place over more than eighteen months and was designed to explore and document the process of enabling a group of semi-skilled blast-furnace operators and other steelworkers to take control of and improve their health.

The method

Certain elements had to be present if this research would do what I wanted it to do. First, it was only going to work if I as researcher could work *with* participants rather than do research *on* them; the element of control was a central issue. Second, I wanted to address concerns raised by participants rather than by those in decision-making positions senior to them. In particular, I realized that the delineation between occupational-health and personal-health issues existed only in the minds of the authorities. Third, I wanted to document all aspects of a detailed case study. I was not interested in comparisons between different groups with controlled variables, but preferred instead to explore all collective particulars within a chosen, specific setting. I was concerned, finally, not only in documenting what is, but in moving with participants to what should be.

The research method that I felt met all the above requirements was participatory action research. As Maguire puts it so succinctly: 'the purpose of participatory research is not only to describe and interpret social reality, but radically to change it' (Maguire 1987:28). I wanted to describe the work setting both in my terms and in those of my partners in the project, and to interpret the meanings arising from this description. I found it important to work with small groups to address issues causing concern and see if we could make changes. All three components of my intended research appeared in Maguire's statement.

McTaggart (1992) discusses the phrase 'participatory action research' which he sees as a convergence of two terms: 'action research' and 'participatory research'. Action research, he suggests, has grown from the work of Lewin and has been actively pursued in Australia, especially in education and in management research. Participatory research has origi-nated in community development approaches in developing countries. To me, the theoretical basis of both these research approaches in critical social science is identical, focusing as they do on emancipation, collabo-ration and empowerment, but the practice has differed. In this country, more reported action research has been with groups who already have a degree of control and power in their social situation, for example, teachers and managers. In contrast, participatory research has developed with those more obviously disempowered. I see that the major difference between these two types of research lies in the description of the relationship between the instigating researcher and the other partici-pants. In action research with teachers and managers the instigator is most likely to be one of their own kind, with shared values and similar use of language. In participatory research, the instigator may be from a different sub-culture if that person is better resourced and more highly educated than the other participants. Since McTaggart's recent work has been with Aboriginal Australians, where lack of power through colonization is probably extreme, the term 'participatory action research' seems most appropriate for it. I suggest it is most appropriate for this project also.

The research sequence

Having made my decision to undertake participatory action research, I proceeded to pass through a defined sequence of stages that together composed my attempt to answer the research questions posed. These stages are now explained in detail.

Entry. My initial task was to find a research setting. After some exploratory inquiries, I made contact with a range of industrial sites, expecting to take a considerable time to find a setting where I was welcome. Within a very short time however, I was invited by a depart-ment of the large steelworks that has long existed south of Sydney to set up my study with employees on the smallest of the company's three blast-furnaces. This company is the largest employer of blue-collar workers in Australia. The blast-furnace has around forty employees of whom all are male and most are semi-skilled heavy industrial workers employed as blast-furnace operators. Other employees include qualified technical assistants, tradesmen and a few in middle-management positions.

I was determined to take the preparatory steps very cautiously. In the initiation of participatory action research, in an ideal situation the impetus should come from the participants. Since here the impetus had to come from me, as I was instigating the whole project, I wanted it to be absolutely clear that my purpose in being involved was for the benefit of the employees, first and foremost. My personal research aims would have to take second place. So my first piece of groundwork was to submit a document to the organization clarifying my intentions and making it clear that I was working towards getting mechanisms in place for health improvement. If health outcomes improved, this would be a bonus, but the activities were the important aspect. Immediately following on this step, I sought the written agreement, in principle, of senior management and of officials of the major trade union representing these employees. This was given without hesitation by both parties and my confidence rose promptly. I was learning from the start that it paid to phrase my requests regarding the project in words that reflected each stakeholder's perspective. Management agreed with my proposal that *worker participation for health-outcomes* was as important as for *productivity-outcomes*, and the union agreed that a project aiming for the *empowerment of workers* should definitely be supported.

Also as part of my preparation, I had to start becoming accustomed to the culture of this huge, unfamiliar organization. I needed to learn to recognize where I could have freedom to get involved and thus feel part of the place and, very importantly, to observe stringently the physical and organizational limits beyond which I would not be welcome. Help was forthcoming here in the form of the human-resource officer of this department. He proved to be invaluable in giving me all the information I required. I learned the history of the place, the current mission of the organization and the existing management structure. I became aware of the fact that in a hazardous working environment like this one, occupational health and safety issues were a key component of all decisions and activities. I met with a small advisory committee which enabled me to translate my somewhat fanciful goals into down-to-earth, practical reality and which helped me to set a constructive time-frame of eighteen months for the project. I took home books and videos on the iron-making process and I was allocated my own set of protective clothing.

Finally, we arrived at the critical part of the entry phase: inviting the employees to participate. On the advice of the advisory committee, I had prepared a brief presentation, supported with some graphics in cartoon form. Taking advantage of a furnace shut-down for maintenance reasons, I was able to present my case to each of the four teams working the four shifts, and invite their involvement. The degree of interest ranged from enthusiasm to neutral acceptance, with no outward antagonism, for which I was grateful. At the end of the meeting with the last group, the general foreman led me through a safety induction, showing me over the whole furnace and familiarizing me with the aspects I had so far only met from the safe distance of company records or on video. The project was now underway.

Getting to know each other. This phase occurred over the following two months. Not only did I have to continue the familiarization process that had commenced in the first phase, I now had to provide an opportunity for the furnace workers to get to know me. I saw this as an extremely sensitive component of participatory research. Unless I could build enough trust between them and me, the whole project would be a failure. One of the situations I had experienced often in the past as a health professional was feeling different from community members, being well-resourced and highly educated. Those whose health I had found most at risk were more often less-resourced and less-educated. I realized there would be a marked gap between us. This time I was also introducing another barrier, that of gender, since *all* the furnace workers were male. (The only two other females I met in my whole eighteen months of visits were two cleaners, whom I met regularly in the toilet block near the furnace car park.) In the past, I had managed to find ways of overcoming barriers and limitations in order to bridge this sub-cultural gap and was intent on meeting this challenge in this instance.

Every Wednesday, with fear and trepidation, I would leave home before daylight to make the two-hour journey. As I neared the industrial area, I had to be prepared to brave the hazards of mountain fog and processions of coal trucks screaming to deliver their loads to the steelworks at the same time as I arrived. Then, invariably, I would get lost within the works for the first few weeks, reminding myself as I drove round in circles that the culture of the steelworks demanded that one gave way to trains, trucks, cars and pedestrians in that order of priority. Anyone foolish enough to think otherwise was at risk of perishing! Finally I would find the furnace office, rush into the toilet block to don my cotton overalls, steel-toed boots, furnace jacket, glare glasses, ear plugs and hard hat, and at last present myself at the superintendent's office. The most fearful part of the whole day was climbing from there to the furnace itself, as we had to walk past the stoves, literally screaming with compressed gases, and disconcertingly changing pitch just as I walked by them; quite a normal process but one I never accepted with equanimity. I learnt to accept the heat, the glare, the dirt, the dust, the fumes, the gases, but never the stoves. Another very different factor in this project made me fearful, that of the open-endedness of the task. Survey research, with which I was highly familiar, had always been so prescriptive and I knew each step of what had to be done, but here I had to play it by ear.

My confidence returned on arriving at the furnace floor as the men made me feel so welcome. I made it clear that we could not start the project properly until I understood what their jobs entailed. They became quite accepting of me moving from floor to crib-room to control room, asking questions, observing and jotting my opinions in my little blue book. It was a whole new world to me. I became familiar with the steelworkers' jargon, with the physical demands of their jobs and the social relationships that existed. I observed the organizational structures in place, and attended meetings of relevant committees to increase my understanding. I came to regard the furnace as a beneficent dragon; on the one hand, a provider of a living, on the other, a breather of fire and fumes, threatening life and limb if not treated with the utmost respect.

At the same time, the steelworkers were beginning to get to know me. Unless I could gain their trust, I could not progress. Some of them made it clear they had been 'researched upon' in the past, and they regarded me with similar suspicion. I valued their honesty and told them so, which seemed to help. Others immediately opened up and revealed very personal aspects of their lives. It seemed the difference in gender, occupation and living locality allowed them to see me as so different that they could expose themselves, knowing I would have little opportunity of spreading their revelations where they could hurt. I spent time over many cups of tea just chatting to them as they came sweating and red-faced into the crib-room, their responsibilities on the floor temporarily relinquished, unwinding in air-conditioned comfort away from the ubiquitous molten metal which they informed me was at a temperature of a mere 1,500 degrees Celsius. I was now beginning to know them by name and to recognize some of their patterns of daily existence.

Generating concerns. The next phase was to learn from the steelworkers themselves what they perceived as health concerns. It was their suggestion that this be done by individual interview, as they pointed out the difficulty of gaining balanced contributions in a small-group discussion, with each meeting open to potential interruption due to the constancy of the furnace's anticipated demands and the need to be prepared always for unanticipated ones. By this stage, also, they appeared comfortable with me, and I agreed they could possibly raise more personal issues and cover points more expansively on a one-to-one basis. The four teams were working on a rotating-shift schedule, rostered sequentially on day shift, afternoon shift, night shift or off-duty. Over a period of a month, I managed to interview all members of each shift as they worked on the day shift, missing only a few men who were on holiday or sick leave. I tape-recorded and transcribed thirty-five interviews, and then listed the participants' concerns according to how often each item was mentioned. Their collective health concerns fitted into six issue categories, those of: job design, especially shiftwork and stress; job environment, mainly the physical environment; inadequate or inappropriate equipment or re-sources on the job; company policy that they felt had a health impact; personal-health concerns such as smoking, drinking, eating or exercising; and, finally, health issues around living in the vicinity of an industrial township.

These priority concerns were fed back to each shift. In view of the fact that the company had agreed to support the men in addressing any 'reasonable' concerns, I felt it was important to also inform management. Consequently, I sent a brief summary copy to the departmental manager, the blast-furnace superintendent, and the human-resource officer, and gained clearance to proceed from all of them. I also sent a copy to the union representative, as I had promised to keep him informed as we proceeded. By this time I had learnt that this liaising, informing role appeared to be an essential component of enabling; those occasions where I omitted to inform all parties proved to be the most problematic within the project.

Participatory action. The central activity of the project was now about to be an actuality. I prepared to record this phase through field notes that I would jot down briefly during our discussions, intending to expand them immediately on returning home. I realized taping would be out of the question in the noisy conditions of the crib-room. The list of concerns was peered over with interest, and each shift had the opportu-nity of nominating a problem which they would be particularly keen to address. Expressions of interest in being involved came unsolicited from most individuals, and there was no doubt of their willing participation. The biggest barrier was going to be the same hindrance found earlier in the project when attempting to identify concerns as a group: the difficulty in predicting the furnace's needs and the men's obligation to respond instantly when required. I deliberated for days over how best to cope with this situation. Nowhere in the literature did it say what to do if the practicalities of conducting small-group discussions for action research or for participatory research were limited. I decided, in the end, that all I could do would be to regard it as a challenge. It would be impossible within the limitations of the workers' rotating-shift roster to ask any one of them to be involved in their free time; the only alternatives were to grab whatever we could, or to give up. With such positive responses, we refused to give up and chose instead to make the most of difficult circumstances.

Thus I tolerated various degrees of participant involvement in our planning and implementing cycles. This ranged from having all men present except the two on watch (the control room and the furnace floor always demanded supervision), down occasionally to losing all comers to an emergency call and having to sip my cup of tea alone! Despite the limitations, I enjoyed their enthusiasm. Between my visits some of them worked very hard. They explored practices in other divisions or on other worksites, dug out relevant documents, they even undertook surveys across all four shifts to investigate degrees of support for their recommended changes.

Acting on concerns expressed. The day prior to each visit, I would send a fax to remind them of my intention to meet with them. On arrival as predicted, I would report briefly to the superintendent's office before making my way up to the furnace. In using the public address system to request entry permission from the control-room staff, I would further announce my presence. My second reporting would be to the general foreman of the shift on duty. If the furnace was behaving and the men were between castings, we would start our discussion immediately. The crib-room was situated very close to the furnace floor to aid the men's vigilance. It served as a retreat from the fumes, dust and heat, where they could relax under air-conditioning and enjoy tea breaks, consume their lunch, read the papers, or play dominoes and draughts. During their whole eight-hour shift, this was the furthest away from the floor they could go. It was clearly the logical place for our discussions. Through linking my faxes with my field notes, I was able to record and interpret all that occurred.

Over the next eight months, we proceeded to meet for vigorous discussions. The process of our discussions was considerably aided by the company's recent policy of total quality management. Worker participation was an integral component of this approach and was spelt out in detail in the Australian Steel Industry Development Agreement. All employees were offered training in how to contribute to better productivity through small-group actions. It was easy enough to implement the same process for health outcomes instead of productivity ones. In fact, this aspect should not be underestimated in considering whether this project will eventually be deemed to be successful or otherwise. The existence of commitment by management to worker input meant that mechanisms were already in place through which to channel ideas arising from our small groups. My challenge was to get our concerns on to the broad agenda and to try to find ways of keeping them there after I withdrew at the end of the project.

One of the first points for discussion was that the workers had found it easy to voice their health concerns to me during the individual interviews, but they wanted help in clarifying what else might be health problems. They believed expert advice could help here. After much negotiation with the Occupational Health and Safety (OH&S) Department of the company, an opportunity was given to our group to have health risk appraisals carried out by an occupational health nurse. Results were fed back to participants immediately and counselling was provided in the occasional instances when abnormal readings were found. It was interesting that the men did not appear to view the results as a basis on which to make health behaviour changes. Just as I had found in the past, the new knowledge was rarely acted on. Instead, the assessments were seen as providing an indication of being valued by the company in relation to senior executives who were routinely offered this service. For this reason alone, we as a group asked that health risk appraisals continue to be offered on a periodic basis.

Similarly, the small groups discussed the blast-furnace environment and the risks it posed. With me acting as broker between management, the Environment Department and the OH&S Department on behalf of our small groups, we gained agreement for the furnace area to be monitored for fumes, dust, gases and noise levels. Although this was done periodically, it was extremely valuable for it to be done as part of our project so we could take further action where required. We complained about the technical language of the ensuing environment reports and asked if, in future, these could be worded in a form understandable to employees so they could be more useful.

During this period, the groups worked through the cyclical process of posing a problem related to the concerns arising in the interviews, deliberating over issues around the problem and then discussing ways of seeking a solution. They definitely relied on me to turn up and get the ball rolling. It was made perfectly clear when I was not able to appear for a month that everything would come to a stop in my absence.

The range of issues dealt with was considerable. Overcoming the health impacts of shiftwork generated enormous interest in investigating alternative rostering schedules; concerns about company policies in relation to the wearing of protective gear led to the formal appointment of a sub-committee to investigate all heat-resistant clothing; a stop-smoking group asked for assistance from a consultant psychologist and gained permission for this to proceed; alternatives were explored to put more physical exercise into the day of technical assistants who spent all the shift in front of computer screens; an innovative hearing-conservation scheme was set up to promote positive rather than punitive ways of using noise-protective gear; the list went on and on, and time rather than enthusiasm was the limitation.

Reflection and evaluation. Since I had agreed to wind down the project at the end of the eighteen-month period, we considered how best to do this. I drafted a report summarizing my perceptions of what had occurred, and then fed this back to the workers at individual interviews to ascertain if they were in agreement. This draft report also went to the union and to the OH&S Department. The members of this department had now become our close friends and allies, since they were as keen as we were to see health improvements. Most of our solutions were just beginning to be implemented or not yet able to come to fruition. We felt it imperative that our recommendations focus primarily on the sustainability of the project mechanisms rather than on the outcome of each of our action-research cycles. Twenty-four more interviews allowed verification that the report represented the views of all of us collectively.

With the final blessing of the furnace superintendent and the OH&S personnel, we eventually submitted our report to senior management, with copies to all relevant persons who had been involved from the beginning. This brought the project itself to an end. On my final visit to the furnace, I was about to say goodbye to all my friends when there was suddenly a screaming burst of alarms sounding. I rushed in to the control room to discover that it was indicating that a fire had broken out elsewhere on the furnace. In the confusion following, while the men put into practice their well-perfected procedures, I rushed fearfully out of the door and down the stairs, not saying goodbye to anyone. With a sigh of relief, I reached hard ground, hurried to leave a note on the superintendent's desk and made my way to the car to escape. My final ignominious retreat made me recognize the respect and high regard I have developed for the steelworkers, and strengthened my determination to continue to work with them in the future to improve their health and quality of life.

Conclusion

As these words are written, I am attacking my next task, which I have to undertake without the support of the small groups. This is to analyse carefully all my transcribed interviews and field notes in order to identify the attributes of a supportive environment for health and the constituents of the process of enabling, as exemplified in this case study. This will, I hope, contribute to meeting my second objective of imparting this understanding to the health professionals with whom I am privileged to teach and to learn.

References

McTaggart, R. (1992) 'Action research: issues in theory and practice', Keynote address to the Methodological Issues in Qualitative Health Research Conference, Deakin University, Geelong.

Maguire, P. (1987) *Doing Participatory Research: A Feminist Approach*, Center for International Education, University of Massachusetts.

National Health Strategy (1992) *Enough to Make You Sick. How Income and Environment Affect Health*, National Health Strategy Research Paper No.1, Melbourne.

Occupational Health & Safety Act (OH&S) (1983) *New South Wales Legislation*.

Ritchie, J., Herscovitch, F. & Norfor, J. (1994) 'Beliefs of blue-collar workers regarding coronary risk behaviours', *Health Education Research: Theory and Practice*, Vol.9(1).

Terborg, J. (1988) 'The organization as a context for health promotion', in Spacapan, S. & Oscamp S. *The Social Psychology of Health*, Sage Publications, Newbury Park.

WHO (1986) 'The Ottawa Charter for Health Promotion', *Health Promotion*, Vol.1(4):, pp.iii-v.

PART VIII THE ROLES OF UNIVERSITIES AND GOVERNMENT HEALTH SYSTEMS IN PR

19 Experiences and issues in institutionalizing qualitative and participatory research approaches in a government health programme[1]

D. V. Mavalankar, J. K. Satia and Bharati Sharma[2]

Participatory research (PR) and rapid appraisal (RA) methods have evolved in the area of rural development and agriculture, and over the last 8 to 10 years have also been applied in the health care sector. Similarly, qualitative research methods (QRM), based on anthropological research techniques, are also gaining acceptance in health services research. These processes have been supported by international aid agencies (Scrimshaw & Gleason 1992; Tolley & Bentley 1992). PR approaches have several advantages over the conventional survey research methodology. PR can help identify local community needs, people's perception of the health services and reasons for non-use of current programmes; it can also provide direction for improvement of the programmes, as well as help ensure participation at all stages of their implementation, thus empowering the community. Much developmental work in these areas has been done by NGOs in developing countries, including some in India.

The coverage of NGOs working in health is limited, compared to the reach of the government health programmes. PR approaches must be integrated into the government health system and become institutionalized in order to benefit the large majority of the rural people in India. But the government health department is substantially different from most NGOs in terms of structure, functioning and culture. Therefore, PR approaches should be transferred to the government health system with great caution; this will require adaptation on both sides.

This chapter discusses our experiences of qualitative research and rapid assessment methods in government-run primary health centres (PHC) and the progress of an intervention to improve communications between the workers and the community. From our experience of working with government, we discuss the process of institutionalization of PR approaches in the government health system, and other important issues relating to that system.

As part of a research project to develop a micro-level planning system for primary health care that would take into account village-level variations in performance and needs, we experimented with some rapid assessment procedures such as quick surveys and village studies, and with some qualitative research methods, such as focus group interviews, in-depth surveys and participant observations. This was done over a period of three years in three PHCs in north Gujarat. The rapid assessment and qualitative research methodology are described briefly in the following sections along with salient observations.

The quick survey methodology and lessons learnt from it

We developed a quick survey methodology to assess levels of coverage, unmet need and reasons for it for primary health care services in a PHC area. Women were selected by a systematic random sample drawn from the eligible-couple register of the PHC. Data were collected by a short interview and were computerized for analysis. Detailed methodology and results of the quick survey are presented elsewhere (Satia et al. 1993).

The survey showed that unmet needs were substantial for many services and that they varied widely between services and among villages. Unmet needs were concentrated in only some villages. Pareto analysis[3] (also called ABC analysis) showed that, by and large, for most services about 60 percent of the unmet need was accounted for by only 25 percent of the villages. This rapid assessment helped us confirm our belief that in spite of uniform inputs and adequate staffing levels, coverage levels vary substantially between villages. We found also that specific reasons for high unmet need could be identified for most of the villages by discussions with the PHC staff.

This indicated that it is possible to identify problem areas within the PHC system using rapid assessment survey procedures, and that with participatory discussions with PHC supervisors it is possible to identify the causes of such problems. Sharing these data with the community may aid further diagnosis of the problem, suggest possible solutions and increase the take-up of the services by the community. Such survey-based rapid assessment procedures help in estimating the levels and distribution of unmet need, and the reasons for the same. But qualitative investigation will be required to understand people's perceptions of health/disease, their causal understanding and other significant factors affecting possible solutions to the problem of unmet need.

Qualitative research methodology and insights from it

We used QRMs such as focus group discussions and in-depth interviews with women of reproductive age to explore the women's perceptions of and reasons for using or not using public health services like immunization, family planning and antenatal and delivery care. In all, 371 in-depth interviews were carried out and 10 focus group discussions held by a team of 5 female investigators. Here we present important observations and lessons from the research; the details of the research methods and results are presented elsewhere (Mavalankar et al. 1993).

Our qualitative research revealed substantial lack of communication between the multi-purpose workers and the community, giving rise to many misconceptions and inadequate knowledge about health services among the people. The community did not see the workers as multi-purpose health workers. They were perceived as performing only one or two functions, like family planning, malaria treatment and immunization. People did not perceive the need for antenatal care, but have now realized the usefulness of vaccinations, especially that for tetanus. In family planning, demand was still a problem partly because of various misconceptions and fears people have about the contraceptive methods available. People also perceived the quality of government services as poor, leading to the under-utilization of these services. The government's priorities in rural health care, namely family planning and immunization, are not the felt needs of the people, therefore community participation in government programmes is unlikely. Furthermore, the behaviour of the government health centre staff is indifferent and unhelpful to the people, which increases the distance between the clients and the health centre. Our qualitative research provided insights into how people perceived the government health services, and their beliefs regarding various health interventions.

Experience of intervention in the government health system

The focus group discussions, in-depth interviews and participant observations pointed to four major areas for action to improve the health services in this area: community preparation and demand-generation activities; counselling and client management; improving the quality of services; and improving the service-delivery system. In order to address the first two needs, we made attempts to improve the communication and health education skills of the workers and supervisors. To this end, we organized a five-day training programme for health workers, supervisors and PHC doctors. Training made use of participatory and experiential teaching methods as well as field-practice sessions. Many communication concepts were put across through games, role plays and demonstrations where everyone participated. In the field-practice sessions, the health workers conducted health education meetings in the villages nearby. The PHC staff liked this non-conventional training methodology, as it was a pleasant contrast to the usual departmental training programmes they attend. These training programmes use the lecture method in a classroom-like situation which the workers find boring. Following the training, we asked each PHC to draw up a plan for health education sessions in its area which it would conduct and we would observe, providing it with feedback. The experience of this follow-up was mixed and instructive.

Communication training for two PHCs was held in July 1992, after which the PHCs did not organize any health education programmes for several months. PHC staff were of the opinion that most people in the community were busy with agricultural work, owing to the monsoon, and so would not attend any health education programmes. No programmes could be organized even after the monsoon, because intensive campaigning for family planning had already begun. During this time, all the PHC staff are trying to achieve family-planning targets.

Training for the other two PHCs was held in November 1992. Learning from our last experience, we asked these two PHCs to plan their schedule of health education activities during the training itself; we also increased the number of field-practice sessions in this training. Following the training, we had a joint meeting with the PHC medical officers and the district health officer. All the activities had produced better results than had the earlier training. The two PHCs involved organized some village-level health education meetings for women. The medical officers took more initiative and seemed to have grasped important points. After several health education meetings supervised by us, to our disappointment, however, we could see that very little of the training had in fact been understood and put into practice. Some weaknesses observed were: a lack of pre-planning; very little, and improper use of health education material; and lack of skills in organizing the health education information in a proper sequence, choosing the relevant and most important messages, speaking in public with conviction and confidence and encouraging discussion with the women participants in the meeting. When we observed successive meetings held by the same PHC, we could not see much improvement in the competence of the workers, in spite of our feedback after every meeting. Possible reasons for this situation could be:

- The medical officers and the supervisors did not monitor and encourage the workers to practise some of the skills acquired during the communication training. These skills and abilities were new and had not been learnt in the basic training for health workers. A week's training is not sufficient to acquire these skills, and unless the workers were encouraged to practise them, they were likely to forget them.
- Health education and communication were given very low priority among PHC activities. The PHC staff saw them as a separate and special activity. They did not see any direct benefit in it for their goal of achieving sterilization targets.

- The district-level health officers were not involved in the interventions, hence, perhaps, it was seen as a programme of an external agency rather than of the health department; there was, of course, therefore no pressure to implement it at the PHC level.

The above experience indicated that a lot of on-the-field training, supportive supervision and follow-up by the supervisors and medical officers is essential for this communication activity to be institutionalized in the PHC system. It also requires the initiative for this to come from district- or state-level officers in charge of PHC activities. Other efforts on our part to make use of rapid assessment data for health planning were also not very successful, because some of these interventions also required support from the district and state levels, and some flexibility at the PHC level, which were not available.

But some lessons from the quick survey results were picked up by the medical officers and used to improve PHC activities. For example, one PHC strengthened its supervisory system, and another used the data to focus on some poorly performing villages for providing health education. The medical officers who took an interest in this work could do more than others. But most of these efforts were again ad hoc and would probably not be institutionalized in the long run.

Our experience shows that intervening in the government set-up is an extremely slow and time-consuming process. This is especially true for interventions which require behavioural change rather than technological changes. Substantial practice-based training and supervision is required, along with active involvement of district-level supervisors and PHC doctors. Practice of new skills is possible only if the higher-level managers (district-level health officers) actively encourage and monitor it. Target-oriented monitoring hampers innovation and experimentation. But sustained interaction with an outside agency may have a positive impact on the health functionaries and may stimulate some managers to take actions to improve the programmes.

Observations on the functioning of PHCs

Besides the study of the community using rapid assessment and qualitative methods, we also interviewed the health workers and medical officers of the PHCs, to understand their viewpoints. Though we did not make use, as such, of the formal participant-observation method of data collection, our informal observations during various visits to the PHCs and interaction with the PHC staff aided this understanding. We observed some of the meetings conducted at the PHCs, and at the outpatient department (OPD) clinics held while we were visiting the PHC. We also observed a sterilization camp[4] and several health education meetings in the villages, conducted by the multi-purpose workers. These observations gave us substantial insights into functioning of the health centres, the attitudes of the staff, and their capabilities and weaknesses.

Most government workers and managers (PHC doctors) saw data collection as an activity that is required by the higher authorities rather than for local use. Data were not seen, therefore, as a tool for improving management. Most medical officers we interviewed were of the opinion that more resources (workers) were the only way to increase work output. Owing to the country's centralized, authoritarian system of government most lower-level staff, including PHC medical officers, do not show any initiative in trying to understand the needs of the community, and meet these needs. For them, the priority is to keep the superior happy; this is usually done by doing whatever work he wants done. We observed a couple of instances where the urgent needs of the patients were neglected by the medical officers so that they could continue talking to us, whom they saw as some higher authority. In such a set-up, expecting the community to participate actively is a distant dream. Staff attitudes need to be reoriented in order for them to understand that community participation could lead to better performance and help them in their work.

Discussion

The experience of working with a government health system to institutionalize bottom-up planning provided considerable understanding of the process of introducing change into that system.

Most PR approaches have been developed and tried in NGO settings. But government health systems differ from NGOs in many ways, in terms of organizational structures and processes. These differences, as we understand them from our experience of working with government, are presented in table form in Annex 19.1 (see p.227). Several of the characteristics of the functioning of the government system are the result of our observations during the study and of our association with various NGOs. Some characteristics of the government that we observed were: weak leadership, low motivation, no empathy towards the poor, weak outreach, poor training, and a hierarchical structure. These characteristics have an important bearing on the ability of government health systems to internalize the PR approaches and use them effectively. Transferring innovations from NGOs to government systems without regard to difference has led in the past to programme failure. Classical examples of such failures in India are the Community Health Worker Scheme and Traditional Birth Attendant (TBA) training programme. Both these programmes worked well in NGO settings but failed in the government health system. It is important to understand these differences in order to adapt and phase in the institutionalization of the PR process in government. We feel the most important and yet most difficult part is to get the medical officer of the PHC interested enough to take the initiative to innovate.

Participatory research or community participation?

Community participation is a key element of primary health care. Because of centralized planning in the health sector in India, poor people's views and needs do not get reflected systematically in health plans, programme design or programme evaluation. PR can help in making people's voices heard at policy-making levels.

Participatory approaches have four main goals: better community diagnosis of the problem; efficiency action; effective in implementation; and empowering the people to take the initiatives to improve their condition. Paul (1987) has listed a hierarchy of objectives for community participation. These are efficiency, cost-sharing, effectiveness, capacity-building and empowerment. Qualitative research and interventions we tried were aimed at improving efficiency, and the effectiveness and training of the PHC staff. We feel that participatory research is only one component of community participation. Participation could be envisaged in each stage of the planning/management cycle: participatory diagnosis and design of project, participatory implementation, participatory monitoring and evaluation, and participatory control.

Several methods can be used to generate participation in the community. Many of them may not be called research methods and should not be classified as participatory research. I suggest that PR should exclude methods and approaches that would not generate new information. For example, participatory games, joint celebration of community festivals, community action through voluntary labour, role plays and other participatory communication efforts can all generate participation but would not generate new knowledge. Methods such as mapping, focus-group interviews and ranking will generate new information for the researchers and formalize some of the community knowledge in forms that can be used in planning or implementation of programmes. Such participative knowledge-generating or -documenting activities should be called PR. It may be possible that involving communities in programme planning and implementation or evaluation may generate new questions or directions for research and action. But for this to happen, the researchers and implementing agency need both to be very receptive to the communities' points of view and to be flexible enough to accommodate them and modify the programmes accordingly.

Improved participation would lead to more effective, efficient and acceptable solutions to health and development problems, perhaps at a lower cost. Empowerment, which is the highest and ultimate goal of the participatory process, is beyond the reach of these direct programmatic benefits. Empowerment occurs as a result of the participative process itself, increasing the community's capacity to take its own decisions and solve its problems. Rapid assessment procedures, including the one we performed, even though useful are elicitive or extractive and should be differentiated from the real participative process, which is a collaborative effort leading to empowerment of the people (Chambers 1992). From our experience we feel that participatory research methods initiated and controlled by outsiders do become extractive and that participation is achieved only in a participatory process where the community has equal control and power to direct research and action.

Institutionalizing participatory approaches in government

Large surveys are impersonal and results are delayed and aggregated, so that such survey data provide little help for planning at local levels, owing to wide variations in the local conditions. This is why we developed the method of the quick survey and village-level analysis to identify which villages have high unmet needs. We supplemented it by qualitative methods to develop deeper understanding of people's perceptions. But it is difficult to convince health administrators and planners, who are used to working with aggregate-level quantitative, and so-called hard data, that qualitative and participatory approaches might be useful in planning and implementing programmes (even though we suspect that most health planning in developing countries goes on without hard data, usually being based on hunches or on the perceptions of bureaucrats). But good managers, who want to know what is going on in the field situation and want to improve the situation especially at the local level, can learn a lot from rapid assessment, and qualitative and participatory methods. What Tom Peters has called 'management by wandering about (MBWA)' and 'keeping close to the clients' are not very different conceptually from RRA, or PRA, even though settings and contexts may be totally different (Peters & Austin 1992). Unfortunately neither of these ideas has reached the government bureaucracy in India, not only in health matters but in all public systems.

Barriers to implementing participatory approaches

Our experience suggests that participatory and qualitative assessment, or diagnosis, is relatively easier to implement in the government system than is participatory planning or interventions. Participation of communities in planning and implementation is difficult in a government set-up due to the highly centralized health planning process and a hierarchical work culture. For example, even for the communication type of interventions, we could see that PHC medical officers did not take any initiative unless the district officers gave permission and encouragement. Most programme designs are in the form of blueprints developed in national capitals and implemented throughout the country. In this system, community participation is seen as people using services to meet the health worker's targets rather than the service meeting client's needs. PR approaches should go hand in hand with a decentralization process, bottom-up planning and changes in the incentive system. We have seen that, owing to years of centralized planning, lower managers (PHC doctors and, at times, state-level officers) may not initially be willing to experiment with modifications of the blueprint of a programme. A process to kindle their initiative and interest needs to be carried out before decentralization can be implemented. The current culture of the organization, which is inimical to new initiatives, flexibility and goal orientation, has to change. The lower manager's evaluation has to change from the fulfilment of targets fixed by the higher-ups to meeting the community's needs; only then will lower managers want to try out community participation approaches. During our study, we observed that the achievement of targets took priority over everything else so that no other initiative could be followed up between November and March, which is the year-end.

Use of community involvement in diagnosis of problems for which nothing can be done could prove to be a frustrating exercise. NGOs, being more flexible, can respond to the emerging needs of the community, which will itself encourage participation and empower the community. Flexibility at lower levels to adapt the programmes to meet community needs is vital to encouraging community participation.

We feel that prerequisites for successful PR in government are: training of the field staff and lower managers; sensitization to community needs of the middle- and higher-level managers; decentralization of planning and management; giving encouragement to flexibility of operations and experimentation; additional allocation of resources and their flexible and timely use; and changes in monitoring and evaluation.

Phased introduction of participatory research

Trying out PR approaches in government has to be done in stages (Heaver 1992). Methods that can be accommodated easily in the current pattern of working and which require least modification of attitudes and processes should be taken up first. From our experience, we feel that health education meetings (orientation training camps and group meetings), currently carried out by health workers, can be converted into focus group discussions or mapping/charting exercises. Methods such as conversational interviewing can be used during home visits to understand people's perceptions of the health situation and quality of services. Many times our in-depth interviews ended with a demand from the women to explain to them details about family planning or other health matters. This suggests that people do want to learn about health issues, if a proper rapport is established. That rapport could be established in one contact only, as shown by our interviewers who were meeting the clients for the first time. At a later stage, techniques like verbal autopsy, to understand the underlying causes of death and social factors responsible for delays in seeking care, can be built into the death registration system. This technique can serve as a tool to guide and monitor child survival and safe-motherhood programmes. We know of an excellent PHC doctor in the government system who regularly used cases of infant death to motivate his workers to improve their work. Village mapping can be used to point out potential beneficiaries, most-vulnerable groups and non-users. This can help also in planning the home visits (FPMD 1992). These approaches would help in making a diagnosis of the situation, generating interest in the community and planning extension work.

The second stage would be using the knowledge generated from PR to adjust health programmes to meet local health needs. This would require flexibility and decentralization, to modify activities according to the local priorities. Our experience showed that currently such flexibility is not present in the government system. Participatory-programme monitoring would require mechanisms by which the community can communicate regularly with the health team about programme performance. Regular village-level meetings, with the sharing of data and observations, continuously updated village maps, or scoreboards can be tried. A village committee could fulfil this role but the well-known problems of predominance of the élite, or men and committee-on-paper-only have to be guarded against. Currently the government of India is setting up women's groups and committees in villages under various schemes (*Mahila Swasthya sangh, Mahila Samakhya*). Following the new constitutional amendment, one-third of the elected representatives at the village level will be women. Such women's groups could be very useful in generating community participation for health and women's-welfare programmes. Examples of what can be achieved can be seen in the government programme *Mahila Samakhya* (Women's equity), and in NGOs like the Self-Employed Women's Association (SEWA).

The third stage would be research to help develop national or regional strategies and plans for health. These could initially be directed to common problems of the current programmes. These stages need not be followed in order. The order can be changed or any two, or all three, stages can run simultaneously. Based on our work, we feel that the rapid assessment procedures can help segment the villages in a PHC area into three broad groups, based on coverage of services. The top one-third of the villages, where coverage of the current services is good, should be taken up first for increasing community participation through PR approaches (which can help identify new needs). The middle third of the villages, where coverage is unsatisfactory, need the systematization of services delivery and the demand creation necessary for it. In the lowest one-third of the villages where the services coverage is very poor, additional resources and efforts will be needed to establish basic health services. In such villages, PR can help diagnose problems in service delivery which may have to be solved first.

We must, of course, remember that PR approaches are a potential not a panacea. They can't solve problems of bad management or improper policies. We must guard against the dangers which Robert Chambers (1992) has pointed to: faddism, rushing, formalism, to all of which the government system is prone; to this list we would add bureaucratization. Avoiding it would be the greatest challenge. Even though the task of institutionalizing PR approaches in government may seem difficult, small beginnings and perseverance can lead to the start of a process which may finally be self-improving and self-spreading. The most important change required is from the rigid attitude of 'We know all' and 'All is well' to one of a readiness to learn and continuously to improve.

Notes

1. A version of this chapter was presented at the International Symposium on Participatory Research in Health Promotion, held at the School of Tropical Medicine, Liverpool, UK from 17 to 21 September 1993.
2. D. V. Mavalankar and B. Sharma are working with the Public Systems Group, Indian Institute of Management, Ahmedabad, India. J. K. Satia is Executive Director, International Council on Management of Population Programmes (ICOMP), Malaysia.
3. Pareto analysis or ABC analysis is a management technique used to identify which causes or factors contribute most to a particular outcome or effect. In this technique each factor is arranged in descending order of importance and their effects are cumulated. Generally a few factors contribute to 60 or 70 percent of the effect while the rest of the factors contribute only to 30 or 40 percent of the effect..
4. Sterilization camps are specially arranged days, usually once a week, when women who want to undergo sterilization voluntarily are brought to the primary health centre for the sterilization operation, which is usually done using a laparoscope.

References

Chambers, R. (1992). 'Rural appraisal: rapid, relaxed and participatory', *Discussion Paper 311*, Institute of Development Studies, Brighton.

FPMD (1992) 'Use of maps to improve services', *The Family-Planning Manager*, Vol.1(5), Nov/Dec, Family-Planning Management Development, Management Sciences for Health, Boston, USA.

Annex 19.1: Differences between government and NGOs

Dimensions	NGOs	Government PHC system
Organizational structure		
Area covered	small/local	large/universal
Size of organization	small	large
Organizational structure	relatively flat	hierarchical
Organizational process		
Leadership	strong/committed; high motivation	weak/indifferent; low motivation
Commitment of staff	moderate	low
Motivation of the staff	moderate	low
Empathy towards poor	yes	no
System of planning	local level	top-down
Strategic flexibility	moderate/high	low/nil
Operational flexibility	high	low/moderate
Supervision	intensive/supportive	weak/punitive
Financial resources	moderate/flexible	moderate/fixed
Administrative procedure	flexible/informal	rigid/formal
Decision-making	fast	slow
Outreach/extension	strong	weak/nominal
Demand generation	strong	weak
Follow-up	strong	weak
Ability to respond to local needs	yes/quickly	no
Diversification	possible	not possible
Orientation towards:	results	process/rules
Programme strategy	flexible	fixed
Human resource management aspects		
Selection of staff	informal	formal
Qualification	flexible	rigid/formal
Training of staff	continuous/periodic	only once/periodic
Ability to hire and fire	high	low
Rewards and promotions	based on performance	time-bound
Transferability of staff	no/occasional	yes/frequent
Inter-staff relationships	close/warm	formal/impersonal
External environment		
Political interference	minimal	high
Rapport with the community	moderate/strong	weak
Socio-political environment	stable	turbulent

Heaver, R. (1992) 'Participatory rural appraisal: potential applications in family-planning, health and nutrition programmes', *RRA Notes: Special Issue on Applications for Health*, No.16, July, pp.13-21, IIED, London.

Mavalankar, D. V., Satia, J. K. & Sharma, B. (1993) 'Strengthening primary health-care services: insights from qualitative research in West India', Indian Institute of Management, Ahmedabad, *Working Paper No.1078.*

Paul, S. (1987) *Community Participation in Development Projects: The World Bank Experience*, World Bank Discussion Paper No.6, Washington DC.

Peters, T. & Austin, N. (1992) *A Passion for Excellence: The Leadership Difference*, Harper Collins, India.

Satia, J. K., Mavalankar, D. V. & Sharma, B. (1993) 'Micro-level planning methodology using rapid assessment for primary health care services', Indian Institute of Management, Ahmedabad, *Working Paper No.1047* (revised), a shorter version of this paper is published in *Health Policy and Planning*, September 1994, Vol.9(3), pp.318-330.

Scrimshaw, N.S. & Gleason, G.R. (1992) *RAP Rapid Assessment Procedures: Qualitative Methodologies for Planning and Evaluation of Health-Related Programmes*, International Nutrition Foundation for Developing Countries, Boston.

Tolley, E. & Bentley, M. E. (1992) 'Participatory methods for research on women's reproductive health, report of a workshop in Karnataka, India', *RRA Notes: Special Issue on Applications for Health*, No.16, July, pp.63-8, IIED, London.

20 Introducing participatory research to university and government health systems: some experiences from India[1]

Shubhada J. Kanani

From the perspective of improving the health of the population, the historic mission of universities is a very suitable one: assist, through education, with programmes for human resource development, advance knowledge through research, and provide services through constant community interaction (Khanna 1987).

The term 'participatory research' is operationally defined here as research conducted with community groups with the aim of enhancing awareness, facilitating problem analysis, and planning future programmes or improving ongoing ones.

Empowerment, an important aim of PR, can be seen as a process which enhances knowledge, changes attitudes and develops skills such that action is ultimately facilitated at the field level. Although empowerment is mostly seen as important for groups with less power at community level, I would like to emphasize that in the hierarchical work climate of most universities and government institutions it is equally important to initiate a process of empowerment for students and workers. The role of the university in facilitating PR is akin to the ripple effect seen in a pond: we at university first get empowered by using PR in our discipline and subsequently facilitate the empowerment of students, NGO and government workers, the potential users of PR. These, in turn, are helped to pass on the initiative to groups in the community, enabling them to think through their problems, and possible solutions, through the PR process.

In this chapter I will look at why the introduction of PR at universities and the use of PR by government institutions is important. Two case studies are presented. One outlines the workshops conducted to sensitize university staff, students and NGO representatives to the philosophy and methods of qualitative and participatory research, and to develop skills in the application of selected methods. The other gives examples of studies which use qualitative and participatory methods to investigate selected issues relevant to the implementation of two government programmes. I will close by discussing some of the problems and constraints that may be encountered when trying to introduce PR into the work climate of universities and governments.

PR in the university context

PR is an appropriate methodology for university-level teaching and research for several reasons:

- In both developed and developing countries, a need for linkages between research organizations and institutions which implement programmes, such as government and non-government organizations (NGOs), is being expressed (CORT 1993; John 1992). PR can be an effective link between research and action.
- The principles of participatory research and the attitudes required to apply them – openness, flexibility and adaptability – are perhaps best introduced early in the young minds of university research students.
- PR can provide students with the tools to test out in complex field situations the concepts and theories learnt in the classroom.

Unfortunately, available reports suggest that PR has made little impression on universities and training institutions. In the few places where it has had some impact, its applications have been in agro-forestry systems (Chambers 1992). Examples in health and nutrition are scarce.

The philosophy and methods of PR can help overcome two basic problems besetting the university community, which Berg (1991) has highlighted: emphasizing inappropriate research issues and lack of appropriate training to students.

Emphasizing inappropriate research issues

The research community continues to conduct research which is extractive and controlled by the researcher rather than looking at more participatory approaches. We have to give a lot more attention to how research can assist in developing and implementing programmes and how it can be responsive to people's perceptions and needs. PR can help enormously in this direction if it is built into the teaching, research and fieldwork of university departments.

Lack of appropriate training

There is lack of appropriate training available to students. This is especially the case for training which will produce people who can understand the nuts and bolts of a programme in its cultural setting and figure out how to make it work better. Currently, many universities disable students who pass through them, conditioning them with attitudes and behaviour based on a feeling of superiority and teaching methods which then have to be unlearned as they prove ineffective in field situations (Chambers 1992). Central to the use of PR is the development of appropriate personal demeanour and attitudes: openness, critical self-awareness, iterative learning, humility, patience, respect and empathy towards the community. This dimension of student development has not been addressed adequately in university training. Students in public health and allied disciplines are usually oriented to quantitative methodologies, and need to enrich the basket of methods with qualitative and participatory approaches. When universities include PR in their teaching and research, over time, the future generations of professionals will be trained in its applications and will help spread its use.

Training in the university context: an example

In the Department of Foods and Nutrition, M S University of Baroda (where the author is a faculty member), graduate students are being trained in PR during their master's and doctoral research work. PR figures as a topic in courses related to community nutrition and health, and research methods. Seminars and workshops on PR methods have been organized in the department. Of particular interest are two workshops on PR organized during the 1993–94 academic year for doctoral students, young staff members of some university departments and field representatives of regional NGOs. One workshop was organized by the Department of Foods and Nutrition and the other by a university-based group called Women's Health Advocacy Cell (WHAC), which is part of a resource centre called Women Household Development Studies Information Centre (WHODISC) at M S University. The objectives of both the workshops were to sensitize the participants to the philosophy and methods of qualitative and participatory research, and to develop skills in the application of selected methods.

The participants experimented with focus group discussions, community mapping, matrix-ranking, seasonality-diagramming, body mapping and drawing-as-dialogue methods. These methods were first tried out in small groups at the workshop venue, with some participants playing the roles of observers, facilitators and recorders. Subsequently, the same groups initiated the use of these methods for separate groups of men, women and adolescent girls in the slums around Baroda. They also recorded the sessions. The community groups generated rich information on various topics like seasonal occurrence of illnesses (seasonality diagram), household information and resources in the community (community mapping), and cultural perceptions of female anatomy/physiology (body mapping). Each session of guided practice, which was carried out by the small groups in the classroom and in the field, was subsequently shared with the larger group. In the group, experiences and difficulties were discussed and feedback was obtained from the resource persons.

Practice sessions were interspersed with theory sessions, which dealt with: the historical roots and philosophy of PR; complementarity of PR and qualitative research with quantitative epidemiological research; issues of validity and reliability; and an overview of selected PR methods and their applications.

The feedback from the participants regarding the workshops was encouraging. Participants said that they realized that the role of the facilitator and the recorder are not easy. In the words of some participants:

> After actually using these tools, I can apply them with more confidence in the field.
> I realized after field training that the roles of the facilitator and recorder are not easy. Practice and skills are required.

Several participants, particularly those from the disciplines of medicine and nutrition, stressed that they developed a positive attitude towards qualitative and participatory research and realized its potential. As one participant said:

> The attitude that I had earlier towards qualitative research in general was not very positive ... after the workshop I now have a totally changed view... I may in future work in this area of research.

A general comment was that PR methods encouraged creativity, were 'fun to use' for them *and* community people; and much more interesting than 'boring questionnaires'. However, a major misgiving was expressed regarding the 'how to' of documenting and using the voluminous, textual data that emerged from these methods. Some participants questioned the usefulness of using qualitative and participatory methods without quantitative back-up, though they acknowledged that for community-based action research, these methods alone may suffice.

PR and the government

While universities are strategically vital in providing professionals trained in PR, the implementing organizations (NGOs and government) are the ones which will put PR into action. As Murphy (1992) has said, implementing agencies need to integrate qualitative and rapid assessment procedures into their normal diagnostic, monitoring and evaluation activities before sustainable participatory development can occur. Development and research institutions should work with the implementing agencies to promote and facilitate this process. Chambers (1992) has pointed out that, to the government officials, PR provides an opportunity for direct-learning experiences and gives a far more accurate and true assessment of the relevance and community acceptance of government health programmes than do the mechanistic, often misleading official reports. In other words, PR brings government officials and field-level functionaries in close contact with the people, especially recipients of government services, and enables them to be more responsive to community perceptions and needs. PR can potentially also be a means for introspection by government personnel regarding their *own* perceptions of their roles and responsibilities, and how these affect programme implementation and outcome.

Two examples are provided below of the author's experiences with the government and qualitative, participatory research.

Management of primary health-care and nutrition programmes in Indore (Madhya Pradesh)

A study was carried out in urban and rural Indore in the State of Madhya Pradesh using a mix of qualitative and quantitative methods (direct observation, preference-ranking, narratives, scenarios, interviews, and impact assessment on beneficiaries through clinical examination and biochemical assessment of haemoglobin). The research methods used made it possible to look closely at selected management components (training, supervision, management information system, work organization and time management) in the context of the implementation of government primary health care (PHC) and national nutrition programmes. Examples of such programmes are family planning, immunization, nutritional anaemia prophylaxis and vitamin A prophylaxis. Insights were obtained into the perspectives on these programmes of providers and receivers of services. In terms of inputs given, time expended and difficulties encountered, family planning and immunization tended to rank higher than other programmes. Field-level functionaries focused on those programmes which were supervised and monitored. A majority of the programmes' intended beneficiaries did not avail themselves of the services because these were not available close enough to their homes owing to poor community outreach by functionaries, or were not adequate (for example, irregular supply of iron or vitamin A supplements), or were not good enough (for example, post-sterilization complications and poor follow-up of tubectomized women). The virtual absence of information, education and communication (IEC) also accounted for people's insufficient awareness, especially of the benefits of the programme. In a nutshell, three central issues appeared to affect programme performance:

- *The human factor*

Even in the present set-up, some functionaries and supervisors showed far more sincerity towards their work than others. The variability in the work performance was not so much situation-related – urban versus rural, subcentre versus main centre – as it was person-related. Thus even if the hardware of the management system is improved, it will not effectively function unless the software, i.e. human development, is given equal emphasis.

- *Attitudes towards primary health care in general, and towards specific programmes in the PHC set-up*

Often a casual or indifferent attitude was seen among the functionaries towards primary health care and the people who need it. Also, those programmes which have important long-term but less visible benefits, such as health education and nutrition supplementation, were taken less seriously than the 'visible' and 'important' programmes like family planning and immunization. This will markedly reduce the chances that a balanced holistic and need-based government health-service system is made available to the people.

● *Priority assigned to specific PHC programmes, and to quality or quantity of work done*

Programmes perceived to be less important, such as the long-term, less visible programmes mentioned above, were given less priority and hence less time and financial/material resources in implementation. Functionaries prioritized certain tasks, such as record-keeping and curative care, at the expense of community contacts, and gave quantity of work done far greater importance than its quality. The issue of priority emerges at the policy-makers' and programme-planners' level, and cascades downwards to the grassroots functionaries. Therefore advocacy efforts are required at the senior decision-makers' level to promote those programmes neglected by the system.

The above insights could not have been gained if qualitative and PR tools had not been used in the study.

The mid-day meal (MDM), or school-feeding programme in Baroda (Gujarat)

Disadvantaged children studying in government-administered primary schools receive a freshly cooked meal in the school every day under the MDM programme. The authorities implementing the programme (the Baroda Municipal Corporation and the MDM Programme Secretariat) requested the Department of Foods and Nutrition to give recommendations to improve the scheme. As a first step, an external evaluation of the programme was carried out jointly by the department and a government agency Urban Basic Services (UBS), with the full support and involvement of the MDM Programme Secretariat.

Out of 163 schools under the programme, 40 schools were randomly selected for this participatory evaluation. School-children, teachers, parents and MDM programme staff gave their perspective on the programme through methods such as preference-ranking of the various meals liked and disliked by the children, focus group discussions and open-ended interviews. Direct observations by the students of the Department of Foods and Nutrition and the UBS investigators were made of the meals as they were cooked and served to the children. The observations provided valuable information for field-level implementation of the programme.

The findings of this joint evaluation will form the basis for improving the programme by the MDM authorities. Some improvements, such as change in the cyclic menu to include more often those foods liked by the children, have already been made. However, producing the report after joint analysis of the data has been a slow process. Further, the deputy director in charge of the MDM programme, who was enthusiastic about the evaluation, retired from service. Renewed efforts will have to be made, therefore, to orient the new officer to this study and to convince him of the importance of implementing its recommendations. Fortunately, the executing officers are still the same, which will make this task less difficult. Our experience supports the experience of Mavalankar et al. (1993) that participatory diagnosis is easier to implement in the government system than are participatory interventions.

Constraints and problems

Despite the potentials of PR, the spread and acceptance of PR in government and university systems has been slow and hesitant, and perhaps will continue to be so, until some far-reaching measures are taken:

- Basic changes in the work culture in both systems are required. The important changes needed are a move from top-down and macro-level planning to more decentralized and micro-level planning and execution of programmes, and from hierarchial decision-making to a type that encourages team work, equality and experimentation. Workers and lower-level supervisors in government have to be empowered to solve local problems (Mavalankar et al. 1993). Similarly, academic freedom should find a place at all levels in the university, from the heads and deans, to the junior-level lecturers and assistants.
- Another measure would be a willingness to admit that we do not have all the answers, that we may not even know which are the real questions. It is not easy to acknowledge that the people in impoverished communities do have something to contribute; that they know the real questions and solutions and the truth about how we function, no matter how embarrassing it may be. A harassed government official may not want to add to his woes and risk his 'reputation' by having to listen to what people have to say. An academic researcher may be concerned more about what research is publishable rather than to conduct research on issues which the people really care about. Besides, it is not easy to conduct research across disciplinary boundaries, something which PR necessitates.
- Finally to institutionalize PR either in universities or in the government, the framework, within which research, teaching or

programmes are carried out, has to have in-built supportive mechanisms from the senior-management level onwards. This will enable PR practitioners to work without anxiety as regards their professional advancement, and to work on a sustained basis. PR is not a matter of one research project or a temporary action programme; it implies empowerment and change, which takes time. A supervisor in a government programme, for example, should be rewarded for work carried out by his team which is both qualitatively or quantitatively satisfactory, and which has come about with active support from the people.

In university departments which belong to applied disciplines with a strong community orientation, research and teaching should not be the only criteria for judging professional achievements of faculty members. Professional advancement and promotions should also be based on their links with the community, and the government and voluntary organizations, for it is through these links that students are enabled to have live contact with real field situations, something which classrooms cannot provide. The three corners of the triangle comprising the work of a university professional should be teaching, research and community service, so that all-round growth of the university system may be facilitated.

None of us in applied health and allied disciplines, whether in the government or in the university, can afford to isolate ourselves from the people. Participatory research can bring us closer to them.

Note

1. Participatory research results from team effort. My special thanks to Priti Khanna and Kavita Sharma of the Department of Foods and Nutrition, M S University; Rahul Bhatt and Hasmukh Patel of the Baroda Municipal Corporation, for their involvement in the evaluation studies of government programmes. I thank my friends of the WHAC group: Renu Khanna, Shagufa Kapdia, Sandhya Barge, Anima Anand, Sandhya Joshi, Urvi Shah and Amrit Chohan, who were a part of the organizing team of the PR workshop. I appreciate the assistance of Daksha Solanki in preparing the manuscript of this chapter.

References

Berg, A. (1991) 'Sliding toward nutrition malpractice: time to reconsider and redeploy', National Council for International Health 1991 International Conference on Women's Health, Martin Forman Memorial Lecture, Crystal City, USA.

CORT (Centre for Operations Research and Training) (1993) 'The need of establishing linkage between voluntary organizations and research institutions', Proceedings of a National Workshop, Baroda.

Chambers, R. (1992) 'Rural appraisal: rapid, relaxed and participatory', *Institute of Development Studies Discussions Paper 311*, University of Sussex, Brighton, England.

John, H.M. (1992) 'In true partnership with the people: participatory action research and the poor', *Search News*, Vol.VII(1).

Khanna, S. (1987) *Health for All – Leadership Initiative of the World Health Organization*, World Health Organization, Geneva.

de Koning, K. (ed.) (1994) *Proceedings of the International Symposium on Participatory Research in Health Promotion*, Education Resource Group, Liverpool School of Tropical Medicine, UK.

Mavalankar, D.V., Satia, J.K. & Sharma, B. (1993) 'Framework for institutionalizing participatory research approaches in government health programmes', in de Koning, K. (ed.) (1994), pp.73-75.

Murphy, J. (1992) 'Institutionalizing the use of rapid assessment procedures in Rural Service Agencies', in Scrimshaw, N.S. & Gleason, G. R (eds), *Rapid Assessment Procedures – Qualitative Methodologies for Planning and Evaluation of Health-related Programmes*, International Nutrition Foundation for Developing Countries, USA.

Index